AF819939

All in One

Recommended by **Teachers**
Trusted by **Toppers**

PSYCHOLOGY
Class 11

EVERYTHING YOU NEED TO SCORE

- Simplified Theory
- NCERT & Other Important Questions
- CBQs; MCQs, A-R, Source Based
- Sample Question Papers

CBSE Exams 2026

All in One®

Recommended by **Teachers**
Trusted by **Toppers**

PSYCHOLOGY
Class 11

EVERYTHING YOU NEED TO SCORE

- Simplified Theory
- NCERT & Other Important Questions
- CBQs; MCQs, A-R, Case Based
- Sample Question Papers

CBSE Exams 2026

Author
Charu Tripathi

arihant
SUCCESS AND NOTHING LESS

ARIHANT PRAKASHAN
(School Division Series)

卐 *ADMINISTRATIVE & PRODUCTION OFFICES*

Regd. Office

'Ramchhaya' 4577/15, Agarwal Road, Darya Ganj, New Delhi -110002
Tele: 011- 47630600, 43518550; Fax: 011- 23280316

卐 *Head Office*

Kalindi, TP Nagar, Meerut (UP) - 250002, Tel: 0121-7156203, 7156204

卐 *SALES & SUPPORT OFFICES*

Agra, Ahmedabad, Bengaluru, Bareilly, Chennai, Delhi, Guwahati, Hyderabad, Jaipur, Jhansi, Kolkata, Lucknow, Nagpur & Pune.

PO No : TXT-XX-XXXXXXX-X-XX

Published By Arihant Publications (India) Ltd.

For further information about the books published by Arihant, log on to www.arihantbooks.com or e-mail at info@arihantbooks.com

Follow us on

卐 *PRICE* ₹300.00

PRODUCTION TEAM

Publishing Managers
Mahendra Singh Rawat & Keshav Mohan

Cover Designer
Rakesh Rawat

Inner Designer
Ankit Tyagi

Project Head
Manju

Page Layouting
Lalit Chaprana

Proof Reader
Bhawna Madhrey

Index *cum* Study Planner

One Book- Endless Features

to Help you Succeed

Complete Theory in Each Chapter

Each chapter has Complete, Easy to Understand and Simplified theory covering latest syllabus and rationalised NCERT Textbook. Theory is developed in such a way that it is suitable for all types of learners.

05

CHAPTER

Learning

Learning may be defined as "any relatively permanent change in behaviour or behavioural potential produced by experience".

YOUR STUDY GOALS

5.1 Introduction
5.2 Meaning and Nature of Learning
5.3 Paradigms of Learning
5.4 Classical Conditioning

5.1 Introduction

- As the child grows and matures, she/he becomes capable of making diverse types of responses. These responses include identifying the images of persons like mother, father or grandfather.

NCERT Folder

1. What is behaviour? Give examples of overt and covert behaviour?

Ans. Behaviour refers to any response of an organism that can be measured.

Behaviours may be overt or covert. Overt behaviour can be outwardly seen or sensed by an observer. Some behaviours are internal or covert. All overt and covert behaviours are associated with or triggered by some stimulus in the environment or changes that happen internally.

Examples of Overt Behaviour

- Blinking of eyes when a stone is hurled at a person.
- Withdrawing the hand immediately after touching a hot pan.

Examples of Covert Behaviour

- The twitching of hand muscles while playing a game of chess.
- Pounding of heart during an interview.

- **Structuralism** The initial approach to study psychology was based on introspection or structuralism in which the individuals were asked to describe their experiences.
- **Functionalism** It was developed by an American psychologist William James. Functionalists studied the working of the mind and the impact of behaviour upon people's interaction with their environment.
- **Behaviourism** It was proposed by John B Watson who viewed psychology as the science of behaviour and behaviour could be described objectively in terms of Stimuli and Responses (S-R). This approach proposed that mentalist concepts such as consciousness, image or mind cannot be measured or studied objectively and scientifically.
- **Gestalt Psychology** It was a revolt against structuralism, founded in Germany by Wertheimer, Kohler and Koffka. It focussed on perceptual organisation (organisation of what we see) and they also demonstrated the laws of

NCERT Folder

Complete explanations of all the questions of NCERT Exercises.

Quick Test 1

1. What is the full form of FMRI?
2. Which are the fast developing brain imaging techniques?
3. What is Hypothetico-Deductive Model (HDM)?
4. Which approach examines human behaviour in social and cultural context?

Quick Test

A set of 4-6 Questions given in between the text, helps students to remain connected with the text while studying. They can instantly assess themselves for their understanding.

One Book- Endless Features

to Help you Succeed

Exam Pattern Questions

Exam Pattern Questions have all types of questions; Objective Type Questions, VSA, SA & LA Type Questions

Exam Pattern Questions

Objective Type Questions

Multiple Choice Questions (MCQs)

1. Scientific knowledge is based on
   (a) counselling
   (b) behaviour
   (c) observation
   (d) consciousness
2. The first Psychological Department in India was set up in
   (a) 1949 (b) 1953
   (c) 1916 (d) 1848
3. The humanistic approach to psychology was developed mainly by
   (a) Abraham Maslow (b) Carl Wright
   (c) JB Watson (d) Max Muler
4. The behaviourist school of psychology was founded by
   (a) JB Watson (b) Wertheimer
   (c) Freud (d) Maslow
7. Which of the following is true about Introspection?
   (a) Individuals are asked to describe in detail, their own physical experiences.
   (b) It is a component of dissociative Identity disorder.
   (c) Individuals are asked to describe in detail, their own mental processes or experiences.
   (d) None of the above
8. An American psychologist, William James, developed functionalist approach to
   (a) study human mind
   (b) to find diversity in society
   (c) analyse the function of psychology
   (d) to explore variety of human feelings
9. In the early 20th century, a new perspective called Gestalt psychology emerged in .... as a reaction to the structuralism of Wundt.
   (a) England (b) Germany
   (c) France (d) USA

SELF ASSESSMENT TEST

Objective Type Questions

1. The behaviourist theory was first offered by
   (a) Freud (b) Watson (c) Skinner (d) Darwin
2. First psychology department in India was established in
   (a) Bombay (b) Delhi (c) Kolkata (d) Chennai
3. Who developed psycho analysis?
   (a) Watson (b) Ivan Pavlov (c) Sigmund Freud (d) Wundt
4. Which of the following is not a scientific knowledge?
   (a) Observation (b) Evidence (c) Data Collection (d) Belief

Sample Question Papers

To make students practice of examination in real sense, there are 3 Sample Question Papers at the end. All these Sample Questions Papers are exactly prepared on the latest syllabus & pattern of examination.

Self Assessment Test

Complete Test of chapter in Exam format.

SAMPLE QUESTION PAPER 1

A Highly Simulated Sample Question Paper for CBSE Class XI

PSYCHOLOGY

General Instructions

- All questions are compulsory except where internal choice has been given.
- Question Nos. 1-14 in Section A carry 1 mark each.
- Question Nos. 15-19 in Section B are Very Short Answer Type-I questions carrying 2 marks each. Answer to each question should not exceed 30 words.
- Question Nos. 20-23 in Section C are Short Answer Questions Type-II carrying 3 marks each. Answer to each question should not exceed 60 words.
- Question Nos. 24-27 in Section D are Long Answer Type I questions carrying 4 marks each. Answer to each question should not exceed 120 words.
- Question Nos. 28 & 29 in Section E are Long Answer Type question carrying 6 marks. Answer to this question should not exceed 200 words.
- Question Nos. 30–33 in Section F are based on two cases given. Answer to each one-mark question should not exceed 20 words. Answer to each two-mark question should not exceed 30 words.

Time : 3 hours **Max. Marks : 70**

Section A

1 Ivy remembers watching the solar eclipse in amazing detail. She is certain, she can remember exactly what she was wearing, who she was with, what music was playing on a nearby radio and even the breed of dog which ran past her just before the eclipse. This is an example of .... (1)
   I. Flashbulb memory
   II. Eidetic image
   III. Procedural memory
   IV. Semantic memory

3 The information related to very recent incidents or very distant events is stored in .... (1)
   (a) short-term memory (b) long-term memory
   (c) sensory memory (d) working memory

4 Which of the following factors affect learning? (1)
   I. Motivation of the learner
   II. Maturation of the learner
   III. Teaching strategies
   IV. Physical and emotional health of the learner

   Codes
   (a) I and II (b) II and III
   (c) I, II and III (d) All of these

Latest Course Structure

One Theory Paper | **3 Hours** | **Marks : 70**

Units	Topics	No. of Periods	Marks
I	What is Psychology?	27	11
II	Methods of Enquiry in Psychology	32	13
IV	Human Development	26	11
V	Sensory, Attentional and Perceptual Processes	18	8
VI	Learning	20	9
VII	Human Memory	19	8
VIII	Thinking	14	5
IX	Motivation and Emotion	14	5
	Total	**170**	**70**

Course Structure

UNIT I What is Psychology?

The topics in this unit are:

1. Introduction
2. What is Psychology?
   - Psychology as a Discipline
   - Psychology as a Natural Science
   - Psychology as a Social Science
3. Understanding Mind and Behaviour
4. Popular Notions about the Discipline of Psychology
5. Evolution of Psychology
6. Development of Psychology in India
7. Branches of Psychology
8. Psychology and Other Disciplines
9. Psychology in Everyday Life

UNIT II Methods of Enquiry in Psychology

The topics in this unit are:

1. Introduction
2. Goals of Psychological Enquiry
   - Steps in Conducting Scientific Research
   - Alternative Paradigms of Research
3. Nature of Psychological Data
4. Some Important Methods in Psychology
   - Observational Method
   - Experimental Method
   - Correlational Research
   - Survey Research
   - Psychological Testing
   - Case Study
5. Analysis of Data
   - Quantitative Method
   - Qualitative Method
6. Limitations of Psychological Enquiry
7. Ethical Issues

UNIT IV Human Development

The topics in this unit are:

1. Introduction

2. Meaning of Development
    - Life-Span Perspective on Development
3. Factors Influencing Development
4. Context of Development
5. Overview of Developmental Stages
    - Prenatal Stage
    - Infancy
    - Childhood
    - Challenges of Adolescence
    - Adulthood and Old Age

UNIT V Sensory, Attentional and Perceptual Processes

The topics in this unit are:

1. Introduction
2. Knowing the world
3. Nature and varieties of Stimulus
4. Sense Modalities
    - Functional Limitation of Sense Organs
5. Attentional Processes
    - Selective Attention
    - Sustained Attention
6. Perceptual Processes
    - Processing Approaches in Perception
7. The Perceiver
8. Principles of Perceptual Organisation
9. Perception of Space, Depth and Distance
    - Monocular Cues and Binocular Cues
10. Perceptual Constancies
11. Illusions
12. Socio-Cultural Influences on Perception

UNIT VI Learning

The topics in this unit are:

1. Introduction
2. Nature of Learning
3. Paradigms of Learning
4. Classical Conditioning
    - Determinants of Classical Conditioning
5. Operant/Instrumental Conditioning
    - Determinants of Operant Conditioning
    - Key Learning Processes
6. Observational Learning
7. Cognitive Learning
8. Verbal Learning
9. Skill Learning
10. Factors Facilitating Learning
11. Learning Disabilities

UNIT VII Human Theory

The topics in this unit are:

1. Introduction
2. Nature of Memory
3. Information Processing Approach : The Stage Model
4. Memory Systems : Sensory, Short-term and Long-term Memories
5. Levels of Processing
6. Types of Long-term Memory
    - Declarative and Procedural; Episodic and Semantic
7. Nature and Causes of Forgetting
    - Forgetting due to Trace Decay, Interference and Retrieval Failure
8. Enhancing Memory
    - Mnemonics using Images and Organisation

UNIT VIII Thinking

The topics in this unit are:

1. Introduction
2. Nature of Thinking
    - Building Blocks of Thought
3. The Processes of Thinking
4. Problem Solving
5. Reasoning
6. Decision-making

7. Nature and Process of Creative Thinking
   - Nature of Creative Thinking
   - Process of Creative Thinking
8. Thought and Language
9. Development of Language and Language Use

UNIT IX Motivation and Emotion

The topics in this unit are:

1. Introduction
2. Nature of Motivation
3. Types of Motives
   - Biological Motives
   - Psychosocial Motives
4. Maslow's Hierarchy of Needs
5. Nature of Emotions
6. Expression of Emotions
   - Culture and Emotional Expression
   - Culture and Emotional Labelling
7. Managing Negative Emotions
8. Enhancing Positive Emotions

Practical (Projects, experiments, small studies, etc.)

The students shall be required to undertake one project andconduct two experiments. The project would involve the use of different methods of enquiry like observation, survey, interview, questionanise small studies and related skills.

Practical would involve conducting experiments and to the topics covered in the course (e.g. Human development, Learning, Memory, Motivation, Perception, Attention and Thinking). Experiment could focus on cause and effect relationship.

Practical Examination

- Practical (Experiments) file 05 Marks
- Project file 05 Marks
- Viva Voce (Project and experiments) 05 Marks
- One experiment 15 Marks*

*(05 Marks for conduct of practical and 10 Marks for report writing)

01 CHAPTER

As a human science, psychology explains consciousness, attention, learning, memory, motivation and more. A unique feature of psychology is the study of internal mental processes, observable only within oneself.

YOUR STUDY GOALS

YOUR PRACTICE GOAL

- Objective Type Questions (33 Qs ; MCQs, A-R,)
- Subjective Questions (14 VSAs, 24 SAs, 3 LAs, 2 Case Based)

What is Psychology?

1.1 Meaning of Psychology

- The word 'Psychology' comes from Greek words: psyche (soul) and logos (study).
- Earlier it was the study of the soul or mind but psychology is now considered a scientific study of the mind and behaviour.
- It explores individual, two-person (dyadic), group and organisational levels, with biological and social bases.
- Psychology uses methods from biological and social sciences to gather data systematically.
- Key terms in psychology
  - **Mental Processes** Internal activities like thinking, remembering.
  - **Experience** Personal and subjective, unique to each person.
  - **Behaviour** Observable actions influenced by internal and external stimuli.

Psychology as a Study of Mental Processes

- Mental processes are internal experiences or states of awareness.
- We use mental processes to think, solve problems, remember and perceive.
- Brain activity reflects mental processes and can be observed through brain imaging.
- Mental and Neural activities overlap but are not identical; the mind has no physical structure.
- The mind evolves through experiences and interactions with the world.
- Consciousness of experiences goes beyond brain activities, as some mental activities continue even during sleep.
- Psychologists study mental processes like remembering and learning to understand how the mind works and to improve mental skills.

Psychology as a Study of Experiences of People

- Experiences are subjective, unique to the person experiencing them and cannot be directly observed by others.
- Experiences are tied to consciousness and awareness. Psychologists study various experiences, such as
  - **Psychological Pain** Feelings of separation or loss.
  - **Esoteric Experiences** States of altered consciousness[1], like meditation or drug induced highs.
- The nature of an experience depends on internal and external conditions; e.g., the same situation may have different experiences on the context and personal state.

Psychology as a Study of Behaviour

- Behaviour refers to the actions or responses of individuals, which may be simple, complex, short or long-lasting.
- Behaviours are overt (visible) or covert (hidden/internal).
- Behaviours are influenced by external and internal stimuli, forming stimulus[2]-response (S-R) associations.

1.2 Psychology as a Discipline

- Psychology studies mental processes, experiences and behaviours.
- Psychologists strive to avoid biases by adopting scientific and objective methods for explaining behaviour.
- Some approaches emphasise subjectivity, acknowledging that personal perspectives are a part of human experience.
- In Indian tradition, self-reflection and conscious experiences are considered essential for psychological understanding.
- Western psychology also values self-knowledge and reflection in understanding human behaviour and experiences.
- Psychology is a relatively new scientific discipline, with the first lab established in 1879 in Leipzig.
- It is often classified as a social science, but in India, it is studied within science faculties both at undergraduate and postgraduate levels.
- Emerging fields like **neuroscience** and **computer science** are influenced by psychology. Brain imaging (e.g., FMRI, EEG) and technologies like AI rely on psychological principles.

1 Consciousness It refers to awareness of the general condition of one's mind, awareness of particular mental contents of self-awareness.
2 Stimulus It refers to any well-defined element in the environment affecting to organism, which may lead to an overt or a covert response.

Psychological Approaches in Science

(i) **Biological Sciences Approach** Psychology uses scientific methods to collect data and identify causes of behaviour. Researchers seek cause-and-effect relationships to predict and control behaviour.

(ii) **Social and Cultural Sciences Approach** Psychology examines behaviour through the interaction of the person with social and cultural contexts. It assumes that behaviour has multiple causes related to social interactions.

Psychology as a Natural Science

- Modern psychology grew from scientific methods influenced by thinkers like Descartes and later by the physics advancements which is called Hypothetico-Deductive Model.

Set of Statements → Deduce/Propose Hypothesis → Testing Hypothesis on the basis of empirical data → Revised Theory

▲ *Hypothetico-Deductive Model*

- Evolutionary theories from biology also explain psychological phenomenons like attachment and aggression.

Psychology as a Social Science

- Psychology recognised more as social science because it studies the behaviour of human beings in their socio-culture contexts.
- Psychology focuses on humans as social beings in cultural contexts irrespective of different socio-culture conditions.
- For example, two girls, Ranjita and Shabnam, share a supportive relationship during a flood illustrating social bonding.
- Such examples show psychology studies both cooperative and anti-social behaviours influenced by context.
- It focuses on the individuals and communities in relation to their socio-culture and physical environment.

1.3 Understanding Mind and Behaviour

- Psychology was once defined as the study of the mind.
- Early scientists avoided studying the mind as it could not be physically defined.
- Neuroscientists Sperry and Penrose linked psychology with the mind.
- The mind cannot exist without brain but has a separate entity, brain injuries often affect behaviour, but mental functions persist.
- For example, people with damaged visual areas may still respond to visual cues. Phantom limb syndrome and cases of mistaken identity (as with duplicates) illustrate mind-brain relations.
- Positive thinking and visualisation can impact physical health and immune response (as shown by Dr. Ornish's research).
- Techniques like mental imagery have helped to treat phobias (irrational fears of objects and situations).
- A field studying the mind's role in strengthening the immune system is called **Psychoneuroimmunology**.

1.4 Popular Beliefs about Psychology

- People often create personal explanations for human behaviour based on common sense.
- Common-sense explanations are usually based on past events and may not predict future behaviour accurately.
- For instance, 'Out of sight, out of mind' vs. 'Distance makes the heart grow fonder' are conflicting beliefs about separation. It depends on one's life experiences.
- Psychology, unlike common sense, uses patterns and scientific data to predict behaviour.
- Examples of psychological findings
  - Men and women's intelligence does not significantly differ, contrary to common beliefs.
  - People may perform better before an audience if they have practised, contrary to the belief that audiences impair performance.
- Studies like Dweck's show that mixed experiences of success and failure help build resilience, contradicting the idea that only success boosts confidence.

Quick Test 1

1. What is the full form of FMRI?
2. Which are the fast developing brain imaging techniques?
3. What is Hypothetico-Deductive Model (HDM)?
4. Which approach examines human behaviour in social and cultural context?

1.5 Evolution of Psychology

- Psychology is influenced by Western developments.
- The first experimental psychology laboratory was established in 1879 by Wilhelm Wundt in Leipzig, Germany.
- Wundt was interested in studying conscious experience and analysing the mind's building blocks.
- Different approaches have contributed to the development of psychology, each with strengths and weaknesses as follows

Structuralist Approach and Introspection

- Structuralism was proposed by Wilhelm Wundt. Structuralists analysed the structure of the mind through introspection.
- Introspection involves asking individuals to describe their own thoughts, feelings and experiences.
- Introspection was criticised for its subjectivity and lack of scientific rigour.
- The limitations of introspection led to the development of new psychological perspectives.

Functionalist Approach

- It was founded by American psychologist William James who had set up a psychological laboratory in Cambridge, Massachusetts, shortly after the Leipzig laboratory was established.
- He developed a functionalist approach to study the human mind.
- He believed that instead of studying the structure of the mind, psychology should focus on what the mind does and how behaviour helps people adjust to their surroundings.
- For example, functionalists studied how behaviour helps people meet their needs.

- According to William James, consciousness is a continuous flow of mental processes that interact with the environment and is the main focus of psychology.
- Another educational thinker, John Dewey, used **functionalism**[3] to argue that people try to work well by adapting to their environment.

Evolution of Gestalt Psychology

- In the early 20th century, a new perspective called **Gestalt psychology**[4] emerged in Germany as a response to Wundt's structuralism.
- It focused on how perceptual experiences are organised.
- Instead of studying the components of the mind, he believed that our experience is more than just the inputs we get from the environment.
- For example, when watching a movie, we actually see a series of quickly moving images of still pictures on our retina.
- Thus, our perceptual experience is more than just the individual elements. Experience is holistic and this is called a Gestalt.

Evolution of Behaviourism

- Another response to structuralism came in the form of **behaviourism**[5].
- Around 1910, John Watson rejected the ideas of mind and consciousness as the subject matters of psychology.
- He was greatly influenced by the work of physiologists like Ivan Pavlov, on classical conditioning.
- For Watson, the mind is not observable and introspection is subjective because it cannot be verified by another person.
- He argued that scientific psychology should focus only on what is observable and can be verified.
- Watson defined psychology as the study of behaviour or responses (to stimuli), which can be measured and studied objectively.

Views of Different Psychologists about Behaviourism

- Behaviourism, as proposed by Watson, was further developed by many psychologists known as **Behaviourists.**
- The most prominent among them was Skinner, who applied behaviourism to many situations and popularised the approach.
- Freud later viewed human behaviour as a dynamic presentation of unconscious desires and conflicts.
- He founded psychoanalysis to understand and treat psychological disorders.
- Freud's psychoanalysis saw human beings as motivated by unconscious desires for the gratification of pleasure-seeking (often sexual) desires.
- The humanistic perspective was proposed by Carl Rogers and Abraham Maslow, that human beings have free will and a natural drive to grow and reach their full potential.
- They argued that behaviourism, with its focus on behaviour shaped by environmental conditions, undermines human freedom and dignity and takes a mechanistic view of human nature.
- These different approaches shaped the history of modern psychology and offered multiple perspectives on its development.
- Aspects of Gestalt psychology and structuralism combined to form the Cognitive perspective, which focuses on how we understand the world.

---

3 **Functionalism** It refers to the school of psychology that emphasised the utilitarian and adaptive functions of the human mind or consciousness.

4 **Gestalt Psychology** It is a branch of psychology in which behaviour is viewed as an integrated whole, greater than the sum of its parts.

5 **Behaviourism** It refers to a school of thought that emphasises objectivity, observable behavioural responses, learning and environmental determinants.

Cognitive Perspective of Psychology

- Cognition is the process of knowing, involving, thinking, understanding, perceiving, memorising and problem-solving.
- It is a collection of mental processes that help to develop our knowledge of the world and how we deal with our environment.
- According to this view, the mind receives, processes, transforms, stores and retrieves information, similar to how a computer works.
- Modern cognitive psychology sees human beings as actively constructing their minds through exploration of the physical and social world. This view is sometimes called **Constructivism.**
- Piaget's theory of child development is considered a constructivist theory of the mind's development.
- Russian psychologist Vygotsky suggested that the human mind develops through social and cultural processes.
- According to Vygotsky, the mind is culturally constructed through joint interactions between adults and children.
- Piaget believed that children actively construct their own minds, while Vygotsky viewed the mind as a joint cultural construction emerging from the interaction between children and adults.

Quick Test 2

1. Who rejected the ideas of mind and consciousness as the subject matters of psychology?
2. Give one point of difference between structuralist and functionalist approaches.
3. Which theory of Piaget considered to be a constructive theory?
4. How behaviourism is evolved?

1.6 Development of Psychology in India

- The Indian philosophical tradition has long focused on mental processes and topics such as human consciousness, self, mind-body relations and various mental functions like cognition, perception, illusion, attention and reasoning.
- However, the development of psychology as a formal discipline in India has been largely influenced by Western psychology.
- The development of psychology in India is outlined below
    - The modern era of Indian psychology began at the Department of Philosophy at Calcutta University in 1916.
    - Here, the first syllabus for experimental psychology was introduced and the first Psychology Laboratory was established in 1915.
    - Calcutta University started the first Department of Psychology in 1916 and another Department of Applied Psychology in 1938.
    - The introduction of modern experimental psychology at Calcutta University was greatly influenced by Dr. N.N. Sengupta, an Indian psychologist trained in the USA in the experimental tradition of Wilhelm Wundt.
    - Professor G. Bose, trained in Freudian psychoanalysis, established the Indian Psychoanalytical Association in 1922.
    - The Departments of Psychology at the Universities of Mysore and Patna were other early centres of teaching and research in psychology.

- Two centres of excellence in psychology, supported by the UGC, are at Utkal University, Bhubaneswar and the University of Allahabad.
- Around 70 universities in India offer courses in psychology.

Phases of Modern Psychological Development

Durganand Sinha, in his book 'Psychology in a Third World Country: The Indian Experience (1986),' traces the history of modern psychology as a social science in India in four phases

(i) **First Phase (Until Independence)**
- This phase focused on experimental, psychoanalytic and psychological testing research.
- It primarily reflected the development of psychology in Western countries.

(ii) **Second Phase (Until the 1960s)**
- This phase saw the expansion of psychology in India into various branches.
- Indian psychologists were seeking to create an Indian identity for psychology, linking Western psychology to the Indian context.

(iii) **Third Phase (Post-1960s)**
- This phase focused on problem-oriented research in India.
- Psychologists began addressing issues specific to Indian society and realised the limitations of relying solely on Western psychology.
- There was an emphasis on research that was relevant to India's social context.

(iv) **Fourth Phase (Late 1970s Onwards)**
- This phase marked the beginning of **indigenisation**[6] in Indian psychology.
- Indian psychologists started to reject Western frameworks and emphasised the need for a culturally and socially relevant understanding of psychology.
- It was characterised by the development of indigenous psychology based on Indian cultural contexts.

Present Context of Psychology in India

- Psychology in India is making significant contributions to global psychology and is increasingly contextualised by emphasising the development of relevant psychological principles.
- New research studies are emerging that involve interfaces with neurobiology and health sciences.
- Psychology in India is now applied in diverse professional fields.
- Psychologists work with children facing special problems such as in hospitals as clinical psychologists, in fields such as corporate organisations, human resources, advertising, sports, development sectors and the IT industry.

Quick Test 3

1. Name the university which started first department of psychology.
2. Who established Indian Psychoanalytical Association?
3. Who wrote the book 'Third World Country: The Indian Experience (1986)'?
4. Which phase focused on experimental and psychoanalytic research?

6 **Indigenisation** Transformation of some service idea etc. to suit a local culture.

1.7 Branches of Psychology

Some important branches of psychology are as follows

Cognitive Psychology

- Cognitive psychology investigates mental processes involved in the acquisition, storage, manipulation, transformation and communication of information received from the environment.
- Major cognitive processes include attention, perception, memory, reasoning, problem-solving, decision-making and language.
- Psychologists conduct experiments in laboratory settings to study these cognitive processes.
- An ecological approach is also followed, focusing on the environmental factors that influence cognitive processes in natural settings.
- Cognitive psychologists often collaborate with neuroscientists and computer scientists.

Biological Psychology

- Biological psychology focuses on the relationship between behaviour and the physical system, which includes the brain, nervous system, immune system and genetics.
- Biological psychologists collaborate with neuroscientists zoologists, and anthropologists.
- **Neuropsychology**[7] has emerged as a field where psychologists and neuroscientists work together to study the role of neurotransmitters or chemical substances responsible for neural communication in different areas of the brain.
- Research is conducted on individuals with normal functioning brain as well as those with damaged brains, using advanced technologies like EEG, FMRI and PET.

Developmental Psychology

- Developmental psychology studies the physical, social and psychological changes that occur at different ages and stages over a lifespan, from conception to old age.
- Initially, developmental psychologists focused mainly on child and adolescent development, but the field later extended to include adult development and ageing.
- Psychologists focus on biological, socio-cultural and environmental factors that influence psychological characteristics such as intelligence, cognition, emotion, temperament, morality and social relationships.
- Developmental psychologists collaborate with anthropologists, educationists, neurologists, social workers, counsellors and experts from various fields and concerned with human growth and development.

Social Psychology

- Social psychology explores how people are affected by their social environments and how people think about and influence others.
- Social psychologists study topics such as attitudes, conformity, obedience to authority, interpersonal attraction, helpful behaviour, prejudice, aggression, social motivation and inter-group relations.

Cross-Cultural and Cultural Psychology

- Cross-cultural psychology examines the role of culture in understanding behaviour, thought and emotion.
- It assumes that human behaviour is not just a reflection of biological potential but also a product of cultural influences. Therefore behaviour should be studied in its socio-culture context.

7 **Neuropsychology** It is the scientific study of behaviour and mental processes as function of brain activity and the nervous system.

Environmental Psychology

- Environmental psychology studies how physical factors like temperature, humidity, pollution and natural disasters influence human behaviour.
- It also investigates how the physical arrangement of workplaces affects health, emotional state and interpersonal relations.
- Current research topics include waste disposal, population explosion, energy conservation and efficient use of community resources, all of which are related to human behaviour.

Health Psychology

- Health psychology focuses on the role of psychological factors (such as stress and anxiety) in the development, prevention and treatment of illnesses.
- Key areas of interest include stress and coping mechanisms, the relationship between psychological factors and health, patient-doctor relationships and ways to promote health and well-being.

Clinical and Counselling Psychology

- Clinical psychology deals with the causes, treatment and prevention of various psychological disorders such as anxiety, depression, eating disorders and chronic substance abuse.
- Counselling psychology aims to help individuals improve everyday functioning by solving problems and coping with challenging situations.
- Clinical and counselling psychologists both address mental health issues, but clinical psychologists often deal with more severe psychological disorders.
- Psychiatrists, in contrast, are medical doctors specialising in mental health and they can prescribe medications and provide treatments like electroshock treatment, whereas clinical psychologists cannot.

Industrial/Organisational Psychology

- Industrial/Organisational psychology focuses on workplace behaviour, examining both the workers' and employers' perspectives.
- It involves training employees, improving work conditions and developing criteria for employee selection.
- For instance, organisational psychologists may recommend management structures that improve communication between managers and staff.
- This field often incorporates knowledge from cognitive and social psychology.

Educational Psychology

- Educational psychology studies how people of all ages learn, help to develop instructional methods and materials for both educational and work settings.
- It also focuses on research related to education, counselling and learning challenges.

School Psychology

- School psychology is a branch of educational psychology that focuses on designing programmes, which promote the intellectual, social and emotional development of children, including those with special needs.
- School psychologists apply psychological principles in the school environment.

Sports Psychology

- Sports psychology applies psychological principles to improve sports performance by motivation and mental preparation.
- Though a relatively new field, sports psychology is gaining global acceptance.

Other Emerging Branches of Psychology

- The interdisciplinary approach to psychology has led to the emergence of various specialised fields, including
  - Aviation psychology
  - Military psychology
  - Rural psychology
  - Managerial psychology
  - Psychology of women
  - Space psychology
  - Forensic psychology
  - Engineering psychology
  - Community psychology
  - Political psychology

Quick Test 4

1. Name some major cognitive processes.
2. Which branch of psychology discusses workplace behaviour including both workers and employers?
3. Name five specialised fields in psychology.
4. Which branch of psychology deals with workplace behaviour?

1.8 Psychology and Other Disciplines

Interdisciplinary Approach Psychology is increasingly recognised as relevant across various disciplines. Researchers and scholars in fields such as science, social science and humanities value psychology in understanding human behaviour.

Major Disciplines Linked to Psychology

Philosophy

- Until the late 19th century, philosophy was responsible for exploring topics like the nature of the mind and understanding motivations and emotions, now studied in psychology.
- In the 19th century, psychologists like Wundt adopted an experimental approach to these topics, leading to the emergence of modern psychology.
- Despite the emergence of psychology as science, it greatly draws from philosophy particularly with respect to methods of knowing and various domains of human nature.

Medicine

- The concept of a healthy mind supporting a healthy body has led to the employment of psychologists in hospitals.
- Psychology and medicine collaborate to prevent health hazards and support treatments.
- Psychologists play a crucial role in counselling patients with critical illnesses (e.g., cancer, AIDS) and those in intensive care or post-operative recovery.

Economics, Political Science and Sociology

- **Economics** Psychology has contributed to understand micro-level economic behaviour, especially in areas like consumer behaviour, savings and decision-making.
- **Political Science** Psychology has helped explore political issues related to power, authority, political conflicts, resolutions and voting behaviour.

- **Sociology** Psychology and sociology together study individual behaviour within different socio-cultural contexts. The collaboration helps address socialisation, group dynamics, collective behaviour and intergroup conflicts.

Computer Science

- Psychology and computer science intersect in the study of the human mind, influencing the development of computer systems.
- Both fields have advanced cognitive sciences, as computer scientists work on making computers more intelligent, capable of sensing and feeling, similar to human experiences.

Law and Criminology

- Lawyers and criminologists rely on psychology in many aspects such as to find reliability of witness memory, signs of guilt/deception, fair punishment, factors influence jury decisions.
- Psychologists conduct research to address these issues, providing valuable insights that may guide legal systems in the future.

Mass Communication

- Psychology plays a role in understanding how the media shapes children's attitudes and behaviours.
- Psychological principles also help improve communication strategies, making media messages more effective. For instance, a news story supported by psychological insights can have a greater impact.

Music and Fine Arts

- Music and psychology intersect in various areas, such as the use of music to enhance work performance.
- A significant area of research is the relationship between music and emotions.
- In India, musicians have started Music Therapy, using different ragas for curing certain physical ailments.

Architecture and Engineering

- Architects use psychological principles to design spaces that meet both mental and physical needs of clients.
- Engineers incorporate human habits and behaviour into their designs, ensuring safety and functionality.
- Psychological knowledge is also valuable in the design of mechanical devices and displays to enhance user experience.

1.9 Psychology in Everyday Life

- Psychology is not just an academic subject but a practical tool for solving various personal and social problems.
- These problems can range from individual challenges (e.g., dealing with an alcoholic parent or a difficult child) to broader societal issues (e.g., lack of family communication, terrorist groups, socially isolated communities).
- Problems in areas like education, health, the environment, women's issues, social justice and intergroup relations often have psychological roots. They stem from unhealthy thinking, negative attitudes and undesirable behaviour patterns.
- A psychological analysis can help to deepen the understanding of these problems and to find effective solutions.

Role of Media in Solving the Problems of Everyday Life

- The media plays a crucial role in addressing everyday problems. Counsellors and therapists on TV offer solutions to various issues faced by children, adolescents, adults and the elderly.
- The media also tackles important social problems, including issues related to social change, population, poverty, violence and environmental degradation.
- Psychologists now contribute actively by designing and implementing intervention programmes that help improve people's quality of life. They work in various settings like schools, hospitals, prisons, military organisations and businesses to address their issues.

Defensive Behaviour and Importance of Psychology in Everyday Life

- Some individuals have an inflated sense of self-worth and reject feedback that contradicts their self-image, leading to defensive behaviour.
- Conversely, some people develop a habit of constantly putting themselves down, which hinders personal growth.
- A balanced, positive understanding of oneself is essential for growth. Psychological principles can be used positively to develop good study habits, enhance memory and improve decision-making.
- Psychology also helps in managing stress, particularly in high-pressure situations like exams.
- Overall, knowledge of psychology is beneficial in daily life, promoting both personal development and social harmony.

Quick Test 5

1. When did psychology emerge as a separate discipline from philosophy?
2. Name the economists who used data on consumer sentiments to predict economic growth.
3. Who developed the experiment as an approach towards philosophy?
4. Name the factors that together explain and understand the behaviour of individuals.
5. Which discipline can help in developing strategies for better communication?

NCERT Folder

1. What is behaviour? Give examples of overt and covert behaviour?

Ans. Behaviour refers to any response of an organism that can be measured.

Behaviours may be overt or covert. Overt behaviour can be outwardly seen or sensed by an observer. Some behaviours are internal or covert. All overt and covert behaviours are associated with or triggered by some stimulus in the environment or changes that happen internally.

Examples of Overt Behaviour

- Blinking of eyes when a stone is hurled at a person.
- Withdrawing the hand immediately after touching a hot pan.

Examples of Covert Behaviour

- The twitching of hand muscles while playing a game of chess.
- Pounding of heart during an interview.

2. How can you distinguish scientific psychology from the popular notions about the discipline of psychology?

Competency Based Que.

Ans. Following are the distinctions between scientific psychology and popular notion about psychology

	Scientific Psychology	Popular Notion about Psychology
(i)	It is based on scientific study of psychological phenomenon.	It uses common sense knowledge to understand behaviour.
(ii)	It explains the psychological phenomenon systematically on the basis of empirical data.	It explains the phenomenon on the basis of experiences, sayings or beliefs.
(iii)	It studies the patterns of behaviour that can be predicted before they occur.	It explains events in hindsight after they occur.

3. Give a brief account of the evolution of psychology.

Ans. Psychology is influenced to a large extent by Western developments. It grew out of ancient philosophy concerned with questions of psychological significance. Formal beginning of modern psychology is traced back to 1879 when the first experimental laboratory was established in Leipzig, Germany by Wilhelm Wundt.

It emerges as a scientific discipline in the following phases

- **Structuralism** The initial approach to study psychology was based on introspection or structuralism in which the individuals were asked to describe their experiences.
- **Functionalism** It was developed by an American psychologist William James. Functionalists studied the working of the mind and the impact of behaviour upon people's interaction with their environment.
- **Behaviourism** It was proposed by John B Watson who viewed psychology as the science of behaviour and behaviour could be described objectively in terms of Stimuli and Responses (S-R). This approach proposed that mentalist concepts such as consciousness, image or mind cannot be measured or studied objectively and scientifically.
- **Gestalt Psychology** It was a revolt against structuralism, founded in Germany by Wertheimer, Kohler and Koffka. It focussed on perceptual organisation (organisation of what we see) and they also demonstrated the laws of perceptual organisation.
- **Psychoanalysis** It was proposed by Dr. Sigmund Freud. He viewed human behaviour as a dynamic manifestation of unconscious desires and conflicts of which we are not aware at present.
- **Humanism** It was advocated by Carl Rogers and Abraham Maslow. They emphasised on the free will of human beings i.e. people are free to do whatever they choose to do and their natural striving to grow and unfold their inner potential.
- **Cognitive Perspective/Constructivism** This perspective is a combination of Gestalt approach and structuralist approach. This approach focuses on cognition i.e. how we know the world through thinking, understanding, perceiving, memorising and problem solving, etc.

4. What are the problems for which collaboration of psychologists with other disciplines can be fruitful? Take any two problems to explain.

Ans. Psychologists acknowledge the relevance of other disciplines in understanding human behaviour. It is located at the intersection of many fields of knowledge pertaining to human functioning. The problems for which collaboration of psychologists with other disciplines can be fruitful are as follows

- The psychologists play significant role in preventing people from engaging in health hazardous behaviours and in adhering to the prescribed doctors' regimen. A successful doctor looks at the psychological as well as physical well-being of the patients.

- While dealing with a criminal case, it is important for a lawyer or a criminologist to understand the psychology of a witness or the criminal. It is also necessary to decide the degree of punishment valid for a crime. Thus, it is important for a lawyer or a criminologist to have the knowledge of psychology in order to regulate the legal system of a country.

Hence, psychology contributes to the growth of other disciplines and draws subject matter from them as well. In the study of brain and behaviour, psychology shares its knowledge with neurology, physiology, biology, medicine and computer science.

In studying the meaning, growth and the development of human behaviour in a socio-cultural context, psychology shares its knowledge with anthropology, sociology, social work, political science and economics.

5. Differentiate between

(i) A psychologist and a psychiatrist

(ii) A counsellor and a clinical psychologist

Ans. (i) The differences between psychologist and psychiatrist are as follows

Psychologist	Psychiatrist
A psychologist deals with the psychological phenomenon.	A psychiatrist deals with serious mental problems.
His/her main work is research in psychology and formulation of psychological conclusions that are derived on the basis of data.	A psychiatrist studies the causes, treatment and prevention of psychological disorders.
A psychologist holds a masters degree in psychology and is mainly into academic and research fields.	A psychiatrist holds a medical degree and he/she can use medical treatment to cure the patients.

(ii) Following are some differences between counsellor and a clinical psychologist

Counsellor	Clinical Psychologist
A counsellor deals with the causes, treatment and prevention of different types of psychological disorders, which are related to motivational and emotional problems.	A clinical psychologist provides therapy for behavioural problems, which are related to mental disorders.
Counsellors help people in vocational rehabilitation programmes, making professional choices and adjusting to new situations in life.	Clinical psychologists conduct interviews and administer psychological tests to diagnose various problems.
A counsellor deals with different types of psychological disorders in everyday life of the patient.	A clinical psychologist deals with specific and complicated psychological disorders.

6. Describe some of the areas of everyday life where understanding of psychology can be put to practice.

Ans. Some of the areas of everyday life where understanding of psychology can be put into practice are as follows

- Psychology helps to understand various personal problems like family, marriage and work sphere. It also helps to deal with larger problems related to community and society.
- Psychology enables an individual to understand oneself in a balanced and positive way without being reactionary, in order to deal with everyday challenges and meet with personal expectations.
- Understanding of psychology further helps in analysing the various social, economic and political problems that affect an individual's life and their solution at individual and collective level.
- Psychology helps in understanding the cause of violence and need for cooperation that makes people wise, which improves the societal relationships by avoiding conflict, frustration and aggression.
- Psychological analysis also enables in decision-making for various spheres and cultivating healthy lifestyles. Therefore, the understanding of psychology enables a person to build stronger relationships at community level and improves the strength at individual level in order to meet daily challenges and obstacles.

7. How can knowledge of the field of environmental psychology be used to promote environment friendly behaviour?

Ans. Environmental psychology studies the interaction between natural and man-made environment and human behaviour. The knowledge of environmental psychology is helpful to promote environment friendly behaviour because

- It studies the interaction of physical factors such as temperature, humidity, pollution and natural disaster on human behaviour.
- It analyses the influence of physical arrangements at work place on the health, emotional state and interpersonal relations of the individual.
- Issues like disposal of waste, population explosion, conservation of energy, etc. are related with behaviour of human beings as well as its consequence.
- Thus, an understanding of human behaviour in relation to environment generates awareness and inculcates safe environmental practices.

8. In terms of helping solve an important social problem such as crime, which branch of psychology do you think is most suitable. Identify the field and discuss the concerns of the psychologists working in this field. Competency Based Que.

Ans. Crime is a social problem, therefore social psychology is most suitable branch for the purpose of solving the problem of crime. It explores the thought process of people and their influence upon others and evaluates the impact of social environment upon the actions of an individual.

Social psychologists are concerned with topics like attitudes, conformity and obedience to authority, interpersonal attraction, helpful behaviour, prejudice, aggression, social motivation and inter-group relations.

A skilled lawyer and a criminologist must have clear knowledge about the factors important in holding a culprit responsible for his action, how well the witness remembers an accident, what are the dependable signs of guilt and falsehood, the degree of punishment for a criminal act etc.

Now a number of psychologists are researching on such issues which will help the legal system of the country in future.

Exam Pattern Questions

Objective Type Questions

Multiple Choice Questions (MCQs)

1. Scientific knowledge is based on

(a) counselling
(b) behaviour
(c) observation
(d) consciousness

2. The first Psychological Department in India was set up in

(a) 1949 (b) 1953
(c) 1916 (d) 1848

3. The humanistic approach to psychology was developed mainly by

(a) Abraham Maslow (b) Carl Wright
(c) JB Watson (d) Max Muler

4. The behaviourist school of psychology was founded by

(a) JB Watson (b) Wertheimer
(c) Freud (d) Maslow

5. The School of Structuralism was established by

(a) Wilhelm Wundt (b) JB Watson
(c) Elton Meyo (d) William James

6. The famous book 'Principles of Psychology is written by

(a) Wilhelm Wundt
(b) JB Watson
(c) Elton Meyo
(d) William James

7. Which of the following is true about Introspection?

(a) Individuals are asked to describe in detail, their own physical experiences.
(b) It is a component of dissociative Identity disorder.
(c) Individuals are asked to describe in detail, their own mental processes or experiences.
(d) None of the above

8. An American psychologist, William James, developed functionalist approach to

(a) study human mind
(b) to find diversity in society
(c) analyse the function of psychology
(d) to explore variety of human feelings

9. In the early 20th century, a new perspective called Gestalt psychology emerged in ……… as a reaction to the structuralism of Wundt.

(a) England (b) Germany
(c) France (d) USA

10. Rahul has a very high thinking, understanding, perceiving, memorising, problem-solving and a host of other mental processes by which his knowledge of the world develops. Which of the following term best describe Rahul's ability?

(a) Smartness
(b) Sharpness
(c) Constructivism
(d) Cognition

11. Nowadays psychologist play an active role in designing and executing intervention programmes in order to provide people CBSE DIKSHA

(a) better quality of life
(b) negative attitude
(c) undesirable patterns of behaviour
(d) social justice

12. Popular theories often conflict against those based on scientific knowledge as they are based on CBSE DIKSHA

(a) Common sense (b) Scientific theories
(c) Social theories (d) Psychological theories

13. Which branch of psychology studies the physical, social and psychological changes that occur throughout life? CBSE DIKSHA

(a) Biological psychology (b) Health psychology
(c) Social psychology (d) Development psychology

14. Which of the following in compasses the work of community psychologists? CBSE DIKSHA

(a) Problems related to community mental health
(b) Selection of employees to work for agencies and organisations
(c) Drug rehabilitation programmes for community and establishing mental health centre
(d) Both (a) and (c)

15. Rita is in a difficult situation while playing chess. She is thinking of various moods she can experiment with. What kind of behaviour is she demonstrating? CBSE DIKSHA

(a) Simple behaviour (b) Covert behaviour
(c) Complex behaviour (d) Overt behaviour

16. .... provide the theories through research where as basic psychology is related to application according to needs. CBSE DIKSHA

(a) Applied psychology (b) Clinical psychology
(c) Social psychology (d) Organisational psychology

17. Due to some issue Aroma visited a Psychologist in her society. Psychologist focused on the relationship between behaviour and the physical system, including the brain and the rest of the nervous system etc. Identify the branch to which the Psychologist belongs to ....

(a) Cognitive psychology
(b) Biological psychology
(c) Developmental psychology
(d) Social psychology

18. Which of the following is/are true regarding the relationship between mind and behaviour?

(i) Using positive visualisation techniques and feeling positive emotions, one can bring about significant changes in bodily processes.

(ii) A new discipline called psychoneuroimmunology has emerged which emphasises the role played by the mind in strengthening the immune system.

(iii) Psychological counsellor treat patients suffering from AIDS and the physically challenged or handling patients in the intensive care unit and during post operative case.

Codes

(a) Only I is true
(b) I and II are true
(c) I, II and III are true
(d) II and III are true

19. Which of the following best describes children's hardiness in the study conducted by Alex?

(a) Commitment, control, challenge
(b) Challenge, control, calmness
(c) Commitment, confidence, control
(d) Control, commitment, conviction

20. Which of the following is associated with the study conducted by Alex?

(a) Past experience (b) Common sense
(c) Future perspectives (d) None of these

21. After conducting the study Alex found out which of the following points?

(a) The scientific knowledge generated by psychology often runs against common sense.
(b) Common sense is always true.
(c) Psychology and common sense have same notions.
(d) All of the above

22. Which of the following is true about the study conducted by Alex?

(a) Alex took three groups of children for study.
(b) All the groups were equal in intelligence.
(c) The first group was much smarter that the rest.
(d) The first group was given easy problems which they were always able to solve.

23. Which of the following statements is/are true regarding Gestalt psychology?

I. Gestalt psychology emerged in reaction to the structuralism of Wundt.

II. It emphasises the study of consciousness as an ongoing mental stream.

III. It argues that our experience is more than the sum of its parts.

IV. It focused primarily on unconscious desires and conflicts.

Codes

(a) I and III (b) II and IV
(c) I and IV (d) III and II

24. Which one of the following is true regarding behaviourism?

I. Behaviourism was introduced by Sigmund Freud in response to Gestalt psychology.
II. John Watson emphasised the study of observable and measurable behaviours.
III. It rejected introspection as unscientific.
IV. Skinner applied the principles of behaviourism to a wide range of situations.

Codes

(a) I and III (b) II and III (c) II and IV (d) III and IV

25. Which of the following correctly describes the cognitive perspective of psychology?

I. It emphasises understanding mental processes like thinking, perception and problem-solving.
II. Cognitive psychologists view the human mind as a biological structure only.
III. It includes studying how knowledge develops through interaction with the environment.
IV. Vygotsky suggested that social and cultural processes play no role in mental development.

Codes

(a) I and II (b) I and III (c) II and IV (d) III and IV

26. A psychologist collaborates with neuroscientists to study how neurotransmitters influence behaviour. Which branch of psychology is involved?

I. Cognitive Psychology
II. Biological Psychology
III. Neuropsychology
IV. Health Psychology

Codes

(a) II and III (b) I and IV
(c) II and IV (d) III and IV

27. A school psychologist designs programmes to enhance the emotional and intellectual development of children with special needs. This field is related to

I. Educational psychology
II. Health psychology
III. Clinical psychology
IV. School psychology

Codes

(a) I and IV (b) III and IV
(c) II and III (d) I and III

Assertion-Reason Questions

Direction (Q. Nos. 28-33) In the following questions, a statement of Assertion (A) is followed by a statement of Reason (R). Mark the correct choice from the options given below.

(a) Both A and R are true and R is the correct explanation of A.
(b) Both A and R are true, but R is not the correct explanation of A.
(c) A is true, but R is false.
(d) A is false, but R is true.

28. **Assertion** (A) Psychology can be defined as a scientific discipline which deals with processes (mental processes) underlying human experience and behaviour.

Reason (R) It studies the range of phenomena spread over several levels, *viz.* individual, dyadic (two person) group and organisational.

29. **Assertion** (A) Theory is a set of statements about how a certain complex phenomenon can be explained with the help of interrelated propositions.

Reason (R) Theory that offers a tentative explanation of how a certain phenomenon takes place.

30. **Assertion** (A) Psychology uses methods primarily from biological sciences to explain mental processes and human behaviour.

Reason (R) Psychology is categorised as a social science discipline, making it primarily focused on socio-cultural phenomena.

31. **Assertion** (A) Cognitive psychology views the human mind as similar to a computer that processes and stores information.

Reason (R) Cognitive psychology is based on the constructivist theory, which emphasises that the mind actively constructs itself through exploration.

32. **Assertion** (A) Indian psychology was initially dominated by Western psychological traditions.

Reason (R) Indian psychologists were significantly influenced by Western theories, particularly in experimental psychology and psychoanalysis.

33. **Assertion** (A) Psychology can be a significant tool for solving personal and interpersonal problems.

Reason (R) The study of psychology helps individuals make better decisions, improve learning and memory, and deal with stress, such as that caused by exams.

Answers

1. (c) observation
2. (c) 1916
3. (a) Abraham Maslow
4. (a) JB Watson
5. (a) Wilhelm Wundt
6. (d) William James
7. (c) Individuals are asked to describe in detail, their own mental processes or experiences.
8. (a) study human mind
9. (b) Germany
10. (d) Cognition
11. (a) better quality of life
12. (a) Common sense
13. (d) Development psychology
14. (d) Both (a) and (c)
15. (b) Covert behaviour
16. (a) Applied phychology
17. (b) Biological psychology
18. (c) I, II and III are true
19. (a) Commitment, control, challenge
20. (b) Common sense
21. (a) The scientific knowledge generated by psychology often runs against common sense.
22. (d) The first group was given easy problems which they were always able to solve.
23. (a) I and III
24. (c) II and IV
25. (b) I and III
26. (a) II and III
27. (a) I and IV
28. (b) Both A and R are true, but R is not the correct explanation of A.
29. (c) A is true, but R is false.
30. (b) Both A and R are true, but R is not the correct explanation of A.
31. (b) Both A and R are true, but R is not the correct explanation of A.
32. (a) Both A and R is true and R is the correct explanation of A.
33. (a) Both A and R are true and R is the correct explanation of A.

Subjective Questions

Very Short Answer Type Questions

1. What is Psychology? **CBSE DIKSHA**

***Or* Define the term psychology.**

Ans. The term psychology is derived from two Greek words 'psyche' meaning soul and 'logos' meaning science or study of a subject. Thus, psychology is a study of the soul or mind.

Now psychology can be defined as a scientific discipline which deals with processes (mental processes, experiences and behaviour) dealing with human experience and behaviour.

2. Suppose you are a psychologist, how would you define experiences in psychology? **Competency Based Que.**

Ans. According to psychologists experiences are subjective in nature. We cannot directly observe or know someone else's experience. Only the experiencing person can be aware or conscious of her or his experiences. The nature of experience is influenced by internal and the external conditions of the experiencer.

3. What do you know about introspective methods?

Ans. Introspection was a procedure in which individuals or subjects in psychological experiments were asked to describe in detail their own mental processes or experiences.

4. What was the focus of Gestalt psychology?

Ans. It focussed on the organisation of perceptual experiences. Instead of looking at the components of the mind, the Gestalt psychologists argued that our experience is more than the inputs received from our environment.

5. Define psychology in term of Watson.

Ans. Watson defined psychology as a study of behaviour or responses (to stimuli) which can be measured and studied objectively.

6. What do you mean by cognitive perspective?

Ans. Cognitive perspective is the process which involves thinking, understanding, perceiving, knowing, memorising and problem-solving. It is a host of other mental processes by which our knowledge of the world develops and make us able to deal with the environment in specific ways.

7. Define evolutionary psychology.

Ans. Evolutionary psychology is a branch, in which social and natural sciences examines psychological structure from a modern evolutionary perspective.

8. Define the beginning of modern era of Indian psychology.

Ans. The modern era of Indian psychology began in the Department of Philosophy (1916) at Calcutta University where the first syllabus of experimental psychology was introduced and the first psychology laboratory was established in 1915.

9. What is biological psychology?

Ans. Biological psychology focuses on the relationship between behaviour and the physical system. It includes the brain and the rest of the nervous system, the immune system and genetics.

10. Explain the importance of health psychology.

Ans. Health psychology focuses on the role of psychological factors (e.g. stress, anxiety) in the development, prevention and treatment of illness. Areas of interest for a health psychologist are stress and coping, the relationship between psychological factors and health, patient-doctor relationship and ways of enhancing or promoting health factors.

11. What is school psychology?

Ans. School psychology focuses on designing programmes that promote intellectual, social and emotional development of children, including those with special needs. The knowledge of psychology was applied in school setting.

12. Define the concept of sport psychology.

Ans. Sport psychology applies psychological principles to improve sports performance by enhancing their motivation. Sports psychology is a relatively new field but is gaining acceptance worldwide.

13. How did modern psychology begin?

Ans. Formal beginning of modern psychology is traced back to 1879 when the first experimental laboratory was established in Leipzig, Germany by Wilhelm Wundt.

14. Write the application of psychology in the field of medicine.

Ans. Doctors use psychological counselling for treating patients suffering from cancer and the physically challenged or handling patients in the Intensive Care Unit and patients during post operative care.

Short Answer Type Questions

1. Explain the mental processes and its significance in study of psychology.

Ans. Mental processes are activities of the mind and brain, related to cognition. We use mental processes when we think or remember something or solve a problem.

However, these mental activities are different from neural activities, though they are mutually overlapping processes. The mind emerges and evolves as our interactions and experiences in this world get dynamically organised in the form of a system which is responsible for the occurrence of various mental processes.

Significance of Mental Processes

Mental processes, such as remembering, learning, knowing, perceiving, feeling are of interest to psychologists. They study these processes to understand how the mind works and to help us improve the uses and applications of these mental capacities.

2. Describe the term experiences.

Ans. Experiences can be defined as the learning acquired through everyday life situation.

It is described as follows

- Experiences are subjective in nature and different for every individual.
- We cannot directly observe or know someone else's experience.
- Only the experiencing person can be aware or conscious of his/her experiences. Thus, experiences are embedded in our awareness or consciousness.
- Experiences are influenced by internal and external conditions of the experiencer.
- The nature of the experience can only be understood by analysing a complex set of internal and external conditions.
- Experiences are important because most of our learning is based on experiences.

3. Explain the emergence of psychology as a science.

Ans. Although psychology is a very old knowledge discipline but it is a young science. The first laboratory of psychology was founded in 1879 in Leipzig. However, what kind of science is psychology, still remains a matter of debate, particularly because of the new interfaces of it, that have emerged in recent times.

Along with other countries, in India, psychology is a subject of study offered in the faculty of science, both at the undergraduate and post-graduate levels. Neuroscience and Computer Science are two emerging disciplines from psychology. EEG, FMRI, etc. are the fast developing brain imaging techniques which make it possible to study brain processes in real time.

Similarly, in IT areas, both human-computer interaction and artificial intelligence cannot possibly grow without psychological knowledge in cognitive processes.

4. Discuss the humanistic perspective on human behaviour.

Ans. Humanists, such as Carl Rogers and Abraham Maslow emphasised on the free will of human beings and their natural striving to grow and unfold their inner potential. They argued that behaviourism with its emphasis on behaviour as determined by environmental conditions undermines human freedom and dignity and takes a mechanistic view of human nature.

These different approaches filled the history of modern psychology and provided multiple perspectives to its development. There are strengths as well as weaknesses in each approach. Some of these approaches have led to further developments in the discipline.

5. How educational psychology and school psychology differ from each other?

Ans. Educational psychology studies how people of all ages learn. Educational psychologists primarily help develop instructional methods and materials used to train people in both educational and work settings. They are also concerned with research on issues of relevance for education, counselling and learning problems.

Whereas school psychology focuses on designing programmes that promote intellectual, social and emotional development of children, including those with special needs. Psychologists try to apply knowledge of psychology in a school setting.

6. Discuss the role of mass communication in psychology.

Ans. The print and the electronic media have affected our lives in many ways. It has a major influence on our thinking, attitudes and our emotions.

The impact of the media on the formation of attitudes of children and their behaviour is a domain where both these disciplines come together. Psychology helps in developing strategies for better and effective communication. A story reported by a journalist will be more penetrating if it is based upon a background of psychological knowledge and insight.

7. Varisha studies in senior secondary and wants to be a journalist. How the knowledge of psychology would help her to become a professional journalist? **Competency Based Que.**

Ans. To become professional journalist, Varisha must have knowledge of psychology. It is because with the help of psychological knowledge she would capture the events in which people are more interested. In mass communication industry, a journalist in reporting news must know the reader's interests in the story.

Every person has a different taste and interest thus, being a journalist it is needed that he/she must be acquainted about peoples' interests and demands. As psychology studies behaviour, experience and mental processes of people thus, its knowledge helps people and organisations to grow and become professionals.

8. Discuss the various streams in psychology.

Ans. Psychology as a discipline today has two parallel streams

- It makes use of the method in physical and biological sciences. In this case, psychology considers itself as a discipline, which focuses largely on biological principles to explain human behaviour.

  It assumes that all behavioural phenomena have causes which can be discovered if we can collect data systematically under controlled conditions. Here the aim of the researcher is to know cause and effect relationship so that a prediction of the behavioural phenomenon can be made and behaviour can be controlled.
- It makes use of the method of social and cultural sciences in studying various psychological and social phenomena. Psychology as a social science focuses on how behavioural phenomena can be explained in terms of the interaction that takes place between the person and the socio-cultural context of which she/he is a part. Each behavioural phenomenon is assumed to have multiple causes.

9. Explain the development of psychology as natural science.

Ans. Psychology has its roots in philosophy. However, modern psychology has developed because of the application of the scientific method to study psychological phenomenon. Science places a great deal of emphasis on objectivity.

Psychology influenced by Descartes and later on by the developments in physics has grown by following a Hypothetico-Deductive Model. The model suggests that scientific advancement can take place if you have a theory to explain a phenomenon.

For example, physicists Big-bang theory to explain how the universe came to be formed. Theory is nothing else but a set of statements about how a certain complex phenomenon can be explained with the help of propositions which are interrelated.

Based on a theory, scientists deduce or propose a hypothesis that offers a tentative explanation of how a certain phenomenon takes place. The hypothesis then is tested and proved true or false based on empirical data that one has gathered. The theory is revised if data gathered point in a different direction than the one suggested by the hypothesis.

10. How psychology is recognised as a social science?

Ans. Psychology is recognised more as a social science because it studies the behaviour of human beings in their socio-cultural contexts. Humans are not only influenced by their socio-cultural contexts but they also create them. Psychology as a social science discipline focuses on humans as social beings. If there are two different persons who grew up in different families under complex social and cultural conditions i.e. we can see some regularity in the relationship of their nature, experience and mental processes with their social and physical environment.

But at the same time, there may be some variations in their behaviours and experiences which would be difficult to predict using the known psychological principles. Psychology deals with human behaviour and experience in the context of their society and culture.

11. Explain briefly the concept of Gestalt psychology.

Ans. In the early 20th century, a new perspective called Gestalt psychology emerged in Germany as a reaction to the structuralism of Wundt. It focused on the organisation of perceptual experiences. Instead of looking at the components of the mind, the Gestalt psychologists argued that when we look at the world, our perceptual experience is more than the sum of the components of the perception. In her words, what we experience is more than the inputs received from our environment.

For example, when light from a series of flashing bulbs falls on our retina, we actually experience movement of light. When we see a movie, we actually have a series of rapidly moving images of still pictures falling on our retina. Thus, our perceptual experience is more than the elements.

12. Explain the modern era of Indian psychology in brief.

Ans. The Indian philosophical tradition is rich in mental processes and reflections on human consciousness, self, mind-body relations and a variety of mental functions. The development of psychology as a discipline in India continues to be dominated by Western psychology. The development of psychology as a discipline in India is explained below

- The modern era of Indian psychology began in the Department of Philosophy (1916) at Calcutta University. Here the first syllabus of experimental psychology was introduced and the first psychology laboratory was established in 1915.
- Another Department of Applied Psychology in Calcutta University was set up in 1938.
- The beginning of modern experimental psychology at Calcutta University was greatly influenced by the Indian psychologist Dr N.N. Sengupta who was trained in USA in the experimental tradition of Wilhelm Wundt.
- Professor Bose was trained in Freudian psychoanalysis. He established Indian Psychoanalytical Association in 1922. Departments of psychology in the Universities of Mysore and Patna were other early centres of teaching and research in psychology.
- There are two centres of excellence in psychology supported by the UGC at Utkal University, Bhubaneswar and at the University of Allahabad. About 70 universities in India offer courses in psychology.

13. Discuss the significance of clinical and counselling psychology.

Ans. Clinical and counselling psychology deals with causes, treatment and prevention of different types of psychological disorders such as anxiety, depression, eating disorders and chronic substance abuse.

Counselling aims to improve everyday functioning by helping people to solve problems in daily living and cope more effectively with challenging situations. A counselling psychologist sometimes deals with people who have less serious problems.

In many instances, counselling psychologists work with students, advising them about personal problems and career planning. Like, psychiatrists, clinic psychologist also study the causes, treatment and prevention of psychological disorders.

14. Describe the evolutionary psychology in brief.

Ans. Evolutionary psychology is an approach in social and natural sciences that examines psychological structure from a modern evolutionary perspective.

This approach is described below

- It seeks to identify which human psychological traits are involved in adaptations i.e. the functional products of natural selection or sexual selection.
- The goal of research in evolutionary psychology is to discover and understand the design of the human mind.
- It is a theoretical approach to psychology that attempts to explain useful mental and psychological traits such as memory, perception or language as adaptations i.e. as the functional products of natural selection.
- The purpose of this approach is to bring the functional way of thinking about biological mechanism such as the immune system into the field of psychology.
- It focussed on how evolution has shaped the mind and behaviour.

15. Explain the linkage of economics, political science and sociology with psychology.

Ans. Economics, political science and sociology have drawn considerably from psychology and have enriched it as well.

- Psychology has contributed a great deal to the study of micro-level economic behaviour, particularly in understanding consumer behaviour, savings behaviour and in decision making. American economists have used data on consumer sentiments to predict economic growth. Three scholars who have worked on such problems have received the Nobel Prize in Economics, namely H Simon, D Kahneman and T Schelling.
- Like economics, political science too draws considerably from psychology, particularly, in understanding issues related to exercise of power and authority, nature of political conflicts and their resolutions and voting behaviour.
- Sociology and psychology come together to explain and understand the behaviour of individuals within different socio-cultural contexts. Issues related to socialisation, group and collective behaviour and intergroup conflicts gain from both these disciplines.

16. "Psychology like other sciences attempts to develop principles of behaviour and mental processes." Discuss. Competency Based Que.

Ans. Understanding and explanation of behaviour, mental events and processes is the main concern in research nowadays.

The psychologists draw conclusions which are supported by data. They design and conduct experiments or studies under controlled conditions on a wide range of psychological phenomena to develop general principles about behaviour and mental processes. The conclusions drawn on the basis of such studies are universal. Experimental, comparative, physiological, developmental, social, differential and abnormal psychology are generally regarded as domains representing basic psychology.

17. The Euro-American psychological models and theories are not accepted by all. Explain the statement in context of human psychology.

Ans. There are psychologists who believe that most psychological theories and models are Euro-American in nature and therefore, do not help us in understanding behaviours in other cultural settings. Psychologists from Asia, Africa and Latin America have been critical of Euro-American approaches which are propagated as universal.

A similar critique is made by feminists who argue that psychology offers a male perspective and ignores the perspective of women. They argue in favour of a dialectical approach which will accommodate both male and female perspectives in understanding human behaviour.

18. "Human behaviour can be controlled and modified through the application of psychological principles." Elucidate. Competency Based Que.

Ans. Concern of psychologists arises from their desire to develop techniques or methods that will improve the quality of human life.

It requires removal of certain difficulties or adverse conditions that individuals experience in different phases of their life. Consequently, psychologists make certain interventions into the lives of needy people.

Applied role of psychologists has brought the subject closer to the life of people in general than other social science subjects and in knowing the limits of the applicability of its principles.

Thus, several independent branches of psychology have emerged that try to use psychological theories, principles and facts to diagnose and resolve problems related to industrial and organisational settings, clinical services, education, environment, health, community development and so on.

19. Praveen is a student of Class XI and he thinks that he is weak in studies as compared to others. He cannot perform good in any field. How psychologist can help Praveen in solving this problem? Competency Based Que.

Ans. In order to help Praveen, psychologist may use different method and approach. First of all psychologist must analyse the problem of Praveen.

He is mainly suffering from inferiority and poor self-confidence. Therefore, he must talk to him and try to realise him that he is not inferior or weak than any one in his class.

The most important thing psychologist should help in regarding his self-confidence. He should acknowledged about his immense potential.

This can be done with the help of giving lot of example of about successful and other personal experience of life.

20. How psychology helps to develop good habits of study for improving one's learning and memory? CBSE DIKSHA

Ans. Psychology helps to develop good habits of study for improving once learning and memory in the following ways

- **Improves Focus** Psychological principles help individuals concentrate better on their studies, reducing distractions.
- **Effective Memory Techniques** Psychology provides strategies like spaced repetition and mnemonic devices to enhance memory retention.
- **Time Management** It offers methods for organising study time efficiently, ensuring optimal learning.

- **Motivation Enhancement** Psychological approaches help increase motivation to study, making learning more consistent and focused.
- **Stress Management** It teaches how to manage stress and anxiety related to studying, helping improve cognitive functioning.

21. Explain how psychology helps in solving one's personal and interpersonal problems. CBSE DIKSHA

Ans. Psychology helps in solving one's personal and interpersonal problems in the following ways

- **Self-Awareness** Psychology promotes self-awareness, helping individuals understand their own emotions and behaviour patterns.
- **Communication Skills** It provides tools for effective communication, improving personal and interpersonal relationships.
- **Conflict Resolution** Psychology helps in resolving conflicts by offering strategies for compromise and understanding different perspectives.
- **Emotional Regulation** It teaches how to manage and express emotions in healthy ways, leading to better personal interactions.
- **Problem-Solving Techniques** It equips individuals with decision-making skills, aiding in the resolution of personal challenges.

22. What are the ways by which psychology helps to reduce or alleviate the stress of examination? CBSE DIKSHA

Ans. Psychology helps to reduce or alleviate the stress of examination in the following ways

- **Relaxation Techniques** Psychology offers stress-relief methods such as deep breathing and progressive muscle relaxation.
- **Cognitive Restructuring** It helps individuals reframe negative thoughts about exams, reducing anxiety and boosting confidence.
- **Time Management** Effective study planning and time management techniques help prevent last-minute cramming and reduce exam stress.
- **Positive Reinforcement** Psychology promotes positive thinking, helping students approach exams with a calm, confident mindset.
- **Stress Awareness** It helps individuals understand the nature of stress and how to manage it, leading to a more relaxed approach to exams.

23. How does psychology help in analysing and understanding yourself in relation to others? CBSE DIKSHA

Ans. Psychology help in analysing and understanding yourself in relation to others in the following ways

- **Self-Reflection** Psychology encourages introspection, allowing individuals to understand their thoughts, emotions and behaviours.
- **Perspective-Taking** It helps individuals see situations from other people's viewpoints, improving empathy and social interactions.
- **Social Comparison** Psychology explains the role of comparing oneself to others, helping individuals gain insights into their own behaviours and attitudes.
- **Interpersonal Skills** It teaches skills such as active listening and conflict management, improving relationships with others.
- **Identity Formation** It helps individuals understand their own identity in relation to the social environment, fostering better self-understanding.

24. How does psychology help to maintain a positive and balanced understanding of ourselves? CBSE DIKSHA

Ans. Psychology help to maintain a positive and balanced understanding of ourselves in the following ways

- **Positive Self-Concept** Psychology promotes the development of a healthy self-esteem and self-image.
- **Emotional Balance** It provides techniques to regulate emotions, leading to a more balanced view of oneself.
- **Cognitive Behavioural Strategies** Helps individuals challenge negative thoughts and replace them with positive affirmations and realistic self-appraisal.
- **Stress Reduction** By managing stress effectively, psychology aids in maintaining emotional balance and avoiding negative self-judgement.
- **Goal Setting and Achievement** Psychology teaches goal-setting techniques that foster a sense of accomplishment, further supporting a positive self-view.

Long Answer Type Questions

1. Discuss the phases of development of modern psychology in India.

Ans. Durganand Sinha in his book 'Psychology in a Third World Country: The Indian Experience', published in 1986 traces the history of modern psychology as a social science in India in four phases. These were

(i) **First Phase** This phase remained till independence. It was a phase with emphasis on experimental, psychoanalytic and psychological testing research. It primarily reflected the development of the discipline in Western countries.

(ii) **Second Phase** This phase remained till the 1960s. It was a phase of expansion of psychology in India into different branches. During this phase, Indian psychologists showed a desire to have an Indian identity by seeking to link Western psychology to the Indian context.

(iii) **Third Phase** It was the post 1960s phase of problem-oriented research in India. In this phase, psychologists became more focused on addressing the problems of the Indian society. Further, the limitations of excessive dependence on Western psychology for our social context were also realised. Leading psychologists emphasised the significance of research, which is of relevance to our situation.

(iv) **Fourth Phase** It was started during the late 1970s and led to search for a new identity of psychology in India. Besides rejecting the Western framework, Indian psychologists stressed the need for developing an understanding based on a framework, which was culturally and socially relevant. This phase is characterised by development in indigenous psychology.

2. Varuna thinks that there are many beliefs and understanding of human behaviour which are not true. Give an example which justifies this statement. Competency Based Que.

Ans. It is true that there are many beliefs and understanding of human behaviour, which are not true. Scientific knowledge generated by psychology often runs against common sense. One such example is a study performed by Dweck (1975). She was concerned with children who gave up too easily when faced with a difficult problem or failure. She wondered how they could be helped.

Common sense tells us to give them easy problems in order to increase their success rate so that their confidence goes up. Only later should we give them difficult problems which they will be able to solve because of their new found confidence. Dweck's study tested this. She took two groups of students who were trained for 25 days in solving math problems. The first group was given easy problems which they were always able to solve. The second group had a mix of easy and difficult problems. Obviously in case of difficult problems, they failed. Whenever this happened Dweck told them that their failure was because they had not tried hard enough and persuaded them not to give up and keep trying. After the training period was over, a new set of math problems were given to the two groups. What Dweck found goes against common belief. Those who had always succeeded because they were given easy problems, gave up much faster when they faced failure than those who had experience of both success and failure and were taught to attributes failure to their lack of effort.

3. How does psychology help in offering solutions in everyday life? CBSE DIKSHA

Ans. Psychology help in offering solutions in everyday life in the following ways

- **Addresses Personal Problems** Psychology helps individuals cope with personal issues like dealing with an alcoholic father or a problem child.
- **Improves Family Dynamics** It helps resolve family-related problems such as lack of communication and interaction among family members.
- **Tackles Social Issues** Provides insights into larger issues like terrorist groups or socially isolated communities, contributing to social cohesion.
- **Educational and Health Issues** Offers solutions for challenges in education, health and environment, helping individuals and communities improve.
- **Promotes Positive Change** Encourages positive thinking and changes in negative attitudes or undesirable behaviours at both individual and group levels.
- **Psychological Interventions** Through psychological analysis, solutions are found for complex problems, helping people understand and manage them better.
- **Media's Role** Media channels, such as television, involve psychologists and therapists who provide guidance on various social problems, benefiting viewers.
- **Professional Support** Psychologists work across various sectors (schools, hospitals, prisons, industries) to design intervention programmes that enhance people's quality of life.
- **Defensive Behaviour Management** Helps in overcoming defensive behaviour or negative self-image by promoting a balanced and positive understanding of oneself.
- **Improvement of Learning and Memory** Psychology offers techniques to improve study habits, learning, and memory, contributing to personal development.
- **Stress Reduction** Provides strategies to manage stress, particularly in high-pressure situations like exams.

Case Based Questions

1. Read the case and answer the questions that follow.

John Watson rejected the ideas of mind and consciousness as subjects of psychology, believing that scientific psychology should focus on observable and verifiable behaviour. He defined psychology as the study of behaviour or responses to stimuli that could be measured objectively. Watson was influenced by Ivan Pavlov's work on classical conditioning, which further supported his view that psychology should examine the relationship between external stimuli and observable behaviour, rather than subjective mental processes.

(i) **According to John Watson, what should psychology focus on? Which of the following best defines Watson's view of psychology?**

(ii) **How did Watson's view of psychology differ from traditional views of psychology?**

Ans. (i) Watson believed that psychology should focus on observable and measurable behaviour. The following points define his view

- Psychology is the study of behaviour.
- Behaviour is a response to stimuli.
- Psychology should examine verifiable responses, not subjective mental processes.
- It focuses on the interaction between stimuli and observable responses.

(ii) Watson's view of psychology differed from traditional approaches like structuralism and introspection because

- Traditional psychology focused on internal mental processes like consciousness.
- Watson rejected the study of the mind and consciousness, arguing that only observable behaviour should be studied.
- He emphasised the importance of behaviour that could be objectively measured and verified, rather than subjective introspection.

2. Read the case and answer the questions that follow.

Psychology is not only a field of study that satisfies our curiosity about human nature, but it also offers solutions to a wide range of problems in everyday life. These problems can range from personal issues, such as a daughter dealing with an alcoholic father, to larger societal issues like terrorism or social isolation. These psychological problems often arise from unhealthy thinking, negative attitudes and undesirable behaviour patterns. By applying psychological principles, we can gain a deeper understanding of these issues and find effective solutions to improve personal and social well-being. Psychologists play an active role in various settings, helping people deal with problems and enhance their quality of life.

(i) **According to the passage, what are some common psychological problems people face in everyday life? Which of the following best summarises these problems?**

(ii) **How do psychologists help in addressing these problems?**

Ans. (i) The passage highlights several psychological problems, including

- Personal problems like a daughter facing an alcoholic father.
- Issues related to unhealthy thinking and negative attitudes.
- Problems at a societal level, such as social isolation or involvement in terrorist groups.
- Behavioral issues like defensive behaviour or poor self-image.

(ii) Psychologists help by

- Applying psychological principles to understand and address these problems.
- Providing interventions to improve personal well-being and behaviour.
- Working in various organisations like schools, hospitals and businesses to enhance people's quality of life.
- Designing programmes to address societal issues such as violence, poverty and social change.

SELF ASSESSMENT TEST

Objective Type Questions

1. The behaviourist theory was first offered by

(a) Freud (b) Watson (c) Skinner (d) Darwin

2. First psychology department in India was established in

(a) Bombay (b) Delhi (c) Kolkata (d) Chennai

3. Who developed psycho analysis?

(a) Watson (b) Ivan Pavlov (c) Sigmund Freud (d) Wundt

4. Which of the following is not a scientific knowledge?

(a) Observation (b) Evidence (c) Data Collection (d) Belief

Very Short Answer Type Questions

1. What is psychology?

2. What do you understand by mental processes?

3. Define the term Gestalt psychology.

4. What is environmental psychology?

5. Define cognition.

Short Answer Type Questions

1. Describe humanistic perspective on human behaviour.

2. Discuss organisational psychology.

3. Differentiate between basic and applied psychology.

4. Explain main fields of specialisation in psychology.

Long Answer Type Questions

1. Differentiate between social psychology and cross-cultural psychology.

2. "Psychology is also recognised more as a social science." Elucidate.

3. Explain some of the themes which provide direction to research and application of psychology.

Case Based Questions

Read the case and answer the questions that follow.

Psychology is also recognised as a social science because it studies the behaviour of human beings in their socio-cultural contexts. For example, Ranjita and Shabnam are classmates from a village. Ranjita comes from a farmer's family, while Shabnam's father works in an office in a town. During the rainy season, Shabnam's house is flooded and she moves into Ranjita's house with her mother and brother. Ranjita helps them feel comfortable in her home and when the floodwaters recede, Ranjita's mother and grandmother help Shabnam's mother set up their house again. This example shows how individuals in communities can be helpful and self-sacrificing in times of crisis. However, this is not always the case, as some people may act in an anti-social manner in similar situations. Psychology, therefore, examines human behaviour in the context of society and culture.

(i) In the given case, what was Ranjita's response when Shabnam's house was flooded? Which of the following defines Ranjita's behaviour?

(ii) What does the passage suggest about human behaviour in crises?

02

CHAPTER

Methodology is what makes psychology a scientific discipline. Psychologists employ various research methods as human behaviour is complex and no single method can address all aspects of it. Common methods in psychological research include observation, experimental research, correlational studies, surveys, psychological testing and case studies.

YOUR STUDY GOALS

2.1 Goals of Psychological Enquiry
2.2 Nature of Psychological Data
2.3 Methods in Psychology
2.4 Analysis of Data
2.5 Limitations of Psychological Enquiry
2.6 Ethical Issues

YOUR PRACTICE GOAL

- Objective Type Questions (24 Qs ; MCQs, A-R)
- Subjective Questions (18 VSAs, 23 SAs, 8 LAs, 3 Case Based)

Method of Enquiry in Psychology

2.1 Goals of Psychological Enquiry

Like all scientific research, psychological inquiry has specific goals. These goals guide the study of human behaviour.

Description

- The primary goal is to describe behaviour accurately for better understanding.
- In a psychological study, behaviours are distinguished from one another through detailed descriptions.
- For instance, if the researcher is observing 'study habits,' they will break it down into observable behaviours like attending classes regularly, submitting assignments on time, sticking to a study schedule, and revising daily.
- Proper description requires recording specific behaviours to understand them more clearly.

Prediction

- The second goal is to predict behaviour.
- By understanding and accurately describing behaviour, psychologists can study the relationship between behaviours and other phenomena.
- Once these relationships are established, psychologists can predict future behaviours under specific conditions.
- For example, a researcher might find a positive relationship between the amount of study time and academic achievement. Based on this, if a student devotes more time to study, it can be predicted that the student will likely perform better in exams.
- Prediction accuracy increases with the increase number of person observed.

Explanation

- The third goal of psychological enquiry is to understand the causal factors or determinants of behaviour.
- Psychologists seek to identify the factors that influence or cause specific behaviours, as well as the conditions under which certain behaviours may not occur.
- For example Why are children more attentive in class than others? Why do some children spend less time studying compared to others? Psychologists aim to identify the conditions (determinants) that lead to certain behaviours, help to establish a cause-effect relationship between variables or events.

Control

- Control refers to the ability to influence behaviour by altering its antecedent conditions. This goal involves
  - Making a behaviour occur (e.g., encouraging more study time)
  - Reducing behaviour (e.g., decreasing study hours)
  - Enhancing behaviour (e.g., increasing study time)
  - For example A student can adjust their study hours based on the desired outcome or psychological treatments and therapies can be used to modify behaviour.

Application

- The final goal is to apply psychological findings to bring about positive changes in people's lives. Psychological research aims to solve real world problems and improve people's quality of life.
- For example, the application of yoga and meditation can help to reduce stress and enhance efficiency in daily life.
- Psychological research also contributes to the development of new theories and constructs, further advancing the field and improving methods for practical applications.

Steps in Conducting Scientific Research

Scientific research follows a systematic and objective approach to study phenomena, ensuring that the findings are testable and reliable. The process involves several key steps

1. Conceptualising a Problem

- Research begins by selecting a topic for study, followed by developing specific research questions or problems. These problems often arise from past research observations or personal experiences.
- The research problems may involve
  - Understanding individual behaviour (e.g. Why do we forget?)
  - Understanding others' behaviour (e.g. Why does someone procrastinate?)

- Studying group influences on behaviour (e.g. Why does performance change when working in a group?)
- Investigating group behaviour (e.g. Why does risk-taking increase in groups?)
- Organisational behaviour (e.g. Why are some organisations more successful than others?)

- The researcher then forms a hypothesis, a tentative answer to the problem, which can later be tested (e.g. "The more time children spend watching violent television, the more aggressive they become").

2. Collecting Data

- The second step involves gathering data. This requires creating a research design or blueprint for the study, addressing the following aspects
  - **Participants** Deciding who will be the part of the study, such as children, adolescents, teachers or patients.
  - **Methods of Data Collection** Choosing methods like observation, experiments, surveys or case studies.
  - **Tools** Deciding on tools (e.g., interviews, questionnaires, observation schedules) for gathering data.
  - **Procedure** Determining how the data will be collected (e.g., individually or in groups).

3. Drawing Conclusions

After collecting data, researchers analyse it using statistical tools and methods, such as graphs, pie charts, and bar diagrams. The goal is to understand the data's meaning and verify whether it supports the hypothesis.

4. Revising Research Conclusions

- Research is an ongoing process. Researchers analyse if their conclusions support the hypothesis. If the conclusions do not support the hypothesis, they revise it or propose an alternative hypothesis.
- Further tests and analysis are conducted and the results are open for verification by future researchers. Thus, research is continuous process, with conclusions and subject to revision and confirmation.

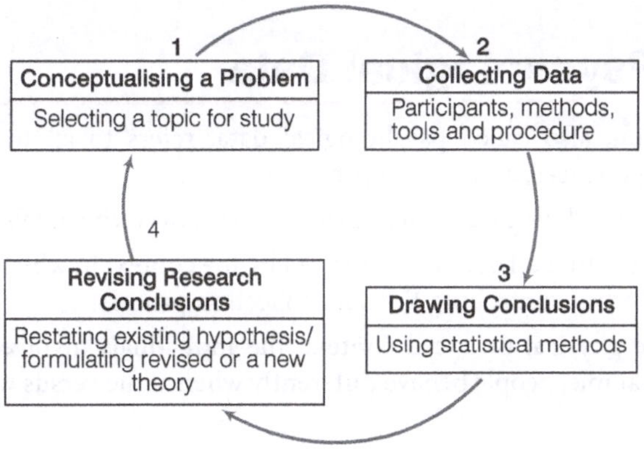

▲ *Steps in Conducting Scientific Enquiry*

Alternative Paradigms of Research

- Psychologists suggest that human behaviour can be studied using methods from sciences like physics, chemistry and biology.
- The key assumption behind this approach is that human behaviour is predictable and influenced by both internal and external forces and can be observed, measured and controlled.
- In most of the twentieth century, psychology focused on the study of overt behaviour and did not focus on personal feelings, experiences or meanings.

Interpretive Method

- The interpretive method is a recent approach that focuses more on understanding than on explaining or predicting behaviour.
- According to this method, the investigation of human behaviour should differ from the methods used in the physical sciences due to the complex and variable[1] nature of human experiences.
- This viewpoint emphasises the importance of how humans interpret events and actions within a specific context.

Examples of this Approach

- The interpretive method is particularly useful in situations involving unique experiences, such as
  - People suffering from external factors like natural disasters (e.g. tsunamis, earthquakes, cyclones).
  - People suffering from internal factors like prolonged illness.
- In such cases, objective measurement of experiences is neither possible nor desirable.
- Everyone interprets reality in their own way, based on their past experiences and the context they are in.
- The mainpurpose of this interpretive approach is to understand the subjective interpretation of reality and to explore different aspects of human experiences and behaviour without disturbing their natural flow.

Quick Test 1

1. Name the goals of psychological enquiry.
2. What is the third goal of psychological enquiry?
3. What is the aim of the interpretive method?
4. Name the second step in scientific research.

2.2 Nature of Psychological Data

- Psychological information, also called psychological data, refers to an individual's covert or overt behaviour, subjective experiences, and mental processes.
- Data plays a crucial role in psychological enquiry as they allow us to verify or falsify our ideas and notions.
- Data are not independent entities. They are influenced by the context in which they are collected and are tied to the method and theory controlling the data collection process.
- Data are affected by the physical or social context, the individuals involved and the time when the behaviour occurs. For example, people behave differently when alone versus when in a group or at home versus at work.
- The method of data collection (e.g. survey, interview, experiment) and the characteristics of the respondents (e.g. individual or group, young or old, male or female, rural or urban) also impact the nature and quality of the data.
- Another important feature of data is that it does not represent absolute reality. Inferences or assumptions are made based on the data.

Types of Psychological Data

- **Demographic Information** This includes personal details such as name, age, gender, birth order, number of siblings, education, occupation, marital status, number of children, locality of residence, caste, religion, parental education, occupation and family income.

1 **Variable** It refers to any measurable conditions, events, characteristics or behaviours that are controlled or observed in a study.

- **Physical Information** This category includes data related to ecological conditions (e.g. hilly, desert, forest areas), economic conditions, housing conditions, room size, facilities available at home, in the neighbourhood and in the schooland modes of transportation.
- **Physiological Data** In some studies, both physical and physiological data are collected. This may include height, weight, heart rate, fatigue levels, Galvanic Skin Resistance (GSR), brain electrical activity (measured by EEG), blood oxygen levels, reaction time, sleep duration, blood pressure, patterns of dreams, salivation rates and running or jumping rates (for animal studies).
- **Psychological Information** This type of data relates to the areas like intelligence, personality, interests, values, creativity, emotions, motivation, psychological disorders, illusions, delusions, hallucinations, perceptual judgement, thought processes, consciousness and subjective experiences.
- **Measurement of Information** The data collected may be crude, in forms like categories (e.g. high/low, yes/no), ranks (e.g. first, second, third) or scores (e.g. 10, 12, 15, 18). Verbal reports, observation records, personal diaries, field notes and archival data are also used. Such types of information are often analysed separately using qualitative methods.

2.3 Methods in Psychology

Psychologists use various methods like observation, experimentation, correlation, surveys, psychological testing and case studies to collect data for different research purposes.

Observational Method

- Observation is a powerful and effective tool for describing behaviour in psychological research.
- Scientific observation differs from everyday observation in several ways.

(i) **Selection** Psychologists do not observe all behaviours they encounter but select specific behaviours for observation. Example If a researcher is interested in how children in Class XI spend their time in school, they might either
  - Prepare a list of activities to observe based on prior knowledge.
  - Observe without preconceptions to discover the activities that occur.

(ii) **Recording** While observing, a researcher records the selected behaviour using different methods, such as marking tallies, taking notes, clicking photographs, recording videos etc.

(iii) **Analysis of Data**
  - After observations are made, psychologists analyse the recorded data to derive meaning.
  - Good observation is a skill; a good observer knows what to look for, who to observe, when and where the observation should be made, how it will be recorded and the methods used for analysing the observed behaviour.

Types of Observation

1. Naturalistic Observation Vs. Controlled Observation

- In naturalistic method the observations are made in natural or real life settings without manipulating or controlling the situation. It is conducted in places like hospitals, homes, schools or daycare centres.
- Many times certain factors that determine behaviour are controlled by the people that are not the focus of their study. This type of observation is called Controlled Laboratory observation which is obtained in laboratory experiments.

2. Non-Participant Observation Vs. Participant Observation

- In non-participant observation, the observer watches the behaviour from a distance and the person being observed may not be aware that they are being observed. Recording a video or sitting at the corner can help in observation.
- The negative aspect of non participant observation is that the presence of an outsider can alter the behaviour of those being observed.
- In participant observation, the observer becomes part of the group being observed, establishing rapport with the group members to be accepted as one of them.

Limitation of Observational Method

- The observer's degree of involvement may vary depending on the study focus.
- The observational method is labour-intensive and time-consuming.
- It is susceptible to the observer's bias, as our observation is influenced by our values and beliefs about the person or event.
- Due to biases, observations may be interpreted in a different way than what the participant may actually mean.
- The observer should record the behaviour as it happens and should not interpret it at the time of observation.

Experimental Method

- Experiments are conducted to establish cause-effect relationships between two sets of events or variables in a controlled setting.
- The experimental method is a carefully regulated procedure where changes are made in one factor and its effect on another factor is studied, keeping other related factors constant.
- In the experiment, the cause is the event being changed or manipulated, while the effect is the behaviour that changes due to the manipulation.

Example of an Experiment

- Two American psychologists, Bibb Latane and John Darley, conducted a study in 1970. Students from Columbia University participated by arriving individually at a laboratory. They were told they would be interviewed on a certain topic.
- Each student went to a waiting room to complete a preliminary questionnaire. Some students found two other people already seated, while others sat alone.
- Smoke started filling the room through a wall vent. Within four minutes, the room contained enough smoke to interfere with vision and breathing.
- Latane and Darley wanted to know how frequently students would report the emergency.
- 75% of the students who were alone reported the smoke, but only 38% of those in groups reported it. When students waited with two confederates instructed to do nothing, only 10% of students reported the smoke.

The Concept of Variable

- Any stimulus or event that varies, meaning it has different values (or changes) and can be measured, is a variable.
- An object is not a variable, but its attributes (like size, shape, colour) are variables.
- **Examples of variables** The height of individuals (e.g., 5' to 6') and intelligence (which can vary from high, moderate, to low).
- Variation can be in the quality or quantity of objects/events.

Types of Variables

1. Independent Variable

- The variable which can be manipulated or altered by the researcher in an experiment.
- The researcher examines the effect of this change on another variable. For example, in Latane and Darley's experiment, the independent variable was the presence or absence of other persons in the room.

2. Dependent Variable

- This variable is observed to see the effect of the independent variable.
- It represents the phenomenon the researcher desires to explain.
- The independent variable is the cause and the dependent variable is the effect.
- The independent variable is the cause and dependent variable the effect in any experimental situation. Therefore both variables are interdependent.
- There are many other relevant or **extraneous variable**[2] that influence the dependent variable.

Experimental and Control Groups

- **Experimental Group** The group exposed to the manipulation of the independent variable.
- **Control Group** The comparison group treated like the **experimental group**[3] but without the manipulated variable.
- In Latane and Darley's study, there were two experimental groups and one **control group**[4]. Participants in the study were sent to three types of rooms: one with no one present (control group) and two with two persons already seated (experimental groups).
- Of the two experimental groups, one was instructed not to do anything when the smoke filled the room, while the other was not given any instructions.
- After the manipulation, the performance of the control group in reporting the smoke was compared with the experimental groups. The control group participants reported the emergency the most, followed by the first experimental group (with no instructions) and the second experimental group (with confederates) reported the least.
- Conditions such as the speed of smoke entry, the total amount of smoke and physical conditions of the rooms were kept constant across all groups.
- Participants are randomly distributed between the experimental and control groups to avoid systematic bias.
- This ensures that each participant has an equal chance of being included in any group, preventing results from being skewed by participant characteristics (e.g., gender).

Types of Extraneous Variables in Latane and Darley's Experiment

(i) **Organismic Variables** These are variables related to the individual, like anxiety, intelligence, and personality.

(ii) **Situational or Environmental Variables** These variables occur during the experiment, such as noise, temperature and humidity.

(iii) **Sequential Variables** These variables relate to the order in which participants are tested under various conditions.

Multiple exposures can lead to experimental fatigue or practice effects, which could influence results and make interpretation difficult.

---

2 **Extraneous Variable** It is the factor that can affect the outcome of the research study, but is not investigated.

3 **Experimental Group** It refers to the subjects in study who receive some special treatment in regard to the independent variable.

4 **Control Group** It refers to the subjects in a study which do not receive the special treatment given to the experimental group.

Techniques to Control Extraneous/Relevant Variables

- Experimenters use several control techniques to manage relevant variables, such as
  - **Elimination** To minimise external extraneous variables, by eliminating them from the experimental setting. For example, experiments may be conducted in a soundproof and air-conditioned room to eliminate the effects of noise and temperature.
  - **Holding Constant** If elimination is not possible, efforts are made to hold the extraneous variables constant so that their effects remain the same throughout the experiment.
  - **Matching** To control organismic (e.g., fear, motivation) and background variables (such as rural/urban, caste, socio-economic status), matching is used. In this procedure, relevant variables in two groups are equated or held constant by taking matched pairs across conditions.
  - **Counter-balancing** This technique is used to minimise sequence effects. For example, if there are two tasks, the order of tasks may be alternated. Half of the group receives tasks in order A then B, while the other half gets B then A or the same individual may perform tasks in the order A, B, B, A.
  - **Random Assignment** Randomly assigning participants to different groups eliminates potential systematic differences between the groups.

Types of Experiments

Field Experiments

- Researchers conduct experiments in natural settings to increase generalisability or conduct studies which are not possible in laboratory. For example, a researcher might compare the effectiveness of lecture and demonstration methods in a school setting.
- These experiments are less controlled, more time-consuming and expensive than laboratory experiments.

Quasi Experiments

- In some cases, the independent variable[5] cannot be manipulated in a laboratory setting. In such situations researcher adopts Quasi (Latin meaning 'as if') Experimentation.
- For example, experimental group could consist of children who lost their parents in an earthquake, while the control group consists of children who experienced the earthquake but did not loose their parents.
- Quasi experiments attempt to manipulate an independent variable in a natural setting using naturally occurring groups.

Quick Test 2

1. What are the types of extraneous variables?
2. What is the difference between covert and overt behaviour?
3. Which type of psychological data involves ecological conditions?
4. What is naturalistic observation?
5. Name two types of variables.

5 **Independent Variable** It is the event or situation manipulated by an experimenter to see if it will have a predicted effect on some other event or situation.

Correlational Research

- **Correlational research**[6] determines whether two variables are related, or covary or not.
- The strength and direction of the relationship between the two variables is represented by a number, known as **correlation coefficient**.
  - It is a number that represents the relationship between two variables. It can range from +1.0 through 0.0 to -1.0.

Types of Correlation

Positive Correlation

- When the value of one variable (X) increases, the value of the other variable (Y) also increases.
- Similarly, when X decreases, Y also decreases.
- For example, the more time students spend studying, the higher their achievement scores tend to be.
- The correlation value is positive, like, +0.85 indicates a strong positive relationship between study time and achievement.

Negative Correlation

- As the value of one variable (X) increases, the value of the other variable (Y) decreases.
- For example, as study hours increase, the number of hours spent on other activities decreases.
- The correlation value is negative, ranging between 0 and -1.0.

Zero Correlation

- No significant relationship exists between the two variables.
- For example, variables might be unrelated, indicated by correlation values close to zero, such as -0.02 or +0.03.

Survey Research

- Survey research is used to study people's opinions, attitudes and social facts.
- Initially, the focus was to find out the existing reality or baseline data like literacy rates, religious affiliations and income levels.
- Over time, survey research has evolved into a more sophisticated technique used for understanding causal relationships.

Example of Survey Method

- A survey was conducted in December 2004 by 'Outlook Saptahik' magazine to understand what makes people in India happy.
- The survey involved 817 participants in the age group of 25-55 years from eight major cities: Mumbai, Delhi, Kolkata, Bangalore, Hyderabad, Ahmedabad, Jaipur and Ranchi.
- Participants were asked a series of questions to gauge their happiness and views on various factors contributing to happiness.

Findings of the Survey

- **Happiness** About 47% of participants reported being extremely happy, 28% were more or less happy, 11% said they were neither happy nor unhappy and 7% were either more or less unhappy or extremely unhappy.

---

6 **Correlational Research** It is the research with the goal of describing the strength of the relationship between two or more events or characteristics or variables.

- **Money and Happiness** 80% of respondents believed that money cannot buy happiness.
- **Sources of Happiness** More than 50% of respondents cited peace of mind and health as the sources of their happiness. Other factors included success in work (43%) and family (40%).
- **Coping with Unhappiness** When feeling unhappy or sad, 36% of people opted to listen music, 23% found solace in the company of friends and 15% went to a movie.

Techniques of Survey Research

Personal Interviews

- It is the most frequently used method for obtaining information. It involves face-to-face interaction between an interviewer and a respondent, where the interviewer asks questions and the respondent provides answers.
- The list of questions prepared in advance for the interview is called an Interview Schedule.
- Personal interviews are conducted to gather factual information, opinions, attitudes and reasons for specific behaviours.
- This method is commonly used in many fields such as in doctor-patient interactions, employer-employee relations and media-person interviews with national/international figures.

Skills required for Interviewer

- A good interviewer needs to make the respondent feel comfortable, ask clear questions, and be sensitive to the way the person responds.
- The interviewer may need to probe for more detailed answers if the respondent gives vague answers.
- Proper training is important for effective interviewing.

Types of Interviews

(i) Structured or Standardised Interview

- The questions in the schedule are written clearly in a particular sequence.
- The interviewer has little or no liberty to change the wording or order of the questions.
- The responses to these questions are also predetermined and these are close-ended questions.

(ii) Unstructured or Non-Standardised Interview

- The interviewer has the flexibility to decide the questions to ask, the wording of the questions and the sequence of questions.
- The responses are not predefined and the respondent can answer the questions in their own way.
- The questions are open-ended, giving freedom to the respondent to express their views in their own words.
- For example, if a researcher wants to know the happiness level of a person, they might ask, "How happy are you?" and the respondent can answer in any way they choose.

Combination of Participants in Interview

- **Individual to Individual** One interviewer interviews one respondent.
- **Individual to Group** One interviewer interviews a group of people. A variant of it is called Focus Group Discussion (FGD).
- **Group to Individual** One group of interviewers interviews one person. This situation can occur in job interviews.
- **Group to Group** A group of interviewers interview another group of interviewees.

Significance of Interview

- It helps to obtain in-depth information.
- It is flexible and adaptable to individual situations, especially when no other method is suitable.
- It can be used with children and non-literate persons.

Questionnaire Survey

- A questionnaire is a simple, versatile and low-cost self-report method to collect information.
- It consists of a predetermined set of questions, where the respondent answers by marking responses on paper.
- Questionnaires can be distributed in groups, sent *via* mail or filled out online.
- Two types of questions are used in the questionnaire
  (i) **Open-ended Questions** The respondent is free to write any answer they consider appropriate.
  (ii) **Closed-ended Questions** The questions and possible answers are provided and the respondent must select the correct answer. Examples of closed-ended questions include Yes/No, True/False, Multiple Choice or Rating Scales.

Rating Scales

- Respondents are asked to rate statements on a scale, such as
  - 3-point scale (Agree, Undecided, Disagree)
  - 5-point scale (Strongly Agree, Agree, Undecided, Disagree, Strongly Disagree)
  - 7-point, 9-point, 11-point or 13-point scales.
- Respondents may also be asked to rank items in a preferred order.

Uses of Questionnaires

- Collecting background and demographic information.
- Gathering information about past behaviour, attitudes, opinions, knowledge, expectations and aspirations.
- Surveys can be conducted *via* mail, but poor response rates can be a problem.

Telephone Survey

- Telephone surveys help to reduce the time spent on data collection.
- However, respondents may give uncooperative or superficial answers since they do not know the interviewer.
- There is a risk of biassed results, as respondents may differ from non-respondents in terms of age, gender, income, education levels and psychological characteristics.

Advantages and Disadvantages of Survey Research

- **Advantages**
  - Information can be gathered quickly and efficiently from thousands of people.
  - Surveys can be conducted quickly, allowing public opinions on new issues to be obtained almost immediately after the issues arise.
- **Disadvantages**
  - People may give inaccurate information due to memory lapses or reluctance to disclose their true beliefs.
  - People may sometimes provide responses they believe the researcher wants to hear.

Psychological Testing

- Psychologists have developed various types of tests to assess human characteristics such as intelligence, aptitude, personality, interest, attitudes, values and educational achievement.
- These tests are used in contexts such as personnel selection, placement, training, guidance and diagnosis in educational institutions, guidance clinics, industries and defense establishments.
- A test consists of questions (items) with responses related to a particular human characteristic or attribute.
- It is important for the characteristic being tested to be clearly defined and the items should be directly related to that characteristic.
- Many tests are designed for specific age groups and may or may not have a fixed time limit for answering.

A psychological test is standardised and objective, assessing an individual's standing in relation to others on certain mental or behavioural characteristics.

Objectivity of the Test

- Objectivity of the test refers to the fact that two or more researchers administer the same psychological test to the same group, they should get similar results for each person.
- For a test to be objective, items must be worded clearly so that they convey the same meaning to different readers.
- Instructions on how to answer the questions must be clear and the test administration process (such as environment, time limits, and method of administration) must be well-defined.
- The procedure for scoring responses should also be clearly outlined.
- The process of test construction is systematic and involves steps such as analysing items and estimating the reliability, validity and norms of the test.

Reliability of the Test

- Reliability refers to the consistency of test scores over a time or between different versions of the test.
- It measures the temporal stability of the test, indicating whether scores remain consistent over time.
- To compute test-retest reliability, the same test is administered to the same group of people on two different occasions and the correlation between their scores is calculated.

Split-half Reliability

- It measures the internal consistency of the test, checking if the items of the test correlate with each other when divided into two equal halves.
- The test is split into two parts (using odd-even item grouping) and the correlation between the two sets of scores is calculated to assess consistency.

Validity of the Test

- Validity refers to whether a test measures what it was designed to measure.
- For example, a mathematics achievement test should measure mathematical ability, not language proficiency.

Norms of the Test

- A test becomes standardised when norms are developed.
- Norms are the average performance standards based on a large sample of people, considering factors like age, sex and place of residence.
- The performance of an individual can be compared to the norms to understand how they score relative to others in the same group.
- Norms also help in interpreting an individual's score on the test.

Types of Tests

Depending upon the language, tests can be categorised as

(i) **Verbal Test** Requires literacy, as the test items are written in a language.

(ii) **Non-verbal Test** Uses symbols or pictures for items instead of words.

(iii) **Performance Test** Involves physical movement of objects in a specific order.

Depending upon the mode of administration, psychological test can be categories as

(i) **Individual Test** This test is administered by the reseacher to one person at a time. It requires face-to-face interaction and the researcher notes down the responses. It is time-consuming but useful for assessing children or those who are not familiar with the language.

(ii) **Group Test** This test can be administered to a large number of people simultaneously. The instructions are written and the administrator explains them to the group. It is less time-consuming but may result in less motivated responses or fake answers.

Speed and Power Tests

Psychological tests are also classified into following types

(i) **Speed Test** It has a time limit within which the test taker must answer all items. It measures performance based on time taken to answer items accurately and all items are of equal difficulty.

(ii) **Power Test** Assesses the underlying ability of the individual, allowing unlimited time. The items are generally arranged in increasing difficulty. Most tests are a combination of speed and power.

Case Study

- A case study is an in-depth examination of a specific case to gather critical information or new insights about less understood phenomena.
- The case can be an individual, group, institution or event, such as a person with psychological disorders, a group of creative writers, a school or a child affected by a traumatic event like a tsunami or pollution.
- Researchers use multiple methods like interviews, observation and psychological tests from various sources.
- Generalising from a single case study should be done with caution due to potential validity issues. It is advised to gather information using multiple strategies and investigators for a comprehensive view.

Importance of Case Studies

- They help to understand emotions, fantasies, fears and experiences, contributing to understanding a person's mind and behaviour.
- Case studies provide detailed descriptions of significant events in a person's life.
- They are crucial in clinical psychology and human development.
- Famous figures like Freud and Piaget developed theories from case study observations, highlighting their importance.
- They provide deep insights into individual lives and behaviours.

Quick Test 3

1 Explain the difference between positive, negative and zero correlation with examples.
2 Describe the purpose of survey research.
3 What are the advantages of using a questionnaire for survey research?
4 Define reliability and validity in the context of psychological testing.
5 What are the different methods used by researcher for case study?

2.4 Analysis of Data

The are two methodotogical approached use for the analysis of data. These are quantitative and qualitative methods.

Quantitative Method

- Quantitative method is used when the data is collected in numerical form (e.g.,psychological tests, questionnaires, structured interviews).
- The participants provide responses and each response is assigned a value (e.g.,1 for correct, 0 for incorrect).
- The goal is to convert psychological attributes into numerical data (e.g., intelligence levels, academic performance).
- For the purpose of drawing conclusions, a researcher may compare individual's scores with that of the group or compare the scores of two groups.
- Following methods enable the researcher to make inferences and derive meaningful conclusions from the data
  - **Central Tendency** Measures like mean, median and mode help to summarise the data.
  - **Variability** Tools like range, quartile deviation and standard deviation are used to understand data spread.
  - **Correlation** Coefficients of correlation are used to examine relationships between variables.

Qualitative Method

- Psychologists have developed various qualitative methods to analyse data. One of them is Narrative Analysis.
- When the researcher uses the method of participant observation or unstructured interview, the data are generally in a descriptive form.
- These type of data cannot be converted into scores or subjected to statistical analysis.
- The researcher uses the following techniques
  - **Content Analysis** Researchers look for thematic categories and examples within the data to interpret it.
  - **Descriptive Nature** This method is more narrative and descriptive, focusing on the meaning behind responses rather than statistical analysis.
- Quantitative and qualitative methods are complementary rather than contradictory. Combining both provides a more complete understanding of the phenomenon under study.

2.5 Limitations of Psychological Enquiry

Some general problems/limitations faced by psychological measurement are

Lack of True Zero Point

- In physical sciences, measurements start from a true zero point. For example, if a person want to measure the length of the table, he can measure it starting from zero. However, psychological measurements lack a true zero point.
- For example, no person has zero intelligence. Thus, psychologists arbitrarily define a point as zero and proceed from there, meaning psychological scores are not absolute but relative.

- In some cases, ranks are used as scores. The differences between ranks may not be consistent. For instance, the difference between the first and second ranks may not be equal to the difference between the second and third ranks, highlighting the relative nature of psychological measurements.

Relative Nature of Psychological Tools

- Psychological tests are often designed with specific contexts in mind.
- For example, a test developed for urban students may include items related to urban settings (e.g., aeroplanes, metro rail). However, such a test would not be suitable for children in tribal areas who are unfamiliar with urban settings but are familiar with different local contexts.
- This emphasises the need to modify and adapt tests to suit the context in which they will be used.

Subjective Interpretation of Qualitative Data

- Qualitative data, such as from unstructured interviews or participant observations, are inherently subjective as they depend on both the researcher's interpretation and the participants' responses.
- Different researchers may interpret data in different ways. To reduce bias, it is recommended that more than one investigator conduct the fieldwork and discuss their findings to reach an agreement.
- Involving respondents in the interpretation process can further enhance the validity of qualitative studies.

2.6 Ethical Issues

- Psychological research involves studying behaviour, so researchers must adhere to ethical principles to protect participants and ensure fairness.
- Key ethical principles are
  - Respect for person's privacy
  - Choice to participate
  - Beneficence or protecting participants in the study from harm
  - Justice or sharing the benefits of research with all participant

Aspects of Ethical Principles

Voluntary Participation

Participants of the study should have the freedom to participate in the study and the right to withdraw at any point without facing any penalties.

Informed Consent

- The principle of informed consent ensures that participants are fully aware of the study's nature before they participate, enabling them to make an informed decision.
- In some experiments, participants may be exposed to unpleasant stimuli or even electric shocks. In such cases, it is crucial to explain the nature of the study to the participants beforehand, especially when harmful or deceptive methods are used.
- Some studies involve technique of deception, where participants are given false instructions or feedback about their performance. In these cases, it is important to inform participants about the true nature of the study before it begins.

Debriefing

- After the study, participants must be given information to fully understand the research and its purpose, especially if deception was used.
- The debriefing process should aim to restore participants to the same mental and physical state as when they entered the study.
- It should also address any anxiety or concerns caused by the study, particularly in cases where deception was involved, ensuring the participant feels reassured.

Sharing the Results of the Study

- Researchers are obligated to share the results of the study with participants after its completion.
- This fulfills participants' expectations and provides an opportunity for them to express their opinions, which may lead to new insights or improvements in future research.

Confidentiality of Data Source

- Participants have the right to privacy and researchers must ensure that any data collected will remain confidential.
- The information collected should only be used for research purposes and should not be shared with third parties.
- To protect confidentiality, researchers should avoid recording participants' identities and any identification lists should be destroyed after the research is completed.

Quick Test 4

1. What is the purpose of using quantitative methods in psychological research?
2. Name one quantitative method.
3. What are two examples of qualitative data that might be collected in psychological research?
4. Why is it important to obtain informed consent from participants in psychological research?
5. What does the principle of confidentiality in psychological research mean?
6. Mention any two principles of psychological enquiry.

NCERT Folder

1. What are the goals of scientific enquiry?

Ans. Following are the goals of scientific enquiry

Description It is very important in a scientific enquiry to describe the behaviour or a phenomenon accurately in order to be able to deal with it. The description requires recording of a particular behaviour which helps in its proper understanding.

Prediction Scientific enquiry aims at the understanding of a particular behaviour in relationship to other behaviours or events. It tries to predict their occurrences under certain conditions with a margin of error. Prediction becomes more accurate with the increase in the number of persons observed.

Explanation Scientific enquiry is conducted to know the casual factors or determinants of behaviour and the conditions where the behaviour does not occur.

Control Being able to explain behaviour also leads to the control in behaviour by making changes in its antecedent conditions. The control refers to making a particular behaviour happen, reduce it and enhance it.

Application Application of a particular behaviour aims at bringing about positive changes in the lives of people by solving their problems in various settings.

2. Describe the various steps involved in conducting a scientific enquiry.

Ans. The various steps involved in conducting a scientific enquiry are

- **Conceptualisation of Problem** It is important in a scientific enquiry to narrow down the focus and understand the specific problem. It is done by reviewing past research, personal experience and observations. This is further followed by preparing a hypothesis or a tentative solution of the problem.
- **Collecting Data** The second step involves the preparation of a blueprint of the entire study. It consists of four aspects namely, identifying the participants in the study, methods of data collection, tools to be used in research and procedure for data collection.
- **Drawing Conclusions** The data are analysed through statistical procedures and represented graphically in the form of pie-chart, bar-diagram, etc. It helps to verify the hypothesis and draw conclusions by putting them into an appropriate context.
- **Revising Research Conclusions** The existing hypothesis is finally confirmed on the basis of revision of data. The research may also be revised by other researchers, hence making it continuous process.

3. Explain the nature of psychological data.

Ans. Data is related to the individuals' covert or overt behaviour, their subjective experiences and mental processes.

The nature of psychological data can be explained through the following points

- The psychological data are not independent entities. The physical or social context, the persons involved and the time of the behaviour affects the data. For instance, an individual behaves differently in a group than being alone.
- The quality and nature of data is affected by the method of data collection. It is possible that while conducting a personal interview, an individual provides with answers which are different than his/her behaviour as observed by the researcher.
- Data are facts without any meaning. This suggests that data do not represents reality. They only acquire meaning when placed in a context by the researcher.

4. How do experimental and control groups differ? Explain with the help of an example.

Ans. An experimental group is a group in which members of the group are exposed to independent variable manipulation whereas, the control group is a comparison group that is treated in every way like the experimental group except that the manipulated variable is absent in it.

For example, in a study conducted by Latane and Darley, there were two experimental groups and one control group. The participants in the study were sent to three types of rooms.

Room 1 in which the participant was alone formed the control group. **Room 2** and **3,** in which two persons were present with the participant formed experimental groups. The independent variable in this study was the absence or presence of other persons sitting in the room. The remaining factors in the experiment were the same for both kinds of groups.

In experimental groups, two persons were present with the real participant while in the control group, participant was alone. Therefore, it can be said that the manipulated variable is absent in control group.

5. A researcher is studying the relationship between speed of cycling and the presence of people. Formulate a relevant hypothesis and identify the independent and dependent variables.

Ans. Hypothesis The presence of people on a cycling path increases the speed of cyclists, as cyclists may adjust their pace based on the proximity of others.

Independent variable The presence or absence of people on the cycling path.

Dependent variable The speed of cycle.

6. Discuss the strengths and weaknesses of experimental method as a method of enquiry.

Ans. Experimental method is aimed at discovering casual relationship between various factors by manipulating the situation under totally controlled conditions.

Strengths of Experimental Method

- It provides a relatively convincing evidence of a cause-effect relationship between two or more variables. The extraneous variables can be eliminated from the laboratory.
- It can minimise the sequence effect with the help of counter-balancing technique.
- It eliminates any potential systematic differences between groups by giving random assignment to groups of participants.
- This is done to help in framing the conclusion without any assumption.

Weaknesses of Experimental Method

- The highly controlled laboratory situation only stimulates the conditions of the outer world.
- The results of the experiments cannot be generally applied to real situations, thus field experiments are required in such situations.
- It is not always feasible to study a particular problem experimentally. It is difficult to know and control all the relevant variables, particularly in field experiments. Many variables cannot be manipulated in laboratory settings.

7. Dr. Krishnan is going to observe and record children's play behaviour at a nursery school without attempting to influence or control the behaviour. Which method of research is involved? Explain the process and discuss its merits and demerits. Competency Based Que.

Ans. Dr. Krishnan will use non-participant observation method to observe and record children's play behaviour at a nursery school without attempting to influence or control the behaviour.

She will sit in the corner of the play school and will observe the behaviour of children, their interaction with other children and teachers, how they play and react to winning and losing. The children will not be aware that they are being observed. Later, she will record her observations in a file. She will analyse and conclude it and then try to match her conclusion with the hypothesis.

Merits of Non-Participant Observation Method

- The observer get first hand information regarding subject.
- The researcher observes the people and their behaviour in a naturalistic situation as it occurs.

Demerits of Non-participant Observation Method

- This method is time taking, labour intensive and vulnerable to the researcher's bias.
- The observations are influenced by the personal values and interpretations of the observer.

8. Give two examples of the situations where survey method can be used. What are the limitations of this method?

Ans. Survey research came into existence to study opinions, attitudes and social facts. Initially, their main concern was to find out the existing reality or baseline. So it was used to find out facts such as the literacy rate at a particular time, religious affiliations, income level of a particular group of people, etc. The two examples where a survey method can be used are as follows

(i) To find out the attitudes of people on polio eradication programme.

(ii) To record information about the members of a particular population.

The limitations of survey method are as follows

- People may give inaccurate information because of memory lapses or they do not want the researcher to know their real opinions about a particular issue.
- People sometimes respond in a way they think the researcher wants to hear.

9. Differentiate between an interview and a questionnaire.

Ans. The differences between an interview and a questionnaire are

Interview	Questionnaire
It is a form of interaction in which questions are asked directly to the respondents.	It is a framework in which questions of scientific enquiry are written.
Questions may vary in their sequence according to the need of the situation.	Questions are written in an appropriate sequence which are answered in written format by the respondents.
Researcher and respondents are in face-to-face contact.	Researcher and respondents are not required to be in face-to-face contact.

Researcher can visit the respondents or call them at the office.	Researcher can go to the places to distribute the questionnaire or questions can be sent through e-mail and post.
The questions are flexible by nature.	The questions are rigid.
Number of questions can be increased or decreased.	Number of questions cannot be changed.

10. Explain the characteristics of a standardised test.

Ans. The construction of a test is a systematic process and involves certain steps. It involves detailed analysis of items and estimating reliability, validity and norms of the whole test.

Following are the characteristics of standardised test

- **Reliability** This refers to the consistency of scores obtained by an individual on the same test on two different occasions. Test-retest indicates temporal stability and split-half indicates internal consistency of the test.
- **Validity** The test has to be devised to measure what it claims to measure in order to be held as valid and usable.
- **Norms** The test needs to devise norms or the average performance of the group. It helps in comparison and interpretation of an individual's performance in relation to the overall standards of the group.

11. Describe the limitations of psychological enquiry.

Ans. During psychological enquiries researcher face a lot of limitation. Some of the common limitation are as follows

- **Lack of True Zero Point** Psychological measurements do not have a true zero point. For example, no person in this world has zero intelligence. All of us have some degree of intelligence.
- **Relative Nature of Psychological Tools** The tools or method applied in psychological enquiries are relative in nature. For instance, a test developed in the Western countries may or may not be applicable in the Indian context.
- **Subjective Interpretation of Qualitative Data** Data from qualitative studies are largely subjective since they involve interpretation on the part of the researcher as well as the person providing data.

12. What are the ethical guidelines that a psychologist needs to follow while conducting a psychological enquiry?

Ans. The researcher is expected to follow certain ethics (or moral principles) while conducting the studies.

Following are the ethical guidelines that a psychologist needs to follow while conducting a psychological enquiry

- **Voluntary Participation** The person on whom the study has to be conducted has the choice whether to participate or not in the study.
- **Informed Consent** The participants should be informed about the nature of the study and its impact upon them before it starts.
- **Debriefing** The participants have to be provided with information for their understanding of the research and enable them to leave the place or laboratory in the same mental and physical state as before the test was conducted.
- **Sharing the Results** The researcher has to share the results of the study with the participants to fulfil their expectations. The opinion of participants about the results also provides new insights to the researcher.
- **Confidentiality of Data Source** The researcher has to make sure that the information given by the participants is kept confidential and not shared with other interested parties.

Henceforth, it is necessary for the researcher to ensure certain ethics and principles in order to respect an individual's privacy and protect him/her from any harm caused by the research.

Exam Pattern Questions

Objective Type Questions

Multiple Choice Questions (MCQs)

1. Which of the following is the goal of psychological enquiry?

(a) Description (b) Prediction
(c) Explanation (d) All of these

2. The situation where one interviewer interviews another person is called as

(a) Individual to Group
(b) Group to Individual
(c) Individual to Individual
(d) Group to Group

3. The steps of investigation in a scientific research includes

(a) Conceptualisation of a problem
(b) Collection of data
(c) Drawing conclusions
(d) All of the above

4. In psychological information, the data collected relates to

(a) Height (b) Weight
(c) Level of fatigue (d) All of these

5. Naturalistic observation can be conducted in

(a) hospitals (b) homes
(c) schools (d) All of these

6. Identify the 2nd step in conducting scientific research enquiry?

(a) Collecting Data
(b) Conceptualising a Problem
(c) Drawing Conclusions
(d) Revising Research Conclusions

7. The …………………… refers to the fact that if two or more persons independently study a particular event, both of them, to a great extent, should arrive at the same conclusion.

(a) conclusion (b) objectivity
(c) study (d) paradigm

8. Rajan has been appointed as a new Hindi teacher in a school. In order to develop rapport with a students he has understand behaviour of the students. He will utilise ……… method for understanding their behaviour.

(a) correlational (b) experimental
(c) observational (d) survey

9. Anuj has conducted a research to know whether 'the amount of study time' is related to the 'student's academic achievement'. This is an example of which of the following research method?

(a) Experimental (b) Correlational
(c) Survey (d) Observational

10. Rohit and Sahil are working on a common research project, while doing so, they are independently trying to study a particular event. At the end of the research if both of them do not reach a common conclusion, then the research is CBSE DIKSHA

(a) low on validity (b) low on objectivity
(c) high on validity (d) high on objectivity

11. In the process of writing a biography of a famous musician, Nilesh is required to interview the musician, in order to understand his life in detail. He has been handed over a list of questions by his seniors and has been instructed to stick to the question mentioned in the list. What kind of interview is Nilesh expected to conduct? Competency Based Que.

(a) Unstructured (b) Decided
(c) Structured (d) To the point

12. If a researcher, while trying to assess the cognitive development of students residing in rural areas, decides to use a test, which includes questions related to technological and infrastructure advancement in urban areas. Then which limitation of psychological enquiry is he overlooking? CBSE DIKSHA

(a) Lack of true zero point
(b) Relative nature of psychological tools
(c) Informed consent
(d) Lack of empathy

13. While explaining a concept of psychology, students, a counsellor, narrated our case, but refused to tell the name of the person involved. Identify the ethical issue which the counsellor is abiding to. Competency Based Que.

(a) Voluntary participation (b) Debriefing
(c) Sharing the results (d) Confidentiality

14. During an experiment, Prashant shows sensitive videos to the participants, which drained them emotionally. The participants were soon allowed to leave the psychological laboratory, without any further guidance.

Which ethical issue has been violated during the course of experiment? **CBSE DIKSHA**

(a) Debriefing
(b) Informed consent
(c) Voluntary participation
(d) Confidentiality

15. **Which of the following statements correctly describe conceptualising a problem in scientific research?**

I. **It begins with selecting a theme or topic for study.**
II. **It ends with proving a hypothesis using a specific research method.**
III. **Researchers develop specific research questions from observations and past studies.**
IV. **Hypotheses are always proven true during the research process.**

Codes

(a) I and III (b) II and IV (c) I and II (d) III and IV

16. **Which of the following correctly describes correlational research?**

I. **It finds relationships between variables.**
II. **A correlation coefficient indicates the strength and direction of the relationship.**
III. **It always proves causation between variables.**
IV. **It uses positive, negative and zero correlations to interpret relationships.**

Codes

(a) I and III
(b) II and IV
(c) I and II
(d) I, II and IV

Assertion-Reason Questions

Directions (Q. Nos. 17-24) In the following questions, a statement of Assertion A is followed by a statement of Reason R. Mark the correct choice from the options given below.

(a) Both A and R are true and R is the correct explanation of A.
(b) Both A and R are true, but R is not the correct explanation of A.
(c) A is true, but R is false.
(d) A is false, but R is true.

17. **Assertion** (A) Dependent variable is the factor that is measured in an experiment.

Reason (R) It changes because of the manipulation of the independent variable.

18. **Assertion** (A) Data from qualitative studies are largely subjective.

Reason (R) They involve interpretation on the part of the researcher as well as the person providing data.

19. **Assertion** (A) Observational methods in psychology are limited due to the potential influence of observer bias.

Reason (R) The observer's values and beliefs can influence the way they interpret the behaviour, leading to potential distortion of the data.

20. **Assertion** (A) Participant observation involves the researcher becoming part of the group they are observing.

Reason (R) The degree of the observer's involvement varies depending on the focus of the study and they need to establish a rapport with the group.

21. **Assertion** (A) A test is said to be objective if it gives the same results when administered by different researchers to the same group of individuals.

Reason (R) Objectivity in psychological testing can be achieved by ensuring that items are worded clearly and instructions are given in a consistent manner.

22. **Assertion** (A) A psychological test is said to be valid if it accurately measures what it is intended to measure.

Reason (R) Validity of a test is crucial for ensuring that a mathematics achievement test, for instance, truly measures mathematical ability rather than unrelated skills such as language proficiency.

23. **Assertion** (A) Psychological research faces the challenge of a 'lack of true zero point' which limits the absolute nature of psychological measurements.

Reason (R) In psychological tests, arbitrary zero points are often used and this leads to relative rather than absolute measurements, such as ranking students based on test scores.

24. **Assertion** (A) In qualitative research, the interpretation of data is largely subjective and can vary between different researchers.

Reason (R) To ensure objectivity, qualitative research should be done by a single investigator to maintain consistency in the interpretation of the data.

Answers

1. (d) All of these
2. (c) Individual to Individual
3. (d) All of the above
4. (d) All of these
5. (d) All of these
6. (a) Collecting Data
7. (b) objectivity
8. (c) observational
9. (b) Correlational
10. (b) low on objectivity
11. (c) Structured
12. (b) Relative nature of psychological tools
13. (d) Confidentiality
14. (a) Debriefing
15. (a) I and III
16. (d) I, II and IV
17. (a) Both A and R are true and R is the correct explanation of A.
18. (a) Both A and R are true and R is the correct explanation of A.
19. (a) Both A and R are true and R is the correct explanation of A.
20. (a) Both A and R are true and R is the correct explanation of A.
21. (a) Both A and R are true and R is the correct explanation of A.
22. (a) Both A and R are true and R is the correct explanation of A.
23. (a) Both A and R are true and R is the correct explanation of A.
24. (c) A is true, but R is false.

Subjective Questions

Very Short Answer Type Questions

1. What do you know about prediction?

Ans. Understanding and describing the behaviour accurately help to know the relationship of a particular behaviour with other types of behaviours, events or phenomena. After knowing this, it can be predicted that under certain conditions what type of particular behaviour may occur. Prediction becomes more accurate with the increase in the number of persons observed.

2. Define the third goal of scientific enquiry.

Ans. Explanation is the third goal of psychological enquiry which is used to know the casual factors or determinants of behaviour. Psychologists are primarily interested in knowing the factors that are responsible for a particular behaviour.

3. Give an example of control.

Ans. The change brought about in behaviour by psychological treatment in terms of therapy in persons is a good example of control. A student can adjust their study hours based on the desired outcome or psychological treatments and therapies can be used.

4. Define the role of data in psychological enquiry.

Ans. Data form an important input in psychological enquiry. They in fact approximate the reality to some extent and provide an opportunity to verify or falsify our ideas, hunches, notions, etc.

5. Preeti is assigned a task to collect demographic information. What attributes she needs to collect?

Competency Based Que.

Ans. While collecting demographic information, Preeti needs to collect various attributes. Such as personal information like name, age, gender, birth order, number of siblings, education, occupation, marital status, number of children, locality of residence, caste, religion, parental education, occupation and family income, etc.

6. Define the term physical information.

Ans. This category includes information about ecological conditions (hilly/desert/forest), mode of economy, housing conditions, size of rooms, facilities available at home, in the neighbourhood and in the school, mode of transportation, etc.

7. Define the term observation in psychological enquiry.

Ans. Observation is a very powerful tool of psychological enquiry. It is an effective method of describing behaviour. A scientific observation differs from day-to-day observation in the many respects.

8. What are the various methods of observation?

Ans. Observation can be done in two ways

(i) Naturalistic observation Vs Controlled observation

(ii) Non participant observation Vs Participant observation

9. What do you mean by experiments?

Ans. Experiments are generally conducted to establish cause-effect relationship between two sets of events or variables in a controlled setting. It is a carefully regulated procedure in which changes are made in one factor and its effect is studied on another factor, while keeping other related factors constant.

10. Define the use of survey research.

Ans. Survey research came into existence to study opinions, attitudes and social facts. Sociologists' main concern was to find out the existing reality or baseline. So they were used to find out facts such as the literacy rate at a particular time, religious affiliations, income level of a particular group of people, etc.

11. What do you understand by interview?

Ans. An interview is a purposeful activity conducted to derive factual information, opinions and attitudes and reasons for particular behaviour, etc from the respondents. It is generally conducted face-to-face but sometimes it can also take place over the phone.

12. What is questionnaire?

Ans. The questionnaire is the most common, simple, versatile, and low-cost self-report method of collecting information. It consists of a predetermined set of questions.

The respondent has to read the questions and mark the answers on paper rather than respond verbally to the interviewer.

13. What do you mean by objectivity?

Ans. Objectivity refers to the fact that if two or more researchers administer a psychological test on the same group of people, both of them would come up with more or less the same values for each person in the group.

14. What is hypothesis?

Ans. After identification of the problem, the researcher proceeds by developing a tentative answer of the problem, it is called Hypothesis.

15. Define the collection of data in scientific research.

Ans. Data collection requires developing a research design or a blueprint of the entire study.

It requires taking decisions about the following four aspects

(i) Participants in the study.

(ii) Methods of data collection.

(iii) Tools to be used in research.

(iv) Procedure for data collection.

16. How behaviour can be controlled?

Ans. Behaviour can be controlled by making changes in its antecedent conditions. Control refers to three things i.e. making a particular behaviour happen, reducing it or enhancing it.

17. What are the methods used by psychologists to collect data?

Ans. Psychologists use a variety of methods like observation, experimental, correlational, survey, psychological testing and case study to collect data.

18. Why psychological test are constructed?

Ans. Psychologists have constructed different types of tests for assessment of various human characteristics such as intelligence, aptitude, personality, interest, attitudes, values, educational achievement, etc. These tests are used in contexts of personnel selection, placement, training, guidance, etc.

Short Answer Type Questions

1. Explain the role of conceptualising a problem in scientific research.

Ans. **Conceptualising a Problem** The process of scientific research begins when a researcher selects a theme or topic for study. Then she/he narrows down the focus and develops specific research questions or problems for the study. This is done on the basis of review of past research, observations and personal experiences.

In psychology, there are diverse range of problems related to behaviour and experiences. These problems may be related to

- understanding our own behaviour.
- understanding other individual's behaviour.
- group influences on individual behaviour.
- group behaviour.
- organisational level.

2. State the advantage of observational method. Why is there need to take precaution before observation?

Ans. **Advantage of Observation Method** The advantage of the observation method is that it enables the researcher to study people and their behaviour in a naturalistic situation, as it occurs.

Need to Take Precaution

- The observation method is labour intensive, time consuming and is susceptible to the observer's bias.
- Our observation is influenced by our values and beliefs about the person or the event. Because of our biases we may interpret things in a different way than what the participants may actually mean.
- Therefore, the observer should record the behaviour as it happens and should not interpret the behaviour at the time of observation itself.

3. What are the limitations of experiment?

Ans. The limitations of experiment are

- They only simulate situations that exist in the outside world. The results of experiments have low external validity.
- Another limitation of the laboratory experiment is that it is not always feasible to study a particular problem experimentally.
- The third problem is that it is difficult to know and control all the relevant variables.

4. What are the three types of variables in experimental studies?

Ans. All relevant variables in experimental studies that might influence the dependent variable need to be controlled. These are of three major types

(i) Organismic variables (such as anxiety, intelligence, personality, etc).

(ii) Situational or environmental variables operating at the time of conducting the experiment (such as noise, temperature, humidity).

(iii) The sequence related variables assume significance when the participants in experiments are required to be tested in several conditions. Exposure to many conditions may result in experimental fatigue, or practice effects, which may influence the results of the study and make the interpretation of the findings difficult.

5. What are the various participants in interview situation?

Ans. An interview may have the following combinations of participants in an interview situation

- **Individual to Individual** It is a situation where one interviewer interviews another person.
- **Individual to Group** In this situation, one interviewer interviews a group of persons. One variant of it is called a Focus Group Discussion (FGD).
- **Group to Individuals** It is a situation where one group of interviewers interviews one person. One may experience this type of situation when appear for a job interview.
- **Group to Group** It is a situation where one group of interviewers interviews another group of interviewees.

6. Arun wants to conduct a survey research and he opted interview technique to complete his task. Why Arun has chosen interview technique? State its significance.

Ans. The interview technique is best suited while conducting a survey research. Arun has chosen this technique due to following significance

- The interview method helps in obtaining in-depth information.
- It is flexible and adaptable to individual situations and can often be used when no other method is possible or adequate.
- It can be used even with children and non-literate persons.
- However, interviews require time. Often getting information from one person may take an hour or more which may not be cost-effective.

7. Explain the quantitative method of data analysis.

Ans. In this method, the responses to the questions of psychological tests, questionnaires, structured interviews, etc are given in scaled forms. That is, they indicate the strength and magnitude of the response.

The participants' task is to select the most appropriate response. Sometimes there are right and wrong responses. A researcher assigns a number to each answer.

At the end, the researcher calculates the total of all these numbers and arrives at an aggregate score, which tells about the participants' level on that particular attribute (for example, intelligence, academic intelligence, etc). In doing so, the researcher converts the psychological attributes into a quantity (usually numbers).

8. Discuss the advantages and limitations of survey research.

Ans. Advantages of Survey Research

- Information can be gathered quickly and efficiently from thousands of persons.
- Since surveys can be conducted quickly, public opinions on new issues can be obtained almost as soon as the issues arise.

Limitations of Survey Research

- People may give inaccurate information because of memory lapses or they may not want to let the researcher know what they really believe about a particular issue.
- People sometimes offer responses they think the researcher wants to hear.

9. Suggest various methods for collection of data and highlight its significance in psychological enquiry/research.

Ans. All varieties of data cannot be collected through a single method of enquiry. Psychologists use a variety of methods like observation, experimental, correlational, survey, psychological testing and case study to collect data. A number of methods can be used for different research purposes. For example,

- One can observe the behaviour of spectators watching a football match.
- One can conduct an experiment to see if children taking an examination do better in the classroom in which they had studied the subject or in the examination hall (cause-effect relationship).
- One can correlate intelligence with self-esteem (for prediction purposes).
- One can survey students' attitude towards privatisation of education.
- One can use psychological tests to find out individual differences.
- One can conduct a case study on the development of language in a child.

10. Discuss the difference between naturalistic and controlled observation.

Ans. When observations are done in a natural or real-life settings it is called Naturalistic observation. In this case, the observer makes no effort to control or manipulate the situation for making an observation. This type of observation is conducted in hospitals, homes, schools, day care centers, etc.

Whereas many times certain factors that determines behaviour are controlled by the people that are not the focus of their study. Many of these studies in psychology are conducted in the laboratory. This type of observation is called Controlled laboratory observation which is obtained in laboratory experiments.

11. "Human behaviour should be studied following the methods adopted by sciences". Explain the statement.

Ans. Psychologists suggest that human behaviour can and should be studied following the methods adopted by sciences. The key assumption of this view is that human behaviour is predictable, caused by internal and external forces and can be observed, measured and controlled.

In order to achieve these goals, the discipline of psychology, for larger part of the twentieth century, restricted itself to the study of overt behaviour, i.e. the behaviour that could be observed and measured.
It did not focus on personal feelings, experiences, meanings, etc.

12. Discuss why sharing the results of the study is ethically important.

Ans. In psychological research, after collecting information from the participants, it is compulsory for the researcher to go back to the participants and share the results of the study with them. When you go for data collection, the participants develop certain expectations from you. One of the expectations is that you will tell them about their behaviour that you have investigated in the study. As a researcher, it is our moral duty to go back to the participants.

This exercise has two advantages. One, you fulfill the expectations of the participants. Second, the participants may tell you their opinion about the results, which sometimes may help you develop new insights.

13. The researcher wants to know about the happiness level among the students of Class 11th. Describe in brief which combination of participants can be used by researcher for knowing happiness.

Ans. An interview may have the following combinations of participants in an interview situation in order to know about the happiness level among the students of Class 11th.

- **Individual to Individual** It is a situation where one interviewer interviews another person.
- **Individual to Group** In this situation, one interviewer interviews a group of persons. One variant of it is called a Focus Group Discussion (FGD).
- **Group to Individuals** It is a situation where one group of interviewers interview one person.
- **Group to Group** It is a situation where one group of interviewers interview another group of interviewees.

14. If Shyam want to know how a mother feels about the loss of her child then he will utilise which method? Write the salient features of this method.
Competency Based Que.

Ans. In order to know about the feeling of about the loss of her child then he will utilise qualitative method. The salient features of this method are as follows

- Through this method one can understand the complex feeling and behaviour of a person.
- It is complementary to quantitative method.
- Data obtained from this type of method cannot be converted into scores or subjected to statistical analysis.
- It can be applied to multiple situations.
- It is multidimensional in nature.

15. Explain interpretive method of psychological research.

Ans. Interpretive method emphasises on understanding over explanation and prediction. According to it, complex and variable nature of human behaviour and experience method of investigation should be different from the method of investigation of the physical world.

This viewpoint emphasises the importance of how human beings give meaning to events/actions and interpret them as they occur in a particular context.

In every situation, objective measurement is neither possible nor desirable. Everyone interprets reality in her/his own way based on past experiences and contexts. Therefore, people need to understand the subjective interpretation of the reality.

Hence, it is the goal to explore the different aspects of human experiences and behaviour without attempting to disturb its natural flow.

16. Discuss the various aspects of observational methods.

Ans. A scientific observation differs from day-to-day observation in many respects. These are

Selection Psychologists do not observe all the behaviour that they encounter. Rather, they select a particular behaviour for observation.

Recording While observing, a researcher records the selected behaviour using different means, such as marking tallies for the already identified behaviour whenever they occur, taking notes describing each activity in greater detail using short hand or symbols, photographs, video recording, etc.

Analysis of Data After the observations have been made, psychologists analyse whatever they have recorded with a view to derive some meaning out of it. It is important to know that making good observations is a skill.

A good observer knows what she/he is looking for, whom she/he wants to observe, when and where the observation needs to be made, in what form the observation will be recorded and what methods will be used to analyse the observed behaviour.

17. Discuss the control techniques used by experimenters.

Ans. Experimenters use several control techniques to control relevant variables. Some of these are

- To minimise external extraneous variables, the best way is to eliminate them from the experimental setting.
- Elimination is not always possible. In such cases, effort should be made to hold them constant so that their effect remains the same throughout the experiment.
- For controlling organismic (e.g. fear, motivation) and background variables (such as rural/urban, caste, socio-economic status), matching is also used. In this procedure, the relevant variables in the two groups are equated or are held constant by taking matched pairs across conditions of the experiment.
- Counter-balancing technique is used to minimise the sequence effect.
- Random assignment of participants to different groups eliminates the potential systematic differences between groups.

18. Explain the correlational research in psychology.

Ans. Correlational research determines to find out the relationship between the two variables i.e. whether they are associated or not. The strength and direction of the relationship between the two variables is represented by a number, known as correlation coefficient. Its value can range from +1.0 through 0.0 to −1.0.

The coefficient of correlation is of three types

(i) **Positive Correlation** It indicates that as the value of one variable (X) increases, the value of the other variable (Y) will also increase. Similarly when variable (X) decreases, a decrease in (Y) too takes place. The value of positive correlation is +1.0.

(ii) **Negative Correlation** It tells us that as the value of one variable (X) increases, the value of the other (Y) decreases. The value of negative correlation ranges from 0 to−1.0.

(iii) **Zero Correlation** It is also possible that sometimes no correlation may exist between the two variables. This is called Zero correlation. This indicates that no significant relationship exists between two variables or the two variables are unrelated. The value of zero correlation is 0.0.

19. Discuss the various types of interview.

Ans. There are two broad types of interviews

(i) **Structured or Standardised Interview** It is one where the questions in the schedule are written clearly in a particular sequence.
The interviewer has little or no liberty to make changes in the wordings of the questions or the order in which they are to be asked. The responses to these questions are also specified in advance. These are called Close-ended questions.

(ii) **Unstructured or Non-Standardised Interview** In this, the interviewer has the flexibility to take decisions about the questions to be asked, the wording of the questions and the sequence in which questions are to be asked.

Responses are not specified in such type of interviews and the respondent can answer the questions in the way she/he chooses. Such questions are called Open-ended questions.

20. **Ramesh wants to construct a questionnaire. Which types of questions he has to frame to construct this activity? Explain in brief.** Competency Based Que.

Ans. Ramesh has to frame two types of questions to construct a questionnaire. These are as follows

(i) **Open-ended Questions** With open-ended questions, the respondent is free to write whatever answer she/he considers appropriate.

(ii) **Close-ended Questions** In the closed ended type, the questions and their probable answers are given and the respondent is required to select the correct answer. Examples of closed-ended questions require responses like Yes/No, True/False, Multiple choice or using a rating scale. In case of rating scale, a statement is given and the respondent is asked to give her/his views on a 3-point (Agree, Undecided, Disagree), or 5-point (Strongly Agree, Agree, Undecided, Disagree, Strongly Disagree) or 7-point, 9-point, 11-point or 13-point scale.
In some cases, the participants are asked to rank a number of things in a preferential order. The questionnaire is used for collecting background and demographic information, information about past behaviour, attitudes and opinions, knowledge about a particular topic and expectations and aspirations of the persons.

21. **Write a short note on reliability of the test.**

Ans. Reliability of the test refers to the consistency of scores obtained by an individual on the same test on two different occasions as follows

(i) **Test-retest Reliability** It indicates the temporal stability or stability of the test scores over time. It is computed by finding out co-efficient of correlation between the two sets of scores on the same set of persons.

(ii) **Split-half Reliability** It gives an indication about the degree of internal consistency of the test. This is based on the assumption that if the items of a test are from the same domain and should correlate with each other or they are from different domains and should not correlate.

For finding out internal consistency, the test is divided into two equal halves employing odd even method (items 1,3,5 in one group and items 2,4,6 in another group) and correlation is computed between the scores of odd and even items.

22. **Write a short note on case study.**

Ans. In case study method, in-depth study of a particular case is emphasised. Researchers focus on cases which can provide critical information or new learning on less understood phenomena. The case can be an individual with distinguishing characteristics or a small group of individuals having some commonality among them, institutions and specific events.

A case study employs multiple methods for collecting information, such as interview, observation and psychological tests from a variety of respondents who in some way or the other might be associated with the case and can provide useful information.

The problem of validity in a single case study is quite challenging. It is recommended that the information should be collected using multiple strategies from different sources of information by a number of investigators.

Careful planning of data collection is also very necessary. Throughout the process of data collection the researcher is required to maintain a chain of evidence for linking various data sources having bearing on the research questions.

23. **Explain the qualitative method of data analysis.**

Ans. Psychologists have developed various qualitative methods to analyse data. One of them is Narrative Analysis.

Data are not always available in the form of scores. When the researcher uses the method of participant observation or unstructured interview, the data are generally in a descriptive form. They are in participants' own words, field notes taken by the researchers, photographs, interview responses noted by the researcher or taped/video-recorded, informal talks, etc. These type of data cannot be converted into scores or subjected to statistical analysis. The researcher uses the technique of content analysis to find out thematic categories and build those categories taking examples from the data.

Long Answer Type Questions

1. **Discuss in brief the various types of observation.**

Ans. The various types of observation are

- **Naturalistic Observation** When observations are done in a natural or real-life settings it is called Naturalistic observation. In this case the observer makes no effort to control or manipulate the situation for making an observation. This type of observation is conducted in hospitals, homes, schools, day care centers, etc.
- **Controlled Observation** Many times certain factors that determine behaviour are controlled by the people that are not the focus of their study. Many of these studies in psychology are conducted in the laboratory. This type of observation is called Controlled laboratory observation which is obtained in laboratory experiments.

- **Non-Participant Observation** Observation can be done through observing the person or event from a distance. The person being observed may not be aware that she/he is being observed. This type of observation is called Non-participant observation.
- **Participant Observation** In participant observation, the observer becomes a part of the group of people being observed.
  In this, the observer takes some time to establish a rapport with the group so that they start accepting them as one of the group members. However, the degree of involvement of the observer with the group being observed would vary depending upon the focus of the study.

2. Explain in brief the concept of variable.

Ans. In the experimental method, a researcher attempts to establish casual relationship between two variables. Any stimulus or event which varies, i.e. have different values (or changes) and can be measured is a variable.

An object is not a variable. But its attributes are variables. For example, the pen that you use for writing is not a variable. But there are varieties of pens available in different shapes, sizes and colours. All of these are variables. Thus, the variation can be in the quality or quantity of objects/events. There are two types of variables

(i) **Independent Variable** It is that variable which is manipulated or altered or its strength varied by the researcher in the experiment. It is the effect of this change in the variable which the researcher wants to observe or note in the study. The independent variable was presence or absence of other persons in the room.

(ii) **Dependent Variable** The variables on which the effect of independent variable is observed is called dependent variable. Dependent variable represents the phenomenon that researcher desires to explain. It is expected that change in the dependent variable will ensue from changes in the independent variable. Thus, the independent variable is the cause and dependent variable is the effect in an experimental situation. Independent and dependent variables are interdependent. Neither of them can be defined without the other.

3. What do you understand by telephone survey? Also discuss the advantages and limitation of survey research.

Ans. Surveys are also conducted through telephone. The telephone survey helps in reducing time.

However, since the respondents do not know the interviewer, the technique is filled with uncooperativeness, reluctance and superficial answers by the respondents.

There is also a possibility that those responding may differ from those not responding, e.g. on age, gender, income levels, education levels, etc. besides their psychological characteristics.

This will lead to very biased kinds of results. Each method has its own advantages and limitations. The researcher needs to exercise caution in selecting a particular method.

Advantages of Survey Research

- Information can be gathered quickly and efficiently from thousands of persons.
- Since surveys can be conducted quickly, public opinions on new issues can be obtained almost as soon as the issues arise.

Limitations of Survey Research

- People may give inaccurate information because of memory lapses or they may not want to let the researcher know what they really believe about a particular issue.
- People sometimes offer responses they think the researcher wants to hear.

4. Differentiate between field experiment and quasi experiment.

Ans. Field experiment and quasi experiment can be differentiated on the basis of the following points

(i) **Location and Setting**

- **Field Experiment** Conducted in a natural setting, like a school or workplace, to increase generalisability.
- **Quasi Experiment** Also in natural settings but focuses on situations that cannot be created in a lab, like the impact of a natural disaster.

(ii) **Control Over Variables**

- **Field Experiment** Limited control over variables compared to a lab experiment.
- **Quasi Experiment** Very little to no control over variables, as it relies on naturally occurring conditions.

(iii) **Manipulation of Variables**

- **Field Experiment** Researchers can manipulate the independent variable, like teaching methods.
- **Quasi Experiment** Independent variable is not manipulated but is selected based on existing conditions, like children who have experienced an earthquake.

(iv) **Purpose and Use**

- **Field Experiment** Used when high generalisability is needed and the study is not feasible in a lab.
- **Quasi Experiment** Used when studying conditions that cannot be artificially created, such as emotional or environmental impacts.

(v) **Examples**

- **Field Experiment** Comparing lecture and demonstration methods in a school setting.
- **Quasi Experiment** Studying the effects of losing parents during an earthquake on children's well-being.

5. Discuss in brief the various types of psychological test.

Ans. Psychological test can be categorised in following types

(i) **Based on Language**

(a) **Verbal Test** Requires literacy, as questions are written in a specific language.

(b) **Non-verbal Test** Uses symbols or pictures instead of language, making it suitable for those with language limitations.

(c) **Performance Test** Involves moving objects in a specific order to solve problems; literacy is not needed.

(ii) **Based on Mode of Administration**

(a) **Individual Test** Administered face-to-face with one person at a time, allowing personalised responses; time-consuming but suitable for children or people unfamiliar with the language.

(b) **Group Test** Administered to multiple people at once, with written instructions; quicker but may lack the motivation in responses compared to individual tests.

(iii) **Based on Speed and Power**

(a) **Speed Test** Has a time limit for completion; all questions are of similar difficulty, testing quickness and accuracy.

(b) **Power Test** No time limit; questions increase in difficulty, testing an individual's capability rather than speed.

6. Rajpriya is going to study relationship between poverty and unemployment in her locality after the pandemic. She decided to use experiment method for it. Define experiment method and explain different type of variables. Competency Based Que.

Ans. Rajpriya is going to study relationship between poverty and unemployment in her locality after the pandemic and she has decided to use experiment method for it.

Experiments methods are generally conducted to establish cause-effect relationship between two sets of events or variables in a controlled setting. It is a carefully regulated procedure in which changes are made in one factor and its effect is studied on another factor, while keeping other related factors constant.

Variable Any stimulus or event which varies, that is, it takes on different values (or changes) and can be measured is a variable.

Independent Variable Independent variable is that variable which is manipulated or altered or its strength varied by the researcher in the experiment. It is the effect of this change in the variable which the researcher wants to observe or note in the study.

Dependent Variable The variables on which the effect of independent variable is observed is called dependent variable. Dependent variable represents the phenomenon the researcher desires to explain.

7. As a budding psychologist, you have been assigned the task of conducting psychological research on the topic 'impact of online gaming on the well-being of adolescence'. Which ethical issues will you be keeping in mind, while carrying out the assigned task? Competency Based Que.

Ans. Ethical issues to be kept in mind, while carrying out the assigned task are as following

- **Informed Consent** Obtain permission from participants or, if minors, from their parents or guardians.
- Ensure they understand the purpose, procedures and any risks involved in the study.
- **Confidentiality** Protect participants' personal information and keep all responses anonymous.
- Avoid sharing any data that could reveal the identity of individual participants.
- **Avoiding Harm** Be cautious to avoid causing emotional or psychological distress.
- Ensure that the questions and procedures do not negatively affect the participants' well-being.
- **Right to Withdraw** Inform participants that they can withdraw from the study at any time without penalty.
- Respect their choice if they decide to stop participating.
- **Debriefing** After the study, explain the findings and purpose to the participants.
- Address any concerns or misconceptions they may have about the research.
- **Avoiding Bias** Keep personal opinions about online gaming separate from the research.
- Ensure findings are objective and based on data rather than preconceptions.

8. A pharma company, after a detailed testing on some volunteers, has claimed that they have successfully devised a vaccine for curing COVID-19. Describe the method of enquiry that was possibly used for testing the effectiveness of the vaccine.

Ans. The method of enquiry that was possibly used for testing the effectiveness of the vaccine are as following

Experimental Method The vaccine would be tested through a controlled experiment, where a sample group receives the vaccine while another (the control group) may receive a place.

- Researchers would observe and compare health outcomes in both groups.

Use of Volunteers Volunteers would likely be selected and divided into two groups–vaccinated and unvaccinated.

- They would be monitored over time to assess immunity and side effects.

Control and Experimental Groups A control group would not receive the vaccine to compare results with the vaccinated group.

- This helps show if the vaccine is effective or if improvements are due to other factors.

Data Collection Researchers would record data on health status, side effects and antibody levels in participants.

- Data analysis would reveal the vaccine's effectiveness in preventing or reducing COVID-19 symptoms.

Ethical Considerations Participants would need to give informed consent and be aware of any risks.

- Monitoring for adverse effects is essential to ensure participant safety throughout the study.

Case Based Questions

Read the following cases and answer the questions that follow.

1. Psychology is also recognised as a social science because it studies the behaviour of human beings in their socio-cultural contexts. For example, Ranjita and Shabnam are classmates from a village. Ranjita comes from a farmer's family, while Shabnam's father works in an office in a town. During the rainy season, Shabnam's house is flooded, and she moves into Ranjita's house with her mother and brother. Ranjita helps them feel comfortable in her home, and when the floodwaters recede, Ranjita's mother and grandmother help Shabnam's mother set up their house again. This example shows how individuals in communities can be helpful and self-sacrificing in times of crisis. However, this is not always the case, as some people may act in an antisocial manner in similar situations. Psychology, therefore, examines human behaviour in the context of society and culture.

(i) In the given case, what was Ranjita's response when Shabnam's house was flooded? Which of the following defines Ranjita's behaviour?

(ii) What does the passage suggest about human behaviour in crises?

Ans. (i) Ranjita showed empathy and self-sacrifice by helping Shabnam's family during the crisis. The following points define Ranjita's behaviour

- She helped Shabnam's family when their house was flooded.
- She made them feel comfortable in her house.
- After the flood, she and her family helped Shabnam's family set up their house again.

(ii) The passage suggests that human behaviour in crises can vary

- In some cases, people act selflessly and help others in need.
- In other situations, individuals may act anti-socially, refusing to help or even worsening the situation.
- Psychology studies such behaviour within the socio-cultural context of individuals and communities.

2. Ravi is a psychologist who is conducting a study on the study habits of university students. He is interested in understanding what factors contribute to effective study habits and how these habits influence academic performance. Ravi decides to observe a group of students and records their daily study routines, including the number of hours spent studying, how often they attend lectures and their revision schedules. After analysing the data, Ravi establishes that students who attend all their classes regularly and follow a structured study plan tend to perform better academically. Based on his findings, Ravi predicts that students who adopt a disciplined study routine will achieve higher academic success. Ravi also identifies certain environmental and psychological factors that can enhance or hinder study habits, such as motivation levels and study environment.

(i) What is the primary goal of Ravi's research?

(ii) How does Ravi's research relate to the goal of prediction?

Ans. (i) The primary goal of Ravi's research is description, as he is observing and accurately recording the study habits of university students to understand and distinguish different behaviours related to academic performance.

(ii) Ravi's research relates to prediction because based on his observations, he establishes a relationship between study habits and academic success, allowing him to predict that students with disciplined study routines will perform better in exams.

3. In a study conducted at a local school, the researcher aimed to observe the behaviour of children in their natural school setting. The researcher decided to observe how children spend their time during recess. They chose this setting because the children's behaviour during recess is less controlled and more spontaneous, providing valuable insight into their social interactions and peer relationships.

The researcher selected a group of children from different age groups and recorded the activities they engaged in during recess. This involved observing their play, interactions and the nature of their conversations. The data was collected through non-participant observation, where the researcher remained at a distance, using a notebook to record observations.

After collecting the data, the researcher analysed the notes and categorised the behaviours observed into different types of social interactions, such as cooperative play, solitary play and conflict. These findings provided valuable insights into the social dynamics of the children, and helped in understanding the relationships between age and social behaviour during unstructured time.

(i) What method of observation was used in the given case?

(ii) What is the main advantage of non-participant observation as seen in this case?

Ans. (i) The method of observation used in the given case is non-participant observation.

- The researcher did not interfere with the activities of the children.
- The researcher observed the children from a distance, making no attempt to influence or control the behaviour.
- The data was recorded using a notebook to note down the observations.

(ii) The main advantage of non-participant observation in this case is that it allowed the researcher to observe the children's behaviour naturally, without interfering in their activities.

- It provided insights into spontaneous, real-life interactions.
- It helped to study the children's social dynamics without any influence from the researcher.
- The behaviour of the children was likely more authentic as they were unaware of being observed.

SELF ASSESSMENT TEST

Objective Type Questions

1. Which of the following information is not collected as a demographic information?

(a) Galvanic skin resistance (b) Occupation (c) Marital status (d) Religion

2. Which of the following information is not collected as a psychological information?

(a) Creativity (b) Interest values (c) Blood's oxygen levels (d) Subjective experiences

3. The final goal of the scientific enquiry is to bring out .... in the lives of people.

(a) positive changes (b) cultural changes (c) negative changes (d) psychological changes

4. The experiments during which independent variables is chosen instead of varied or manipulated by the experimenter are called

(a) Field experiments (b) Quasi experiments (c) Positive experiments (d) Negative experiments

Very Short Answer Type Questions

1. What is independent variable?
2. Define positive correlation.
3. What are the goals of psychological enquiry?
4. Define the term prediction.
5. Give one example where survey method can be used.

Short Answer Type Questions

1. Define the interpretive method of research.
2. Give four techniques to control extraneous variables.
3. Explain characteristics of a standardised test.
4. Explain the main features of interview method.
5. State any three difference between structured and unstructured interview.

Long Answer Type Questions

1. Discuss in detail the different types of psychological tests.
2. Discuss the factors affecting data collection.
3. How Interview is different from Questionnaire?

Case Based Questions

Read the case and answer the questions that follow.

In the experiment conducted by Latane and Darley, the researchers wanted to examine the effect of the presence of other persons on the reporting of smoke. The experiment was designed to test how the presence or absence of others affected people's willingness to report an emergency situation. In the study, participants were sent to three types of rooms. In one room, no one was present (control group). In the other two rooms, two persons were already seated (experimental groups). The independent variable in this experiment was the presence or absence of other persons in the room, while the dependent variable was whether the participants reported the presence of smoke in the room. The researchers found that participants in the control group, where no one else was present, reported the smoke the most. The experimental group that was not given any instructions reported the smoke less and the group with confederates (who were instructed not to react) reported the smoke the least.

(i) What is the independent variable in the experiment conducted by Latane and Darley?

(ii) What is the dependent variable in this experiment?

03

CHAPTER

Human development involves various changes from birth to old age. Over a span of time, individuals experience physical /biological cognitive and socio-emotional growth. Although each individual's experiences are unique, there are common patterns in development.

YOUR STUDY GOALS

YOUR PRACTICE GOAL

- Objective Type Questions (28 Qs ; MCQs, A-R)
- Subjective Questions (14 VSAs, 15 SAs, 4 LAs, 3 Case Based)

Human Development

3.1 Meaning of Development

- Development refers to the pattern of progressive, orderly and predictable changes that begin at conception and continue throughout life.
- It includes both growth and decline, particularly observed during old age.
- Development is influenced by three interlinked processes
  (i) **Biological processes** Genetic inheritance affects physical traits like height, weight and organ development.
  (ii) **Cognitive processes** It involves mental activities like thinking, preceiving and problem-solving, vital for learning and development.
  (iii) **Socio-emotional processes** It involves changes in interactions with others, changes in emotions and in personality.

Life-Span Perspective on Development

The Life-Span Perspective (LSP) incorporates the following assumptions about development

- **Lifelong Process** Development occurs throughout all stages of life, from conception to old age. It involves both gains and losses, which interact dynamically.
- **Integrated Processes** Biological, cognitive and socio-emotional processes are interconnected in the development of an individual.

- **Multi-directional** Development involves both growth and decline in various aspects. Some dimensions may increase while others decrease. For example, with the increase in age, one's performance is likely to decrease on tasks requiring speed.
- **Plasticity** Development is modifiable throughout life, meaning skills and abilities can be improved at any age. This plasticity varies across individuals.
- **Historical Influences** Development is affected by historical contexts. For example, career expectations for students today differ from those in the past.
- **Interdisciplinary** Human development is studied across various disciplines, such as psychology, anthropology, sociology and neuro-science, to understand development throughout life.
- **Contextual Response** Individuals respond to various contexts, including genetic inheritance, physical environment, social, historical and cultural influences. Life events (e.g., loss of a parent, natural disasters) and positive influences (e.g., awards, job opportunities) can significantly impact one's life course.

Growth, Development, Maturation and Evolution

Growth It refers to the increase in the size of body parts or of the organism as a whole. It is measurable and quantifiable, such as increases in height or weight.

Development It involves the changes that occur throughout an individual's life cycle. These changes have direction and are interrelated, with one change leading to another. Development encompasses growth as one of its aspects but also includes other types of changes in proportions, features and abilities. Not all changes are part of development; temporary changes (e.g., those caused by illness) are not considered part of development.

- Development includes various types of changes
  - Physical growth (increase in size).
  - Proportional changes (e.g., from child to adult).
  - Changes in features (e.g., disappearance of baby teeth).
  - Acquiring new features or abilities.

Maturation It refers to changes that follow a specific sequence, largely dictated by genetic factors. These changes are characteristic of the species and result in common patterns of growth and development. For example, most children sit up by 7 months, stand with support by 8 months, and walk by one year. Maturation occurs when the underlying physical structures are sufficiently developed and proficiency in behaviours requires minimal external help. Special efforts to accelerate maturation (e.g. helping infants walk before they are ready) do not yield successful results if the child is not biologically prepared. The process of maturation 'unfolds from within' based on a genetically determined timetable.

Evolution It refers to species-specific changes over a time. The species **Homo sapiens** (modern humans) is believed to have appeared around 50,000 years ago. **Natural selection** is a key mechanism in evolution, favouring individuals or species that are best adapted for survival and reproduction. Evolutionary changes are passed from one generation to the next within a species. Evolution proceeds at a very slow pace; for example, the emergence of humans from great apes took approximately 14 million years.

3.2 Factors Influencing Development

- People differ in physical and psychological characteristics, but these differences are influenced by the interaction of heredity (genetics) and environment. For example, an individual with short height genes will never be taller than average despite of good nutritional environment.
- Despite variations, all humans belong to the same species due to the influence of genetic and environmental factors.

Genetic Factors

- Genetic transmission is complex, as most characteristics result from combinations of multiple genes.
- Genes provide a unique blueprint for an individual's development, but development occurs in the context of the individual's environment.
- Heredity explains how characteristics are passed down through generations using genetic codes, which are in every cell of our body.
- The genetic code ensures that a fertilised human egg grows into a human baby, not into another species like an elephant or a bird.
- Genotype refers to the genetic material or heritage that a person inherits, not all of this is visible in observable traits.
- Phenotype refers to the expression of the genotype in observable and measurable traits like height, weight, eye colour, skin colour, intelligence, creativity and personality.
- The observable characteristics result from the interaction between inherited traits and environmental influences.

Environmental Factors

- Environmental influences are as complex as genetic factors. While genetics set certain limits, the environment shapes development within those limits.
- **Sandra Scarr** (1992) proposed that parents' genetic predispositions influence the environment they provide for their children.
- For example, intelligent parents might provide books and encourage reading, which would likely lead to their children becoming good readers. Children also actively choose environments that suit their genetic predispositions.
- These interactions between genetics and environment continue to evolve from infancy through adolescence.

Quick Test 1

1 Explain the concept of 'Development'.
2 Mark the difference between genotype and phenotype?
3 Differentiate between Growth, Development, Maturation and Evolution.
4 What are environmental factors that influence individual development?
5 How does the interaction between heredity and environment shape observable traits?

3.3 Context of Development

- Development occurs within a specific socio-cultural context, influenced by biological changes and changing environments throughout an individual's life.
- Major life transitions such as entering school, adolescence, marriage, having children and retirement are shaped by both biological changes and environmental factors.
- The environment may alter at any point during a person's lifespan, influencing development.

Bronfenbrenner's Model of Development

Urie Bronfenbrenner's contextual view of development emphasises the role of environmental factors in the development of an individual. This has been depicted as

- **Microsystem** The immediate environment where a child directly interacts with social agents like family, peers, teachers and the neighbourhood.
- **Mesosystem** Interactions between different contexts, such as the relationship between parents and teachers or the influence of parents' views on an adolescent's friends.
- **Exosystem** Indirect influences where the child is not directly involved but is affected by external factors, such as a parent's job transfer causing family tension, which then impacts the child.
- **Macrosystem** The broader cultural context in which the individual lives, such as societal norms and values.
- **Chronosystem** The influence of events across an individual's life course, including socio-historical changes, such as parental divorce or economic setbacks, which affect development.
- **Implications** Research shows that children in impoverished environments with unstimulating surroundings, lack of educational resources, and ineffective parental role models face developmental disadvantages and difficulties in learning.

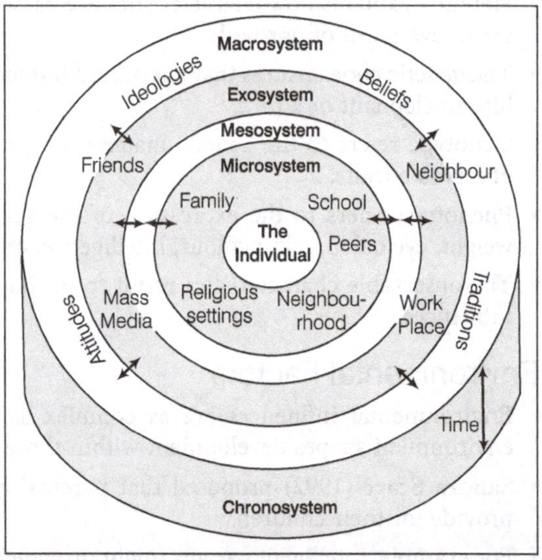

Bronfenbrenner's Contextual View of Development

Durganand Sinha's Model of Development

Durganand Sinha has presented an ecological model for understanding the development of children in Indian context. Ecology of children could be viewed in terms of concentric layers, these are

(i) **Upper Layer** The important ecological factors influencing child's development in the visible upper layer constitute

(a) Home, its condition in terms of overcrowding, space available to each member, toys, technological devices used etc.

(b) Nature and quality of schooling and facilities to which the child exposed.

(c) Nature of interactions and activities undertaken with peer groups.

(ii) **Surrounding Layer** This layer constantly influences the 'upper layer' factors. However, these influences are not always clearly visible. Following are the ecological factors that influence child's development.

(a) General geographical environment which includes space and facilities for play and other activities available outside the home including general congestion of locality.

(b) Institutional setting provided by caste, class and other factors.

(c) General amenities available such as drinking water, electricity, means of entertainment and so on.

- The upper and surrounding layers interact and their combined influence can have different developmental outcomes depending on the individual's experiences.
- The ecological environment can change throughout a person's life, so understanding an individual's development requires considering their unique environmental context and experiences.

3.4 Overview of Developmental Stages

- Human life progresses through different stages, such as adolescence and adulthood, each characterised by a dominant feature or characteristic that defines that stage.
- Developmental stages are considered temporary, with individuals moving towards a specific goal or ability during each stage.
- Certain behaviours and skills are learned more easily during specific stages, becoming social expectations. These are referred to as **developmental tasks**.
- Different stages of development and their main features are described below.

3.5 Prenatal Stage

- The period from conception to birth, lasting around 40 weeks is known as Prenatal stage.
- Genetic blueprint guides development during prenatal and post-birth stages.
- Prenatal development is influenced by maternal characteristics such as age, nutrition and emotional state.
- Diseases and infections carried by the mother can affect prenatal development. For example, rubella, genital herpes and HIV can cause genetic problems in new born.
- Common teratogens including drugs, radiation and pollution that can cause developmental abnormalities or even death. For example
  - **Intake of drugs** Marijuana, heroin, cocaine, alcohol and tobacco can lead to congenital abnormalities.
  - **Radiation** X-rays and industrial chemicals may cause genetic changes.
  - **Pollutants** Carbon monoxide, mercury and lead can harm foetal development.

3.6 Infancy Stage

- The period from birth to two years, marked by rapid brain development and essential life functions like breathing, sucking, swallowing and waste discharge.
- During infancy, **motor development**[1], sensory abilities, cognitive growth and socio-emotional development occur.

Motor Development During Infancy

- The newborn's movements are governed by reflexes which are automatic, built in responses to stimuli.
- Some reflexes present in new born, such as coughing, blinking and yawning, persist throughout life.
- Other reflexes disappear as the brain matures and voluntary control over movements begins.
- As the brain develops, physical development also progresses and the muscles and nervous system mature which lead to the development of finer skills.

1 Motor Development It refers to the progression of muscular coordination required for physical activities.

- Infants develop skills like holding, reaching for objects, sitting, crawling, walking and running.
- Physical (motor) development follows a universal sequence, with minor exceptions.

Some Major Reflexes in the New born

Reflex	Description	Developmental Course
Rooting	Turning the head and opening the mouth when touched on the cheek.	Disappears between 3 and 6 months
Moro	In response to a loud noise, the baby throws its arms outward, arches its back and then brings the arms together as if grasping something.	Disappears in 6 to 7 months, but reaction to loud noises is permanent
Grasp	When a finger or object is pressed against the baby's palm, the fingers close around it.	Disappears in 3 to 4 months, replaced by voluntary grasping
Babinski	When the bottom of the baby's foot is stroked, the toes fan out and then curl.	Disappears in 8 to 12 months

Development of Sensory Abilities During Infancy

- Infants can hear immediately after birth. Newborns can recognise their mother's voice just a few hours after birth.
- Newborns have other sensory capabilities.
- Newborns prefer to look at some stimuli rather than others, such as faces, although these preferences change over the first few months of life.
- The newborn's vision is estimated to be lower than adult vision. Their full colour vision develops by 3 months of age.
- By 6 months, vision improves and by about the first year, it is almost the same as that of an adult.
- Newborns might be able to distinguish between red and white colours but, in general, they are colour deficient.
- Newborns respond to touch and can even feel pain. Both smell and taste capacities are present in newborns.

Cognitive Development During Infancy

- During infancy, the child experiences the world through senses and interactions with objects, i.e. through looking, hearing, touching, mouthing and grasping.
- If something is out of sight, it is out of mind for children at this stage.
- For example, if a person hides the toy in front of the child with which the child has been playing, the young infant would react as if nothing has happened, i.e. the child will not search for the toy.
- According to Jean Piaget, children at this stage do not go beyond their immediate sensory experience, i.e. they lack **object permanence**[2].
- Gradually, by 8 months of age, the child starts pursuing an object partially covered in front of them.
- The basis of verbal communication seems to be present in infants.
- Vocalisation begins with the infant's babbling, sometime between 3 to 6 months of age.
- Jean Piaget stressed that children actively construct their understanding of the world. Information does not simply enter their minds from the environment.
- As children grow, additional information is acquired and they adapt their thinking to include new ideas, improving their understanding of the world.
- Piaget believed that a child's mind passes through a series of stages of thought from infancy to adolescence.
- Each stage is characterised by a distinct way of thinking and is age-related.
- It is important to remember that it is the different way of thinking that makes one stage more advanced than the other and not the amount of information.

2 **Object Permanence** It is the understanding that object and events continue to exist even when they cannot directly be seen, heard or touched.

Piaget's Stages Cognitive Development

Stage	Approximate Age	Characteristics
Sensorimotor	0-2 years	Infant explores the world by coordinating sensory experiences with physical actions.
Preoperational	2-7 years	Children use symbols to represent words, ideas and images; object permanence is established; the child cannot coordinate different physical attributes of an object.
Concrete Operational	7-11 years	The child can reason logically about concrete events and classify objects into different sets. Can perform reversible mental operations on representations of objects.
Formal Operational	11-15 years	The adolescent can apply logic more abstractly; hypothetical thinking.

Socio-Emotional Development During Infancy

- An infant starts preferring familiar faces and responds to the parent's presence by cooing and gurgling (babbling).
- By 6 to 8 months of age, infants become more energetic and show a preference for their mother's company.
- When frightened by a new face or separated from their mother, infants cry or show distress.
- On being reunited with the parent or caregiver, infants reciprocate with smiles or hugs.
- The close emotional bond of affection that develops between infants and their parents (or caregivers) is called attachment.
- A classic study by Harlow and Harlow (1962) involved baby monkeys being separated from their mothers shortly after birth and reared by surrogate mothers.
  - The baby monkeys were placed in experimental chambers and cared for by two surrogate mothers, one made of wire and the other of cloth.
  - Half of the baby monkeys were fed by the wire mother and half were fed by the cloth mother.
  - Regardless of the source of food, the baby monkeys preferred the cloth mother and spent more time with her.
  - The study showed that attachment is not based solely on food but on comfort and contact, indicating the importance of emotional comfort.
- Young children develop strong attachments to comfort objects like toys or blankets, even though they are not their mothers.
- As children grow, they eventually abandon these comfort objects.
- Human babies also form attachments with their parents or caregivers, who consistently and appropriately reciprocate their signals of love and affection.
- According to Erik Erikson (1968), the first year of life is a crucial period for developing attachment, representing the stage of developing trust or mistrust.

Effect of Responsive and Sensitive Parenting on Infant

- Responsive and sensitive parenting plays a key role in building a sense of trust in infants.
- A sense of trust is built on physical comfort, which helps an infant develop an expectation that the world is secure and good.
- If parents are sensitive, affectionate and accepting, it provides the infant with a strong base to explore the environment, leading to secure attachment.
- On the other hand, if parents are insensitive, dissatisfied or critical of the child, it can cause feelings of self-doubt in the child.

- Securely attached infants respond positively when picked up, play more freely and are generally more confident.
- Insecurely attached infants feel anxious when separated from their caregiver, cry out of fear, and get upset.
- A close interactive relationship with warm and affectionate adults is crucial for a child's healthy development.

3.7 Childhood Stage

- Childhood is the stage between infancy and adolescence, typically from 3 to 10 years of age.
- During early childhood, the child's growth slows down compared to infancy.
- The child develops physically, gains height and weight and learns basic motor skills like walking, running, jumping and playing.
- The child's world expands from just the parents to the family, other adults near home, and at school.
- The child begins to acquire concepts of good and bad, developing a sense of morality.
- During childhood, children develop increased physical capacities, can perform tasks independently, set goals and meet adult expectations.

Physical Development During Childhood

- The brain and head grow more rapidly than any other part of the body during this stage.
- The growth and development of the brain are crucial as they help in the maturation of abilities such as eye-hand coordination, holding a pencil and attempts at writing.
- During middle and late childhood, children increase significantly in size and strength.
- The increase in weight is mainly due to the growth of the skeletal and muscular systems, as well as the size of some body organs.
- Early development follows two principles
  (i) **Cephalocaudal Development** Development proceeds from the head (cephalic) to the tail (caudal) region. Children gain control over the upper body before the lower part. This is why an infant's head is proportionally larger than their body during early infancy.
  (ii) **Proximodistal Development** Growth proceeds from the center of the body and moves towards the extremities (distal regions). Children gain control over their upper body before their extremities. For example, infants initially reach for objects by turning their entire body and gradually they extend their arms to reach for things.
- These changes are a result of the maturing nervous system, not limitations. Even visually impaired children show the same developmental sequence.
- As children grow older, they look slimmer as their trunk lengthens and body fat decreases.

Motor Development During Childhood

- Gross motor skills during early childhood involve the use of arms and legs, allowing children to move around confidently and purposefully.
- Fine motor skills (finger skills and eye-hand coordination) improve substantially during early childhood.
- During these years, the child's preference for using the left or right hand also develops.

Age in Years	Gross Motor Skills	Fine Motor Skills
3 Years	Hopping, jumping, running	Build blocks, pick objects with forefinger and thumb
4 Years	Climb up and downstairs with one foot on each step	Fit jigsaw puzzle precisely
5 Years	Run hard, enjoy races	Hand, arm, and body all coordinate with eye movement

Cognitive Development During Childhood

- The brain matures and experiences contribute to the development of children's cognitive abilities.
- The ability to acquire the concept of object permanence helps children to use mental symbols to represent objects.
- However, children at this stage lack the ability to do mentally what they can physically do before.
- Cognitive development in early childhood focuses on Piaget's stage of preoperational thought.
- In this stage, children gain the ability to mentally represent an object that is not physically present, such as drawing designs/figures to represent people, trees, dogs, houses, etc.
- The ability to engage in symbolic thought helps children expand their mental world.

Egocentrism During Childhood

- A key feature of preoperational thought is **egocentrism**[3], where children see the world only in terms of their own selves and struggle to appreciate others' points of view.
- Due to egocentrism, children engage in **animism**[4], thinking that all things are living like themselves.
- Between 4 and 7 years of age, children develop curiosity and begin asking questions about their surroundings, a stage called intuitive thought.
- Children during this stage have a tendency for centration, i.e., focusing on a single characteristic or feature of an event.
- For example, a child may prefer a tall narrow glass over a short wide one, even if both hold the same amount of juice.

Concrete Operations During Childhood

- Concrete operations involve mental actions that allow the child to do mentally what was previously done physically.
- Concrete operations are reversible mental actions.
- Between 7 and 11 years of age, intuitive thought is replaced by logical thought, marking the stage of concrete operational thought.
- In a well-known test, a child is shown two identical balls of clay, one rolled into a thin strip and the other left in its original shape. When asked which has more clay, the child, around 7 or 8 years old, would say both have the same amount, as they can imagine the process of rolling the strip back into a ball.
- Concrete operations allow children to focus on multiple characteristics of an object, rather than just one, reducing egocentrism.
- As a result, children's thinking becomes more flexible and they can think about alternatives when solving problems or mentally retrace their steps if needed.
- However, even though children can see relationships between different properties of objects, they cannot engage in **abstract thinking**[5].

Socio-Emotional Development During Childhood

- Important dimensions of socio-emotional development include the self, gender and moral development.
- Through socialisation, children develop a sense of who they are and whom they want to identify with.
- The developing sense of independence encourages children to do things their own way.
- According to Erikson, the way parents respond to children's self-initiated activities affects the development of a sense of initiative or guilt.

---

3 **Egocentrism** It is the state of being overly interested in oneself and one's own needs, at the expense of others.
4 **Animism** It is the belief that objects have lifelike qualities and are therefore capable of having feelings, intentions and emotions.
5 **Abstract Thinking** It is the ability to understand and think about complex concepts that are not tied to concrete experiences.

- For example, providing freedom and opportunities for play (like cycling, running, skating) and answering their questions supports initiative.
- On the other hand, if their questions are dismissed and their play is ridiculed, children may develop feelings of guilt over self-initiated activities, which could persist throughout life.
- In early childhood, self-understanding is limited to physical characteristics (e.g., 'I am tall', 'I am a girl').
- In middle and late childhood, self-definition shifts to internal characteristics (e.g., 'I am smart', 'I feel proud when teachers give me responsibility').
- Children's self-descriptions also include social aspects, such as identifying with social groups.
- Self-understanding during this stage also involves social comparison, where children assess what they can or cannot do in comparison to others (e.g., 'I got more marks than Atul', 'I can run faster than others in class').
- This shift leads to the recognition of one's differences from others as an individual.
- Once children enter school, their social world expands beyond their families and they spend more time with peers.
- The increased time spent with peers plays a significant role in shaping their development.

Gender and Sex Roles

Sex Differences

- Research shows that males are generally more aggressive than females.
- Men tend to perform better than women on physical tasks such as sit-ups, short-run speeds, and long jumps.
- Women have better fine eye-hand coordination than men and their joints and limbs are more flexible.

Gender Roles

- Sex refers to the biological dimension (male or female), while gender refers to the social dimension (the roles and expectations society assigns to males or females).
- An important aspect of gender is gender identity, which refers to identifying oneself as male or female. Most children acquire this by the age of 3 and can accurately label themselves as boys or girls.

Gender Role Expectations

- A gender role is a set of expectations that prescribes how males and females should think, act, and feel.
- Parents and peers play a significant role in gender socialisation, especially in the early years.
- Through rewards and punishments, parents teach children what is considered gender-appropriate behaviour and assign different types of chores to boys and girls.
- Parents also engage in 'dependence training' for daughters and 'independence training' for sons in everyday interactions.

Media Influence on Gender Stereotypes

- The media, including cartoons and commercials, perpetuate gender stereotypes.
- Research shows that in commercials, authority figures are often portrayed as male, while women are depicted in dependent or domestic roles.

Gender Socialisation and Self-Identification

- Once children learn their gender role, they begin organising their world and socialise themselves based on gender norms.
- Children's behaviour and attention are guided by an internal motivation to conform to gender-based socio-cultural standards and stereotypes.
- After internalising gender standards, children expect gender-appropriate behaviour from themselves.
- For example, young boys may refuse to wear feminine clothes in a fancy dress competition and girls may avoid playing the father's role during games of house.

Gender Typing

- Gender typing occurs when individuals are ready to categorise and organise information based on what is considered appropriate or typical for males and females in a society.

Moral Development During Childhood

- Moral development is an important aspect of a child's growth, involving the ability to distinguish between right and wrong.
- It includes feelings of guilt, understanding others' perspectives and helping others in trouble.
- According to Lawrence Kohlberg, children pass through stages of moral development, similar to cognitive development stages.
- Kohlberg suggests that children think about right and wrong differently at various ages.
- In early childhood (before 9 years), children think in terms of external authority, such as being punished for wrong actions and rewarded for right actions.
- As children grow, they develop moral reasoning based on the rules of others, such as parents or society's laws.
- These rules are internalised by children to be virtuous and to gain approval from others, rather than to avoid punishment.
- Children see rules as absolute guidelines that should be followed.
- Moral thinking in childhood is relatively inflexible.
- As children grow, they gradually develop a personal moral code.
- By the end of childhood, children experience a gradual growth in coordination, balance and logical reasoning.
- Socially, children become more involved in systems like family and peer groups.

Quick Test 2

1. What is Bronfenbrenner's ecological systems theory focused on?
2. Name an example of teratogens.
3. What are the two main characteristics of the prenatal stage of development?
4. At what age do infants typically start developing object permanence?
5. What is attachment in infancy?
6. Name any one source of danger to the unborn child?

3.8 Adolescence

- The term adolescence comes from the Latin word adolescere, meaning 'to grow into maturity'.
- Adolescence is the transitional period between childhood and adulthood, beginning at puberty when sexual maturity and the ability to reproduce are reached.
- While physical changes are universal, social and psychological experiences depend on cultural contexts.
- In cultures where adolescence is seen as problematic, adolescents may have different experiences than in cultures where adolescence is viewed as the beginning of adult behaviour and responsibility.
- Not all cultures have a defined period of adolescence, though most societies recognise some period of adolescence.

Physical Development During Adolescence

- Adolescence is marked by dramatic changes in growth rate and sexual characteristics.
- Puberty is a gradual process, not a sudden event.
- Hormones released during puberty lead to the development of primary and secondary sexual characteristics.
- **Primary sex characteristics**[6] are directly related to reproduction, while **secondary sex characteristics**[7] are signs of sexual maturity.
- In boys, pubertal changes include growth acceleration, facial hair and a deeper voice.
- In girls, rapid growth in height begins about two years before menarche (onset of menstruation).
- Growth spurts generally begin at age 12-13 for boys and 10-11 for girls.
- There are variations in the pubertal sequence. For instance, two children of the same age may experience puberty at different times.
- Both genetics and environment play a role in the timing of puberty.
- Identical twins tend to reach menarche closer in time than fraternal twins.
- Girls from affluent families tend to experience menarche earlier than girls from poor families.
- Historical trends show that the age of menarche is declining in industrialised nations due to better nutrition and medical care.

Psychological Development During Adolescence

- Adolescents show increased interest in members of the opposite sex and sexual matters around puberty.
- This is due to biological changes and the emphasis placed on sexuality by peers, parents and society.
- Many adolescents have misconceptions or lack adequate knowledge about sex and sexuality.
- Parents often find it difficult to discuss sexual matters, leading to secrecy among adolescents, which hinders communication.
- Concerns about adolescent sexuality have intensified recently due to the risk of AIDS and other sexually transmitted diseases.
- The development of sexual identity, including sexual orientation and sexual behaviour, is an important developmental task for adolescents.
- Adolescents are preoccupied with their appearance and develop personal images of how they look.
- Another key task is accepting one's physical self and maturity, which involves forming a realistic and acceptable image of their physical appearance.
- Puberty also involves cognitive and social changes alongside physical changes.

Cognitive Developments during Adolescence

- During adolescence, thoughts become more abstract, logical and idealistic.
- Adolescents become capable of examining their own thoughts, others' thoughts and considering what others think about them.
- The development of logical and reasoning abilities gives adolescents a new level of cognitive and social awareness.
- Formal operational thought, appearing between the ages of 11 and 15, allows adolescents' thinking to expand beyond concrete experiences and become idealistic.
- Adolescents begin to think about ideal characteristics for themselves and others and compare themselves with these ideals.

---

6 **Primary Sex Characteristics** These are the sexual structures necessary for reproduction.

7 **Secondary Sex Characteristics** These are physical featrues that are associated with gender but that are not directly involves in reproduction.

Development of Logical and Moral Thinking

- Adolescent thinking becomes more systematic in problem-solving, considering possible actions and systematically seeking solutions.
- Piaget referred to this logical thinking as **hypothetical-deductive reasoning**.
- Logical thought also influences moral reasoning, leading to more flexibility in considering social rules.
- Adolescents recognise alternative moral courses and explore options, developing a personal moral code.
- This can lead adolescents to not follow societal norms if they conflict with their personal code of ethics.

Adolescents' Egocentrism

- Adolescents develop a unique form of egocentrism, according to David Elkind, which includes two components
  (i) **Imaginary Audience** Adolescents believe that others are as preoccupied with them as they are with themselves. They think people are always noticing them and observing every behaviour, making them self-conscious.
  (ii) **Personal Fable** Adolescents feel a sense of uniqueness and believe no one understands their feelings. To preserve this uniqueness, they may create fantasy stories, leading to a world apart from reality. This often reflects in their diaries.

Identity Formation

- Identity refers to an individual's character, values, commitments and beliefs.
- The primary task of adolescence is to establish an identity separate from their parents.
- A detachment process during adolescence helps individuals to develop a personalised set of beliefs that belongs to them.
- Achieving an identity may cause conflicts with parents and within the adolescent themselves.
- Adolescents who can cope with these conflicting identities develop a new sense of self.
- Those unable to manage this identity crisis may experience confusion, leading to isolation from peers and family or losing their identity in the crowd.
- Adolescents may seek independence but also show dependence on their parents, leading to fluctuations between self-confidence and insecurity.
- They may complain of being treated as a baby sometimes, whereas on other occasions they may seek comfort by depending on parents.
- Seeking an identity involves striving for continuity, responsibility and a clear sense of self.

Factors Affecting Identity Formation

- Identity formation during adolescence is influenced by factors such as cultural background, family and societal values, ethnic background, and socio-economic status.
- Family relationships become less important as adolescents spend more time outside the home and develop a need for peer support and acceptance.
- Increased peer interactions offer opportunities to refine social skills and try different social behaviours.
- Vocational commitment, such as career questions, future planning, and goal setting, also impacts identity formation.
- In some cultures, young people are free to choose their occupation, while in others, the choice is restricted.
- Career counselling in schools helps students evaluate various courses and jobs, offering guidance on career choices.

Major Concerns (Challenges) During Adolescence

- Adolescents often face issues like peer influence, newfound freedom and unresolved problems, which create difficulties during this stage.
- Common emotional challenges include uncertainty, loneliness, self-doubt, anxiety and concerns about their future.
- However, they also experience excitement, joy and feelings of competence as they overcome developmental challenges.

Delinquency

- Delinquency refers to socially unacceptable behaviour, legal offences and criminal acts, including truancy, running away from home, stealing, burglary and vandalism.
- Adolescents with delinquency and behavioural issues tend to have a negative self-identity, decreased trust and low achievement levels.
- Delinquency is often associated with low parental support, inappropriate discipline and family discord.
- Adolescents from impoverished communities or those experiencing unemployment and alienation from middle-class norms may engage in antisocial behaviour to gain attention or be accepted by peers.
- Most delinquent adolescents eventually outgrow these behaviours as they mature and gain a better sense of self-worth, responsibility and positive role models.

Substance Abuse

- Adolescence is a period where individuals are particularly vulnerable to smoking, alcohol and drug abuse.
- Many adolescents start smoking or taking drugs as a way to cope with stress, which interferes with the development of healthy coping skills and decision-making.
- The reasons for smoking and drug use include peer pressure, the desire to seem more adult and the need to escape academic pressure.
- The addictive properties of nicotine make it difficult for adolescents to quit smoking. Adolescents who are impulsive, aggressive, anxious, depressed or unpredictable are more likely to engage in substance abuse.
- Continued drug use can lead to physiological dependency and addiction, which may endanger the adolescent's future.
- Positive relationships with parents, peers and other adults can help prevent drug abuse.

Society for Theatre in Education Programme

- In India, the Society for Theatre in Education Programme in New Delhi is a successful anti-drug initiative.
- It uses street performances to entertain and educate adolescents (13-25 years old) about how to refuse drugs.
- The United Nations International Drug Control Programme (UNDCP) has recognised this programme as a model for other non-governmental organisations in the region.

Eating Disorders

(i) **Anorexia Nervosa** An eating disorder characterised by the relentless pursuit of thinness through starvation. Adolescents may eliminate certain foods or only eat slimming foods, often influenced by media's portrayal of thinness as the ideal image.

(ii) **Bulimia** A binge-and-purge eating disorder where individuals alternate between periods of overeating (bingeing) and purging (self-induced vomiting or laxative use).

3.9 Adulthood

An adult is generally seen as someone responsible, mature, self-supporting and well-integrated into society. However, there is variation in when individuals assume these roles depending on their social context.

Life Events in Adulthood

- Major life events such as marriage, having children and starting a career often occur during adulthood.
- The timing and experiences of these events can vary across cultures, but there is a general similarity in adult development within each culture.

Early Adulthood

- Early adulthood focuses on exploring adult living possibilities and developing a stable life structure.
- This stage represents a fresh phase of adult development.

Challenges During Adulthood

Career and Work

- Entering the workforce is a significant challenge for individuals in their twenties and thirties.
- This stage involves adjusting to new roles, proving competence, coping with competition and managing expectations from employers and oneself.
- Career development becomes a key focus, as individuals aim to establish their professional identity.

Marriage, Parenthood and Family

- Adjusting to marriage and parenthood can be stressful, especially for young adults.
- Parenting experiences vary based on the number of children, the availability of social support and the quality of the couple's relationship.
- The rise of dual-income families, where both parents work, introduces new challenges like balancing work and family responsibilities.
- Despite the stresses, parenting can provide personal growth and satisfaction as individuals guide the next generation.

Physical Changes in Middle Age

- Physical changes during middle ages are caused by maturational changes in body.
- Maturational changes lead to gradual physical decline, such as vision impairment, hearing loss and changes in physical appearance (e.g. wrinkles, weight gain).

Cognitive Changes

- Some cognitive abilities decline with age, especially long-term memory, while others, like wisdom, may improve.
- There are individual differences in cognitive abilities at all ages.

3.10 Old Age

- Key challenges in old age include retirement, widowhood, illness and death in the family.
- The experience of aging is influenced by socio-economic status, healthcare availability, social attitudes, and the support system.
- As individuals age, health becomes the primary concern, replacing work and family as the focal point.
- Retirement is a significant life change and its impact varies. Some view it negatively as a loss of satisfaction and self-esteem, while others embrace it as an opportunity for personal pursuits.
- Older adults who are open to new experiences and maintain active and achievement-oriented behaviours tend to adjust better to retirement.

Dependency in Old Age

- Older adults often need to adjust to changes in family dynamics, such as becoming grandparents and learning new roles.
- Children typically become busy with their careers and families, often setting up independent homes, which can create a sense of isolation for older adults.
- Many older adults depend on their children for financial support and companionship, especially as they experience loneliness.
- This dependency can lead to feelings of hopelessness and depression for some elderly individuals, exacerbated by diminishing health, energy and financial resources.
- In many cultures, including Indian culture, dependency on children in old age is seen as a natural part of the life cycle.
- Elderly parents in many Eastern cultures raise their children with the expectation that they will care for them in their later years.
- It is essential to provide the elderly with a sense of security, belonging and emotional support, especially during times of crisis.

Death in Late Adulthood

- While death is more common in late adulthood, it can occur at any stage of life.
- Death in children and young adults is often perceived as more tragic, usually caused by accidents. In older adults, death is more likely due to chronic illnesses.
- The death of a spouse is considered one of the most significant and difficult losses in late adulthood.
- Survivours often experience profound grief, loneliness, depression, financial difficulties and increased health risks.
- Different cultures have unique beliefs about death. For example, in the Gond culture of India, death is believed to be caused by magic and demons whereas in the Tanala culture of Madagascar, natural forces are thought to cause death.

Quick Test 3

1. What is adolescence?
2. What are secondary sexual characteristics?
3. What are two common challenges faced by adolescents during this stage?
4. What are the key cognitive developments that occur during adolescence?
5. What is the role of identity formation during adolescence?
6. Mention two cognitive changes that occur during middle ages.

NCERT Folder

1. What is development? How is it different from growth and maturation?

Ans. Development is the pattern of progressive, orderly and predictable changes that begin at conception and continue to take place throughout an individual's life.

Differences between growth and development are as follows

Growth	Development
Growth refers to an increase in the size of body parts or of the organism as a whole.	Development refers to a larger process, which is in terms of growth and maturation both.
Growth is measurable and quantified.	Development is not always measurable and quantified.
Any change that does not lead to the decline in age is considered as growth.	The change that leads to decline such as in old age is also considered as development.

Differences between maturation and development are as follows

Maturation	Development
Maturation refers to the changes that follow an orderly sequence.	Development does not necessarily refer to orderly sequence.
Maturation is largely dictated by the genetic blueprint which produces commonalities in the growth.	Development needs not to be identified with genetic changes and growth.

2. Describe the main features of life-span perspective on development.

Ans. The main features of life-span perspective on development are

- Development is life long process i.e. it takes place across all age groups starting from conception to old age. It includes both gains and losses, which interact in dynamic (change in one aspect goes with changes in others) ways throughout the life-span.
- The various processes of human development i.e. biological, cognitive and socio-emotional are mixed together in the development of a person throughout the life-span.
- Development is multi-directional. Some dimensions or components of a given dimension of development may increase, while others may decrease.
- Development is highly plastic within person, modifiability is found in psychological development. This plasticity varies among individuals. This means skills and abilities can be improved or developed throughout the life-span.
- Development is influenced by historical conditions. For example, the career orientation of school students today is very different from those students who were in schools 50 years ago.
- Development is concerned with a number of disciplines like psychology, anthropology, sociology and neuro-sciences. They study human development and try to provide answers to development throughout the life-span.
- An individual responds and acts in contexts, which include what was inherited, the physical environment, social, historical and cultural contexts.

3. What are developmental tasks? Explain by giving examples.

Ans. Developmental tasks refer to a physical or cognitive skill that a person must accomplish during a particular age period to continue development.

For example, the newborn in their first week of life are able to indicate what direction a sound is coming from and can distinguish their mother's voice from the voices of other women sound. As the infants grow, the muscles and nervous system mature which lead to the development of finer skills. Basic physical skills include grasping, walking and running.

The child during infancy experiences the world through senses and interactions with objects through looking, hearing, touching, mouthing and grasping. An infant starts preferring familiar faces and responds to parents presence by cooing and gurgling. They become more mobile by 6 to 8 months of age and starts showing a preference for their mothers company when frightened by a new face or when separated from their mother, they cry or show distress.

4. "Environment of the child has a major role in the development of the child". Support your answer with examples. Competency Based Que.

Ans. Environment of the child has a major role in the development of the child because it includes the surroundings in which a child develops various cognitive and motor skills. It also influences the physical development of the child according to the limits created by genetic characteristics. Further, the socio-economic and cultural environment has a major role in the development of a child's thought process.

For example, a child who is sent to school is able to develop characteristics of confidence and self-reliance more easily than a child who does not receive education. In genetic terms, children having anger genetic quality learn to calm down if they grow in a stable environment. Therefore, environment plays a vital role in the development of a child, it not only develops a particular skill but influences the whole personality.

5. How do socio-cultural factors influence development?

Ans. Following are the socio-cultural factors which influence the development of an individual

- Development is influenced by socio-cultural factors which provides social context to development.
- The various socio-cultural consequences that a child meets with are learnt by him/her. As a result a child develops such personality which is influenced by his/her experiences.
- Every person has different socio-cultural background which impacts his/her interaction with the rest of the society.
- During the developmental period of an individual his variable experiences are dependent upon their social and cultural background.
- These factors include the conditions at home, the quality of schooling and interaction with peer groups.
- Children who have unstable family environment find it hard to learn new things and make their own decisions. Children who are exposed to diverse experiences early in life develop a confident attitude and are more able to face challenges.

6. Discuss the cognitive changes taking place in a developing child.

Ans. The cognitive changes take place during different stages of development in the life of a developing child. These are as follows

- **0-2 Years** This is the age of sensori-motors whereby, infant explores the world by coordinating sensory experiences with physical actions.
- **2-7 Years** In this age, preoperational thinking begins and the child acquires the concept of object permanence that enables him/her to use mental symbols to represent objects. However, the child at this stage lacks the ability that allows her/him to do mentally what was done physically before. The child does not have the ability to judge or assume the consequences of actions before performing them.
- The child gains the ability to mentally represent an object that is not physically present e.g. children draw designs/ figures to represent people, trees, dog, house, etc. The ability of the child to engage in symbolic thought helps to expand her/his mental world.
- **7-11 Years** This age is marked by the development of concrete operational thought.
  As the child grows and is approximately between 7 and 11 years of age (the period of middle and late childhood) intuitive thought is replaced by logical thought. This is the stage of concrete operational thought, which is made up of operation i.e. mental actions that allows the child to do mentally what was done physically before.
- **11-15 Years** The adolescents in this age develop formal operational thought, which leads to a hypothetical thinking and are able to apply logic abstractly. They also develop a special kind of egocentrism of imaginary audience and personal fable.

7. Attachment bonds formed in childhood years have long-term effects. Explain taking examples from daily life.

Ans. The close emotional bond of affection that develops between infants and their parents (care givers) is called attachment. Human babies form an attachment with their parents or care-givers who consistently and appropriately reciprocate to their signals of love and affection.

According to Erik Erikson (1968), the first year of life is the key time for the development of attachment. It represents the stage of developing trust or mistrust. A sense of trust is built on a feeling of physical comfort which builds an expectation of the world as a secure and good place.
An infant's sense of trust is developed by responsive and sensitive parenting.

For example, if the parents are sensitive, affectionate and accepting, it provides the infant a strong base to explore the environment.

Such infants are likely to develop a secure attachment. On the other hand, if parents are insensitive and show dissatisfaction and find fault with the child, it can lead to creating feelings of self-doubt in the child.

It is seen in our daily life that securely attached infants respond positively when picked up, move freely and play whereas insecurely attached infants feel anxious when separated and cry due to fear and get upset. A close interactive relationship with warm and affectionate adults is a child's first step towards healthy development.

8. What is adolescence? Explain the concept of egocentrism.

Ans. Adolescence is commonly defined as the stage of life that begins at the onset of puberty, when sexual maturity or the ability to reproduce is attained. It has been regarded as a period of rapid change, both biologically and psychologically.

Egocentrism The concept of egocentrism deals with self-focus. It is a viewpoint of the world that is centred upon the self. It hinders an appreciation of the viewpoint of others.

This kind of an attitude develops within a child from his/her childhood stage. However, it differs during adolescence. The egocentrism in adolescents comprises the following two elements

(i) **Imaginary Audience** It is adolescent's belief that others are as preoccupied with them as they are about themselves. They imagine that people are always noticing them and are observing each and every behaviour of them which makes them extremely self-conscious.

(ii) **Personal Fable** It is part of the adolescents' egocentrism that involves their sense of uniqueness. Adolescents' sense of uniqueness makes them think that no one understands them or their feelings.

9. What are the factors influencing the formation of identity during adolescence? Support your answer with examples.

Ans. The formation of identity during adolescence is influenced by several factors. Few of these are explained below

- **Cultural Background** The cultural background and the level of their exposure the ideas and opinions of adolescents about the world around them. These factors fix the norms followed by them and hence, their cultural identity. For example, adolescent behaviour varies among Indian and American cultures.
- **Family and Societal Values** Adolescents practice some values of society in which they live and these values shape their identity. For example, teenagers in European countries are conditioned to a materialistic society in contrast to young adults in Tibet who are more spiritually inclined.
- **Ethnic Background** In order to make their own identity adolescents distinguish themselves as members of their ethnic group. For example, expectations of teenage behaviour and responsibilities vary across different ethnicities and tribes.
- **Socio-economic Status** It is seen that the socio-economic background of an adolescent ensures the peer group and the extent of their accessibility to popular lifestyle choices that determine identity.
  For example, accessibility to expensive gadgets and branded clothing that are popular among teenagers are determined by their socio-economic background.
- **Vocational Commitment** Adolescents begin to think of their career as a component of their identity. For example, adolescents choose whether to study arts, or commerce.

10. What are the challenges faced by individuals on entry to adulthood?

Ans. Challenges faced by individuals on entry to adulthood are as follows

Career and Work Earning a living, choosing an occupation and developing a career are important themes for people in their twenties and thirties. Entering work life is a challenging event in anyone's life.

There are apprehensions regarding different adjustments, proving one's competence, performance, dealing with competition and coping with expectations both of the employers and oneself. Developing and evaluating a career becomes an important task of adulthood.

Marriage, Parenthood and Family Adults have to make adjustments when entering in a marriage life like to knowing the other person if not known earlier, coping with each other's likes, dislikes, tastes and choices. If both the partners are working, adjustments are required regarding sharing and performing roles and responsibilities at home.

Parenting experience is affected by different situations such as the number of children in the family, the availability of social support, and the happiness or unhappiness of the married couple. Death of a spouse or divorce creates a family structure in which a single parent either the mother or the father has to take up the responsibility of the children.

Exam Pattern Questions

Objective Type Questions

Multiple Choice Questions (MCQs)

1. **Heredity is determined by**

(a) cells (b) nature
(c) genes (d) neurons

2. **Genes work in**

(a) pairs (b) groups
(c) autosomes only (d) traits only

3. **Piaget called the period of infancy as the**

(a) Formal operational stage
(b) Preoperational stage
(c) Concrete operational stage
(d) Sensorimotor stage

4. **The approximate age of sensorimotor stage is**

(a) 0-2 years (b) 2-7 years
(c) 7-11 years (d) 11-15 years

5. **Distinctly observable characteristics are called**

(a) Genotype (b) Genes
(c) Genetics (d) Phenotype

6. **......... is an evolutionary process that favours individuals or a species that are best adopted to survive and produce.**

(a) Growth (b) Natural selection
(c) Development (d) Evolution

7. **Which of the following factor influence the development of a human being?**

(a) Environmental (b) Genetic
(c) Both (a) and (b) (d) None of these

8. **Identify the correct statement in the contexts of Bronfenbrenner Model of Development.**

(a) Microsystem consists of relations between these contexts family, peers, teachers and neighbourhood.
(b) Exosystem includes immediate environment /setting.
(c) Macrosystem includes the culture in which the individual live.
(d) All of the above

9. **Rituraj is hopping, running and jumping in lobby of his house. These skills are included under**

(a) Fine motor skills
(b) Gross motor skills
(c) Major motor skills
(d) Development motor skills

10. **The genetic blueprint of an individual leading to changes in an orderly fashion is known as ....** **CBSE DIKSHA**

(a) Development (b) Maturation
(c) Growth (d) Evolution

11. **Prerna's parents and friends do not share a healthy bond with each other. This has been leading to a detrimental impact on her overall development. The problem discussed above can be classified under which of the following stages?** **CBSE DIKSHA**

(a) Exosystem (b) Mesosystem
(c) Microsystem (d) Microsystem

12. **Factors such as geographical environment, availability of drinking water, electricity, etcetera, are a part of which layer?** **CBSE DIKSHA**

(a) Surrounding layer (b) Highest layer
(c) Upper layer (d) Peripheral layer

13. **Aastha observed severe abnormalities in her child soon after his birth. After a lot of investigation, she gets to know that this is majorly because of the radiation she was exposed to during her pregnancy. Radiation in this case is an example of ....** **CBSE DIKSHA**

(a) Facilitator (b) Toxicogenic
(c) Inhibitor (d) Teratogen

14. **Risha has been fighting with her sister, as she feels that she is getting less amount of juice than her. This is majorly because of the difference in the shape of the glass. Identify the feature of the thought process that Rishi has been displaying.** **CBSE DIKSHA**

(a) Fixation (b) Centration
(c) Ideation (d) None of these

15. **Kusha has developed a habit of bringing a lot of food from the past few months and since this behaviour leads to feelings of guilt, she has started purging out the food by using medicines. The above mentioned symptoms signify the presence of which of the following disorders?** **CBSE DIKSHA**

(a) Bulimia
(b) Obsessive compulsive disorder
(c) Anorexia Nervosa
(d) Binge

16. Rashmi has of late been finding solutions to her problems by analysing the various possible courses of action. Which of the following concepts related to thinking has she been using? **CBSE DIKSHA**

(a) Centration
(b) Solution Oriented Approach
(c) Imaginary Audience
(d) Hypothetical deductive reasoning

17. Which of the following statements is true about Bronfenbrenner's Ecological Systems Theory?

I. The microsystem involves indirect influences on the child through events outside their immediate surroundings.
II. The mesosystem deals with interactions among contexts such as family, school and peers.
III. The exosystem includes events that the child directly participates in, shaping their immediate experiences.
IV. The macrosystem encompasses cultural influences affecting the child's development.

Codes

(a) I and II (b) II and IV
(c) III and IV (d) I and III

18. Which of the following accurately explains the role of the mesosystem in a child's development?

I. It is composed of direct interactions with family, peers and teachers.
II. It represents the connections between the microsystem's various components.
III. It involves events like the parent's workplace conditions that indirectly affect the child.
IV. It helps shape the individual's relationships with others through linked experiences.

Codes

(a) II and IV (b) I and II
(c) I and III (d) III and IV

19. Which of the following statements is true about Durganand Sinha's ecological model?

I. The visible upper layer includes conditions such as home environment and schooling quality.
II. The surrounding layer refers to factors like caste and geographical settings.
III. The upper and surrounding layers do not interact with each other.
IV. The surrounding layer's effects are clearly visible in a child's development.

Codes

(a) I and II (b) II and III
(c) I and IV (d) III and IV

20. Shreya's father is transferred to a different city and this change affects her schooling and interactions with peers. This scenario is related to which system in Bronfenbrenner's model?

I. Microsystem II. Mesosystem
III. Exosystem IV. Chronosystem

Codes

(a) II and III (b) III and IV
(c) I and IV (d) II and IV

21. In the context of Sinha's model, which layer influences the quality of schooling and the child's play environment?

I. Upper Layer
II. Surrounding Layer
III. Microsystem
IV. Chronosystem

Codes

(a) I and II (b) II and III
(c) III and IV (d) I and III

Assertion-Reason Questions

Directions (Q. Nos. 22-28) In the following questions, a statement of Assertion A is followed by a statement of Reason R. Mark the correct choice from the options given below.

(a) Both A and R are true and R is the correct explanation of A.
(b) Both A and R are true, but R is not the correct explanation of A.
(c) A is true, but R is false.
(d) A is false, but R is true.

22. **Assertion** (A) It is important to note that biological, cognitive and socio-emotional processes are interwoven.

Reason (R) These processes influence changes in the development of the individual as a whole through the human life-span.

23. **Assertion** (A) Genes do not exist in isolation and development occurs within the context of an individual's environment.

Reason (R) Genes provide a distinct blueprint and timetable for the development of an individual.

24. **Assertion** (A) Durganand Sinha's ecological model of development focuses on understanding a child's development within the Indian context.

Reason (R) According to Sinha's model, the surrounding ecological factors, such as caste, class and general geographical environment, significantly influence a child's development.

25. Assertion (A) Reflexes in newborns are genetically carried survival mechanisms that disappear as the brain functions mature.

Reason (R) Reflexes, such as grasping and rooting, are essential for motor development and provide the foundation for voluntary control over behaviour in the future.

26. Assertion (A) According to Jean Piaget, cognitive development in infants begins with sensory exploration and gradually progresses to complex abstract thinking.

Reason (R) Piaget's stages of cognitive development are characterised by different ways of thinking, with each stage offering a more advanced understanding of the world compared to the previous one.

27. Assertion (A) The development of sexual identity during adolescence is influenced by factors like biological changes and societal emphasis on sexuality.

Reason (R) Adolescents often lack adequate knowledge of sex and sexuality due to a lack of open communication with parents, which is further complicated by misconceptions.

28. Assertion (A) The perception of retirement can vary, with some individuals viewing it as a negative change and others seeing it as an opportunity for personal growth.

Reason (R) The attitude towards retirement is often linked to one's ability to stay busy and maintain a striving, achievement-oriented behaviour in old age.

Answers

1. (c) genes
2. (a) pairs
3. (d) Sensorimotor stage
4. (a) 0-2 years
5. (d) Phenotype
6. (b) Natural selection
7. (c) Both (a) and (b)
8. (c) Macrosystem includes the culture in which the individual live.
9. (b) Gross motor skills
10. (b) Maturation
11. (b) Mesosystem
12. (a) Surrounding layer
13. (d) Teratogen
14. (b) Centration
15. (a) Bulimia
16. (d) Hypothetical deductive reasoning
17. (b) II and IV
18. (a) II and IV
19. (a) I and II
20. (b) III and IV
21. (a) I and II
22. (b) Both A and R are true, but R is not the correct explanation of A.
23. (d) A is false, but R is true.
24. (a) Both A and R are true and R is the correct explanation of A.
25. (a) Both A and R are true and R is the correct explanation of A.
26. (a) Both A and R are true and R is the correct explanation of A.
27. (a) Both A and R are true and R is the correct explanation of A.
28. (a) Both A and R are true and R is the correct explanation of A.

Subjective Questions

Very Short Answer Type Questions

1. What do you understand by maturation?

Ans. Maturation refers to the changes that follow an orderly sequence and are largely dictated by the genetic blueprint which produces commonalities in our growth and development.

2. Define the term phenotype.

Ans. Phenotype is the way an individual's genotype is expressed in observable and measurable characteristics. It includes physical traits such as height, weight, eye and skin colour and many of the psychological characteristics such as intelligence, creativity and personality.

3. Give the meaning of teratogens.

Ans. Teratogens is a source of threat to prenatal development. Environmental agents that cause deviations in normal development that can lead to serious abnormalities or death.

4. What do you know about intuitive thought?

Ans. As children grow and are approximately between 4 and 7 years of age they develop curiosity and ask questions about the things happening in surrounding. Piaget called this the stage of intuitive thought.

5. Jenna saw a newborn baby in a hospital who was doing some actions. What are called these actions? Give some example of it. Competency Based Que.

Ans. The actions which newborn babies do are called as reflexes. These govern the movement of newborns. These are automatic, built-in responses to stimuli. They are genetically-carried, survival mechanisms and are the building blocks for subsequent motor development.

Some examples of reflexes are like coughing, blinking, and yawning. These are present in the newborns and continue throughout their lives.

6. Define the term attachment.

Ans. The close emotional bond of affection that develops between infants and their parents (care givers) is called attachment.

7. What do you mean by puberty?

Ans. Puberty or sexual maturity marks the end of childhood and signifies the beginning of adolescence, which is characterised by dramatic physical changes in both growth rate and sexual characteristics.

8. Define hypothetical deductive reasoning.

Ans. Adolescent thinking becomes more systematic in solving problems as they think of possible courses of action, why something is happening the way it is and systematically seek solutions. Piaget called this type of logical thinking as hypothetical deductive reasoning.

9. What are the factors that influence identity formation?

Ans. The formation of identity during adolescence is influenced by several factors such as cultural background, family and societal values, ethnic background and socio-economic status. These all prevail upon the adolescents' search for a place in society.

10. Define the term delinquency.

Ans. Delinquency refers to a variety of behaviours, ranging from socially unacceptable behaviour, legal offences to criminal acts. Adolescents with delinquency and behavioural problems tend to have a negative self-identity, decreased trust and low level of achievement.

11. What is sensorimotor stage?

Ans. Sensorimotor is the first Piagetian stage in which infants construct an understanding of the world by coordinating sensory experiences with physical and motor actions.

12. Explain preoperational stage.

Ans. In this stage, the child gains the ability to mentally represent an object that is not physically present e.g. children draw designs/ figures to represent people, trees, dog, house, etc. The ability of the child to engage in symbolic thought helps to expand her/his mental world.

13. Mention the development in concrete operational stage.

Ans. In concrete operational stage, children can perform logical operations and reasoning on concrete examples but cannot deal with abstract things.

14. What are the components of moral development?

Ans. The way children come to distinguish right from wrong, to feel guilty, to put themselves in other people's position and to help others when they are in trouble, are all components of moral development.

Short Answer Type Questions

1. Discuss the genetic factors that influence development.

Ans. The genetic factors that influence development are as follows

- Genes provide a distinct blueprint and timetable for the development of an individual.
- The principles of heredity explain the mechanism for transmission of characteristics by every species from one generation to the next with the help of genetic code. It is because of the human genetic code that a fertilised human egg grows into a human baby and cannot grow into an elephant, a bird or a mouse.

- Genetic transmission is very complex. Most characteristics are combinations of larger number of genes.
- It is also impossible to possess all the characteristics by our genetic structure.

2. Describe the prenatal stage of development.

Ans. The period from conception to birth is known as the prenatal period. It lasts for about 40 weeks. Genetic blueprint guides our development during the prenatal period and after birth. Both genetic and environmental factors affect our development during different periods of prenatal stage.

Prenatal development is also affected by maternal characteristics, which include mother's age, nutrition and emotional state. Disease or infection carried by the mother can adversely affect prenatal development.

3. Jean has assigned a work to write about the effects of teratogens in prenatal development. Write about it in brief. Competency Based Que.

Ans. Teratogens are harmful for human body especially for foetus. Common teratogens include drugs, radiations, and pollution. The effects of these are as follows

- Intake of drugs (marijuana, heroin, cocaine, etc), alcohol, tobacco, etc by women during pregnancy may have harmful effects on the foetus and increase the frequency of congenital abnormalities.
- Radiations (such as X-rays) and certain chemicals near industrial areas can cause permanent change in the genes.
- Environmental pollutants and toxic wastes like carbon monoxide, mercury and lead are also sources of danger to the unborn child.

4. Explain the development of sensory abilities in new borns.

Ans. Newborn can recognise their mother's voice just a few hours after birth and have other sensory capabilities. The newborn's vision is estimated to be lower than the adult vision. By 6 months it improves and by about the first year, vision is almost the same as that of an adult. They might be able to distinguish between red and white colours but in general they are colour deficient and full colour vision develops by 3 months of age.

Infants can hear immediately after birth. As the infant develops, proficiency at localising sound improves. Newborns respond to touch and they can even feel pain. Both smell and taste capacities are also present in the newborn.

5. Describe briefly the development of child in childhood stage.

Ans. The child's growth slows down during early childhood as compared to infancy. The child develops physically, gains height and weight, learns to walk, runs, jumps and plays. Socially, the child's world expands from the parents to the family and adults near home and at school.

The child also begins to acquire the concepts of good and bad i.e. develops a sense of morality. During childhood, children have increased physical capacities, can perform tasks independently, can set goals and meet adult expectations.

The increasing maturation of the brain along with opportunities to experience the world, contribute to development of children's cognitive abilities.

6. Discuss the environmental factors that influence development.

Ans. The environmental factors that influence development are as follows

- Genes set the limit and within that limit the environment influences development.
- Genes also play an important role in determining the type of environment their children will encounter.
- Sandra Scarr (1992) believes that the environment which is provided by parents for their children depends to some extent on their own genetic predisposition.
- Children themselves choose certain environments based on their genotype. These interactions with environment keep changing from infancy through adolescence. Environmental influences are as complex as the genes one inherit.

7. Differentiate between genotype and phenotype.

Ans. **Genotype** It is known the actual genetic material or a person's genetic heritage. However, not all of this genetic material is apparent or distinctly identifiable in our observable characteristics.

Phenotype It is the way an individual's genotype is expressed in observable and measurable characteristics. It includes physical traits such as height, weight, eye and skin colour and many of the psychological characteristics such as intelligence, creativity and personality.

These observable characteristics of an individual are the result of the interaction between the person's inherited traits and the environment.

8. "Adolescence is definitely a vulnerable period." Comment.

Ans. During adolescence, peer influence, new gained freedom and unresolved problems may create difficulties for youth. Conforming to peer pressure can be both positive and negative. Adolescents are often confronted with decisions regarding smoking, drugs, alcohol and breaking parental rules, etc.

These decisions are taken without much regard to the effect they can have. Adolescents may face periods of uncertainty, loneliness, self-doubt, anxiety and concern about themselves and their future. They are also likely to experience excitement, joy and feelings of competence as they overcome the developmental challenges. Therefore, it is true that adolescence is definitely a vulnerable period.

9. "The myth of old age as an incapacitating is changing." Discuss the statement in context of old aged challenges.

Competency Based Que.

Ans. Now people are living longer, age of retiring from work is changing and the cut-off point for the definition of 'old age' is moving upward.

Some of the challenges, which the aged have to cope with include retirement, widowhood, illness or death in the family. The image of old age is changing in certain ways. Now there are people who have crossed seventy years of age or so and are quite active, energetic and creative.

They are competent and are therefore, valued by society in many walks of life. In particular, we have aged people in politics, literature, business, art and science. Hence, the myth of old age as an incapacitating and therefore, frightening phase of life is changing.

10. Explain in brief the socio-emotional development of children.

Ans. Socio-Emotional Development of Children can be explained as following

(i) **Self-Identity and Socialisation** Children start developing a sense of who they are and whom they want to be identified with. Growing independence leads them to do things in their own way.

(ii) **Role of Parental Response** Positive responses from parents (like encouraging play and answering questions) build a child's sense of initiative. Negative responses (such as dismissing questions or activities) can lead to feelings of guilt, impacting confidence even later in life.

(iii) **Self-Understanding** Children define themselves by physical traits and in middle and late childhood children begin to identify with internal traits (e.g., 'I am smart') and social aspects, comparing themselves with others (e.g., 'I got more marks than Atul').

(iv) **Social Comparison** Children start to compare their abilities with others, helping them establish individuality.

(v) **Peer Influence** As the children enter school, children's social world extends beyond family and interactions with peers significantly shape their socio-emotional development.

11. What are major challenges faced by adolescents? Discuss the challenge of substance abuse.

Ans. Some major challenges faced by adolescents are delinquency, substance abuse and eating disorders.

Adolescent years are especially vulnerable to smoking, alcohol and drug abuse. Some adolescents take recourse to smoking and drugs as a way of coping with stress which can interfere with the development of coping skills and responsible decision-making.

The reasons for smoking and drug use could be

- Peer pressure and the adolescents' need to be accepted by the group.
- Desire to act more like adults.
- Feel a need to escape the pressure of school work.

The addictive powers of nicotine make it difficult to stop smoking. Adolescents who are more vulnerable to drugs, alcohol and nicotine use are impulsive, aggressive, anxious, depressive, and unpredictable, have low self-esteem and low expectation for achievement.

Drug use if continued long enough can lead to physiological dependency, i.e. addiction to drugs, alcohol or nicotine may seriously jeopardise the rest of the adolescents' lives.

12. Explain eating disorders in adolescents.

Ans. The eating disorders in adolescents are as follows

- **Anorexia nervosa** is an eating disorder that involves relentless pursuit of thinness through starvation. It is quite common to see adolescents eliminate certain foods from their diets or to eat slimming foods only. The media also projects thinness as the most desirable image and copying such fashionable image of thinness leads to anorexia nervosa.
- **Bulimia** is another form of an eating disorder in which the individual follows a binge-and- purge eating pattern. The bulimic goes on an eating binge, then purges by self induced vomiting or using a laxative at times alternating it with fasting. Anorexia nervosa and bulimia are primarily female disorders and are more common in urban families.

13. What is ecology of the child? Explain the ecological factors that influence development.

Ans. Ecology of the child could be viewed in terms of two concentric layers

(i) **Upper Layer** The most important ecological factors influencing development of the child in the visible upper layer constitute the following

- Home, its conditions in terms of overcrowding, space available to each member, toys, technological devices used, etc.

- Nature and quality of schooling and facilities to which the child is exposed.
- Nature of interactions and activities undertaken with peer groups from childhood onwards.

(ii) **Surrounding Layer** The elements of the surrounding layer of ecology constitute the following

- General geographical environment which includes space and facilities for play.
- Institutional setting provided by caste, class and other factors.
- General facilities available to the child like drinking water, electricity, means of entertainment and so on.

14. Explain the Bronfenbrenner's Model of Development.

Ans. In following way, Bronfenbrenner's Model of Development explains how a child's growth is influenced by different layers of their environment.

- According to Bronfenbrenner, the immediate surroundings in which a child interacts, known as the microsystem, have a strong impact. This includes daily interactions with family, friends, teachers and neighbours.
- Next is the mesosystem, which represents the connections between these immediate environments, such as the relationship between a child's parents and their teachers. For example, if parents and teachers communicate well, it can positively impact the child's school experience.
- The exosystem includes larger social settings where the child isn't directly involved but that still affects them. For instance, a parent's job transfer may lead to family stress, indirectly impacting the child. Beyond these layers is the macrosystem, which refers to the child's cultural and societal environment, including shared beliefs and values that influence their behaviour and outlook.
- Lastly, the chronosystem accounts for events and changes over time, such as family dynamics like divorce or economic shifts, which can have long-lasting effects on the child's development.
- Bronfenbrenner's model also points out that children who grow up in deprived environments, with limited resources like books or educational activities, may struggle with learning and development. This model helps us understand that a child's growth is shaped not only by close interactions but also by broader social and cultural factors, as well as life events.

15. Mansi is doing a research work on old age people. She finds that there are many challenges at this stage but the most common is dependency. Why dependency mostly affects the old age people? **Competency Based Que.**

Ans. Dependency is the common issue/challenge found among old age people. It is because old adults may depend on their children for financial support and to overcome their loneliness (after children have moved out). This might trigger-off feelings of hopelessness and depression in some people.

In old age feeling of loss of energy, and dwindling of health and financial assets, lead to insecurity and dependency. The elderly tend to look towards others to lean on and to care for them.

Indian culture favours dependency of elderly on their children, for old age needs caring. In fact, parents in most oriental cultures rear their children with the fond hope that they will care for them during old age.

It is important to give the elderly sense of security and belonging, a feeling that people care for them (especially in the time of crisis) and to remember that we all have to grow old one day.

Long Answer Type Questions

1. Describe the cognitive developmental changes in adolescence.

Ans. The cognitive developmental changes in adolescence are as follows

- Thoughts of adolescents become more abstract, logical and idealistic. They become more capable of examining their own thoughts, others' thoughts and what others are thinking about them. Developing logical and reasoning ability of adolescent gives them a new level of cognitive and social awareness.
- Formal operational thought appears between the age of 11 and 15 years. During this stage, adolescents thinking expands beyond actual concrete experiences and they begin to think more in abstract terms and reason about them.
- In addition to being abstract, adolescent thought is also idealistic. Adolescents begin to think about ideal characteristics for themselves and others and compare themselves and others with these ideal standards.
- Adolescent thinking becomes more systematic in solving problems as they think of possible courses of action, why something is happening the way it is and systematically seek solutions. Piaget called this type of logical thinking as hypothetical deductive reasoning.
- Logical thought also influences the development of moral reasoning. Social rules are not considered as

absolute standards and moral thinking shows some flexibility.

2. Describe in brief the identity formation in adolescence.

Ans. • Identity refers to distinguishing character or personality of an individual like her/his values, commitments and beliefs. The primary task of adolescence is to establish an identity separate from the parents.

- In the process of achieving an identity the adolescent could experience conflict with parents and within herself or himself. Seeking an identity involves searching for continuity and sameness in oneself, greater responsibility and trying to get a clear sense of who one is i.e. an identity.
- The formation of identity during adolescence is influenced by several factors such as cultural background, family and societal values, ethnic background and socio economic status. Family relationships become less important as the adolescent spends more time outside the home and develops a strong need for peer support and acceptance.
- Vocational commitment is another factor influencing adolescent identity formation. It includes question related to career, the ability to think about the future and to be able to set realistic and achievable goals. In some cultures, freedom is given to the young people to choose an occupation, whereas in certain other cultures the option of making this choice is not given to the children. Here parents' decision is likely to be accepted by the children.

3. Discuss the challenges faced by old aged people.

Ans. Some of the challenges, which the aged people have to cope with include the following

- Older adults may depend on their children for financial support and to overcome their loneliness. This might trigger-off feelings of hopelessness and depression in some people.
- In old age, feeling of loss of energy and diminishing of health and financial assets lead to insecurity and dependency.
- The deaths, especially of children and younger adults, are often perceived to be more tragic than those of others. In children and younger adults, death is more likely to occur because of accidents but in older adults it is more likely to occur because of chronic disease.
- The death of a spouse is usually seen as the most difficult loss. Those left behind after the death of their partner suffer deep grief, cope with loneliness, depression, financial loss and are also at risk of many health related problems.

4. Discuss the challenges of marriage, parenthood and family faced by adults.

Ans. The challenges of marriage, parenthood and family faced by adults are as follows

- Adults have to make adjustments when entering in a marriage life like, to knowing the other person if not known earlier, coping with each other's likes, dislikes, tastes and choices.
- If both the partners are working, adjustments are required regarding sharing and performing roles and responsibilities at home.
- In addition to getting married, becoming a parent can be a difficult and stressful transition in young adults, even though it is usually accompanied by the feeling of love for the baby.
- Parenting experience is affected by different situations such as the number of children in the family, the availability of social support, and the happiness or unhappiness of the married couple.
- Death of a spouse or divorce creates a family structure in which a single parent either the mother or the father has to take up the responsibility of the children.
- In recent times, women are increasingly seeking employment outside the home thus creating another type of family in which both parents work. The stressors when both parents are working are quite the same as of a single working parent, namely, taking care of children, their schoolwork, illness and coping with workload at home and in the office, etc.

Case Based Questions

1. Read the case and answer the questions that follow.

Amit is a 15-year-old student living in a suburban area with his parents and younger sister. His family lives in a spacious, well-lit house with a small garden and good facilities, such as a library and internet connection. Amit's parents both work full-time, but they ensure that they spend quality time with their children. Amit attends a local high school, where he is an average student, but he enjoys extracurricular activities like sports and music. Although he is relatively happy at home and in school, he sometimes feels the pressure to excel in academics and is unsure about his future career. His friends, who live in the same neighbourhood, have a close relationship with Amit and share similar interests.

(i) In the given case, what type of environment is Amit growing up in? How do his family and school settings influence his development?

(ii) Based on Bronfenbrenner's Model of Development, which system does Amit's social interaction with friends and family fall under?

Ans. (i) Amit is growing up in a Microsystem environment, where his immediate surroundings, such as his family, school and friends, play an essential role in his development.

- His family is supportive, providing a safe and nurturing environment with quality facilities.
- His school provides a balanced environment for academics and extracurricular activities, which contributes to his development.
- Amit's peer relationships are also strong, which positively influences his social skills and emotional development.

(ii) Amit's social interaction with his family and friends falls under the Microsystem.

The Microsystem includes the immediate environments in which a child interacts directly, such as family, peers, and school. Amit's close relationship with his friends and his family's active role in his life directly influence his growth and well-being.

2. Read the case and answer the questions that follow.

An infant starts preferring familiar faces and responds to their parent's presence by cooing and gurgling (babbling). By 6 to 8 months of age, infants show a preference for their mother's company. When frightened by a new face or when separated from their mother, they cry or show distress. Upon being reunited with the parent or caregiver, they respond with smiles or hugs. This emotional bond between infants and their parents or caregivers is known as attachment. In a classic study by Harlow and Harlow (1962), baby monkeys were separated from their mothers and reared by surrogate mothers made of wire or cloth. Regardless of whether the baby monkeys were fed by the wire or cloth mother, they showed a preference for the cloth mother and spent more time with her, emphasizing that contact-comfort is vital for attachment rather than the provision of food.

(i) In the given case, what is the primary characteristic of infant attachment?

(ii) What did the Harlow and Harlow study indicate about infant attachment?

Ans. (i) The primary characteristic of infant attachment is the preference for familiar faces, especially the mother's, and the emotional bond where the infant responds with distress when separated and with joy when reunited. Key points

- Infants prefer familiar faces.
- They respond with cooing and gurgling.
- The attachment is formed with the primary caregiver, especially the mother.

(ii) The Harlow and Harlow study indicated that infant attachment is more influenced by comfort and security provided by the caregiver (such as the cloth mother) rather than just the provision of food. The baby monkeys preferred the cloth mother despite being fed by the wire one, which highlights the importance of contact-comfort in attachment. Key points

- Attachment is based on comfort, not just food.
- The baby monkeys preferred the cloth mother over the wire one.
- The study emphasises the significance of comfort in forming attachment bonds.

3. Read the case and answer the questions that follow.

Adolescence is characterised by dramatic physical changes in both growth rate and sexual characteristics. Puberty is a gradual process where the hormones released result in the development of primary and secondary sexual characteristics. In boys, these changes include acceleration in growth, facial hair, and voice changes, while in girls, a rapid growth spurt usually begins two years before menarche, the onset of menstruation. This process starts around the age of 12 or 13 for boys and at the age of 10 or 11 for girls. These changes vary from individual to individual and are influenced by both genetics and environmental factors.

(i) What are the main physical changes that occur during adolescence?

(ii) What factors influence the onset and progression of puberty?

Ans. (i) The main physical changes during adolescence include

- Acceleration in growth.
- Development of facial hair in boys.
- Change in voice in boys.
- Onset of menstruation (menarche) in girls.
- Rapid growth spurt beginning two years before menarche in girls.

(ii) The onset and progression of puberty are influenced by

- **Genetics** For example, identical twins typically reach puberty at similar times.
- **Environment** Factors like socioeconomic status, with girls from affluent families generally experiencing earlier menarche.

SELF ASSESSMENT TEST

Objective Type Questions

1. Which of the following is a component of egocentrism?
(a) Imaginary audience (b) Personal fable (c) Both (a) and (b) (d) None of these

2. Adolescents who are more vulnerable to drugs, alcohol and nicotine use are
(a) impulsive (b) personal fable (c) anxious (d) None of these

3. The important dimensions of children's socio-emotional development are
(a) self (b) gender (c) moral (d) All of these

4. Concept of Identity crisis was given by
(a) Erikson (b) Harlow (c) Piaget (d) Rogers

Very Short Answer Type Questions

1. What do you mean by socio-emotional process?
2. Define phenotype.
3. Give some examples of delinquency.
4. What is anoxeria nervosa?
5. What is animism?
6. What is concrete operational thought?

Short Answer Type Questions

1. What are the characteristics of adolescence?
2. Describe any two reflexes in the newborn.
3. How can we remove delinquency?
4. How does the environment affect development? Explain in brief.
5. Explain physical development that occurs in an adult.

Long Answer Type Questions

1. Describe with examples maturation and development.
2. Explain the factors that influence the formation of identity during adolescence.
3. Discuss duties of family members towards old aged.
4. Describe the four life skills which you think that will facilitate the challenges faced by adolescence.

Case Based Questions

Read the case and answer the questions that follow.

Kashish is a humanities student who excels in English literature and related activities. She is also good in co-scholastic activities as well. In a session with the counsellor, she expressed that she is fat and conscious about her body since the sixth grade. She disturbed her food habits with the notion to match with her peers and their beauty standards. She experimented with throwing up after the late-night eating and found that she had much more control and believed this would help her to prevent the weight gain. Kashish fell into a vicious cycle of late-night binges followed by making herself throw up.

(i) Name and explain the eating disorder highlighted in the case above.
(ii) Explain other disorder under the same category.

04
CHAPTER

We respond to various external and internal stimuli through our receptors. Some receptors are observable, while others are internal and require devices to detect. These receptors gather a variety of information from both the external world and our internal body. Attention plays a crucial role in helping us notice and process the information our sense organs gather.

YOUR STUDY GOALS

YOUR PRACTICE GOAL

- Objective Type Questions (21 Qs ; MCQs, A-R)
- Subjective Questions (9 VSAs, 12 SAs, 2 LAs, 3 Case Based)

Sensory, Attentional and Perceptual Processes

4.1 Knowing the World

- Our knowledge of objects and their characteristics (e.g., size, shape, colour) depends on our sense organs (e.g., eyes, ears).
- The registered information from these stimuli is sent to the brain, which processes and constructs meaning from them.
- Our understanding of the world around us relies on three key processes: **Sensation, Attention and Perception**.
- These processes are interrelated and together form cognition.

4.2 Nature and Varieties of Stimulus

- The environment around us is filled with various stimuli, which include seeing, hearing, smelling, tasting and touching.
- These stimuli provide different types of information and humans have specialised sense organs for each.
- We have a set of seven sense organs which are known as sensory receptors or information gathering systems as they gather information from different kinds of sources.
- Five senses namely eyes, ears, nose, tongue, and skin collect information from outside world. Eyes are responsible for vision, ears for hearing, nose for smell and tongue for taste.

- Skin is responsible for the experiences of touch, warmth, cold and pain. Specialised receptors of warmth, cold and pain are found inside our skin.
- Besides these five external sense organs, we have two deep senses. They are called kinesthetic and vestibular systems. They provide us with important information about our body position and movement of body part related to each other.
- These seven sense organs register, ten different variety of stimuli, for example, light may be noticed whether bright or dim, whether yellow or green.
- Sound may be noticed whether loud or faint, whether melodious or distracting.
- A light may be noticed whether a bright or dim, whether yellow, red or green and so on.
- Sound may be noticed whether loud or faint, whether, inelodious or distracting and so on.

4.3 Sense Modalities

- The initial experience of a stimulus by a sense organ is known as Sensation.
- Sensation refers to the process of detecting and encoding physical stimuli.
- It involves basic experiences such as hardness, warmth, loudness and colour, resulting from the stimulation of sensory organs.
- Each sense organ is specialised for handling different types of stimuli, known as sense modalities.

Functional Limitations of Sense Organs

- Sense organs have limitations in their functioning. For example,
    - Eyes cannot see very dim or very bright light.
    - Ears cannot hear very faint or very loud sounds.
- Humans operate within a limited range of stimulation. A stimulus must meet a certain intensity or magnitude to be noticed.
- The study of the relationship between stimuli and sensation is known as Psychophysics.

Absolute Threshold/Limen (AL)

- The absolute threshold (or Absolute Limen) is the minimum intensity of a stimulus needed to be detected by a sensory system.
- For example, adding a small amount of sugar to water may not result in sweetness. However, there is a point at which the water will be perceived as sweet. The minimum number of sugar granules required to detect sweetness is the absolute threshold.
- The absolute threshold varies across individuals and situations depending on organic conditions and motivational states.
- Determining the absolute threshold involves conducting several trials, where the stimulus is varied until it is perceived in about 50% of trials.

Difference Threshold/Limen (DL)

- The difference threshold (or Difference Limen) is the smallest noticeable difference between two stimuli.
- For example, after tasting sweet water, if you add more sugar granules, then a point will come where the sweetness will be perceived as different or stronger than before. The number of granules required for this noticeable difference represents the difference threshold.
- The difference threshold is the minimum change in a stimulus required to notice a difference on 50% of trials.

Understanding Sensory Processes

- Sensory experiences depend on both the stimulus characteristics and the sense organs and neural pathways that connect them to the brain.
- Sense organs receive stimuli, convert them into electrical impulses and transmit them to brain centers for processing.
- If there is any damage or defect in the sense organ or its neural pathways, it can lead to partial or complete loss of sensation.

Quick Test 1

1. What is the role of sense organs in detecting stimuli?
2. How does attention help us to process information from our sense organs?
3. What are the five external sense organs?
4. What is sensation?
5. Our knowledge of the world around us depends on which process?
6. What is the difference threshold?

4.4 Attentional Processes

- Attention refers to the process of selecting certain stimuli from a group of others.
- It involves various properties such as alertness, concentration and search.
- Alertness is the readiness to respond to stimuli that appear before him/her.
- Concentration refers to focusing of awareness on specific objects while ignoring others. This requires mental effort, as in searching for a specific person among a crowd. Search is the process of looking for specific stimuli.

Focus and Fringe

- Attention has a focus (centered on a particular object or event) and a fringe (the outer part of the awareness field, where stimuli are less clear).
- The focus is the central part of attention, while the fringe is the less clear, peripheral area of awareness.

Divided Attention

When we can attend two different things at the same time, it is called Divided attention. In day-to-day life we attend several things at the same time. But, this becomes possible only with highly practiced activities, because they become almost automatic and require less attention to perform than new or slightly practised activities. Automatic processing has three main characteristics

- It occurs without intention.
- It takes place unconsciously.
- It involves very little or no thought processes.

Classification of Attention

Attention is classified in several ways, and one process-oriented classification divides it into selective and sustained attention.

Selective Attention

Selective Attention refers to the process of focusing on a limited number of stimuli from a large number of stimuli. Our perceptual system has limited capacity, it can only process a few stimuli at a time.

Factors Affecting Selective Attention

Several factors influence selective attention. These factors generally relate to the characteristics of individuals. These factors classified as external and internal factors.

1. **External Factors**
   - These factors are related to the characteristics of the stimuli.
   - The size, intensity and motion of stimuli are important determinants of attention.
   - Large bright and moving stimuli easily catch attention. Stimuli, which are novel and moderately complex, also easily get into our focus.
   - Rhythmic auditory stimuli are more readily attended than verbal narrations. Sudden and intense stimuli have a wonderful capacity to draw attention.
2. **Internal factors**

   These lie within the individuals. They are divided into two categories

   (i) **Motivational Factors** These are related to our biological or social needs. For example, hunger makes one more sensitive to food related stimuli.

   (ii) **Cognitive Factors** These include factors like interest, attitude and preparatory set. Objects or events, which appear interesting are readily attended by individuals.

Theories of Selective Attention

Several theories explain how selective attention works

1. Filter Theory (Broadbent, 1956)

- According to this theory, multiple stimuli simultaneously enter our receptors and create a 'bottleneck'.
- The stimuli are filtered through the short-term memory system, allowing only one to pass through for further processing, while others are screened out. We become aware only of the stimulus that successfully passes through the selective filter.

2. Filter-Attenuation Theory (Treisman, 1962)

- This theory modifies Broadbent's view, suggesting that stimuli that do not pass through the filter are not completely blocked but are instead attenuated (weakened).
- This means that some weak stimuli may still reach higher levels of processing. For instance, hearing one's name in a noisy environment is an example of weak stimuli slipping through the filter.

3. Multimode Theory (Johnston and Heinz, 1978)

- The Multimode Theory proposes that attention is flexible and involves selecting stimuli at three stages

  (i) **First stage** Sensory representations (e.g. visual images of stimuli) are formed.

  (ii) **Second stage** Semantic representations (e.g., meaning of words or names) are constructed.

  (iii) **Third stage** These sensory and semantic representations enter consciousness.
- More mental effort is required when selection occurs at the later stages (semantic and conscious processing), compared to the early stages (sensory representations).

Sustained Attention

- Sustained attention refers to the ability to maintain focus on an object or event for extended periods.
- This type of attention is also known as **vigilance** and it involves concentration over long durations, often requiring individuals to stay focused on a task for many hours.

Factors Influencing Sustained Attention

These factors highlight the importance of the nature and consistency of stimuli in supporting sustained attention and performance on tasks that require prolonged focus.

- **Sensory Modality** Performance tends to be superior when the stimuli (or signals) are auditory rather than visual. Auditory signals are easier to maintain attention on for longer periods.
- **Clarity of Stimuli** Intense and long-lasting stimuli are more likely to facilitate sustained attention. Clear and persistent signals help in maintaining focus and improve performance.
- **Temporal Uncertainty** Stimuli presented at regular intervals are easier to attend to than those that appear at irregular intervals. A predictable schedule of stimuli helps the individual to remain focused.
- **Spatial Uncertainty** Stimuli that appear at a fixed location are easier to attend to than those that appear at random locations. Fixed locations help in directing and maintaining attention more effectively.

Span of Attention

The span of attention or perceptual span, refers to the number of objects a person can attend to in a fraction of a second. It specifically describes the amount of information an observer can grasp from a complex array of stimuli during a single momentary exposure.

- The tachistoscope is an instrument used to determine the span of attention by presenting visual stimuli for a brief period.
- **Miller's Report** Based on several experiments, psychologist George Miller reported that the span of attention generally falls within the range of seven plus or minus two. This is known as the 'magic number', suggesting that people can typically focus on five to seven pieces of information at once.
- **Exception** Under special conditions, the span of attention can be extended to nine or more.
- **Real-World Example** The four-digit numbers on vehicle number plates are designed to fit within this limit, helping traffic police easily read and record the number along with any alphabets in case of traffic rule violations.

Attention Deficit Hyperactivity Disorder (ADHD)

- ADHD is a behavioural disorder in children, especially those of primary school age, characterised by impulsivity, excessive motor activity, and an inability to maintain attention.
- The disorder is more common in boys than girls. If not managed properly, attention difficulties may continue till adolescence or adulthood.

Main Features of ADHD

- Difficulty in maintaining attention.
- Children with ADHD are often easily distracted, have trouble following instructions, and struggle with interpersonal relationships (e.g., poor interactions with parents and peers).
- They tend to perform poorly in school, despite having normal intelligence.
- There are difficulties in reading and learning basic subjects.

Causes of ADHD

- Studies do not conclusively support a biological basis for ADHD, but some research links dietary factors (such as food colouring) to the disorder.
- Social-psychological factors like home environment and family issues are considered more reliable contributors to ADHD.

Treatment of ADHD

- **Ritalin** It is a widely used drug that decreases hyperactivity and improves attention, although it does not cure ADHD and may cause negative side effects, such as suppressed growth.
- **Behavioural Management Programmes** These programmes use positive reinforcement and structured learning tasks that minimise errors and provide immediate feedback to promote success.

- **Cognitive Behavioral Training** Involves rewarding desired behaviours and teaching self-instructions (e.g., 'stop, think, then do'). This approach helps children focus their attention and behave reflectively, leading to more stable improvements over a time.

Quick Test 2

1 What does attention refer to?
2 What is the difference between the focus and the fringe in attention?
3 State one example of divided attention from your day-to-day life.
4 Which instrument is used to determine the span of attention.
5 How does attention influence our ability to maintain focus over time?
6 List down the causes of ADHD.

4.5 Perceptual Processes

- Perception is the process through which we recognise, interpret, and assign meaning to information received by our sense organs.
- It is not merely the interpretation of the external or internal world, but a construction of objects and events from an individual's unique point of view.
- Perception involves multiple sub-processes such as attention, sensory receptors and the brain's involvement in processing through learning, memory and other psychological functions.

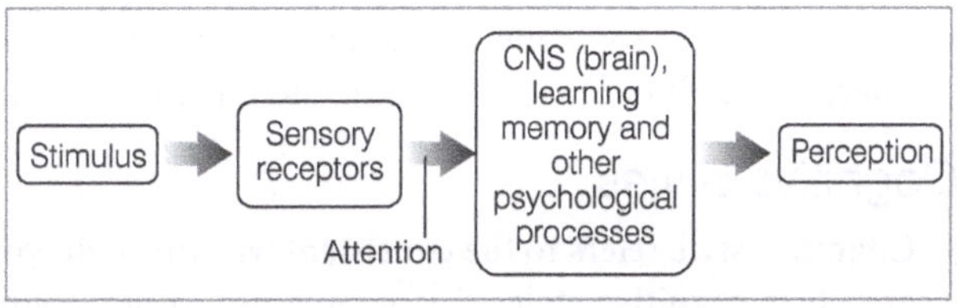

▲ *Sub-processes of Perception*

Processing Approaches in Perception

1. **Bottom-up Processing**
   - The idea that the recognition process starts from the parts, which form as the basis for the recognition of the whole is kwown as bottom-up processing.
   - It emphasises the features of stimuli in perception, where perception is seen as a process of mental construction.
2. **Top-down Processing**
   - The notion that the recognition process begins from the whole, which leads to identification of its various parts is known as Top-down processing.
   - It emphasises the perceiver's knowledge, expectations and experiences, with perception seen as the recognition or identification of stimuli.
   - Both processing approaches work together to help individuals understand and make sense of the world around them.

4.6 The Perceiver

- Human beings are not just mechanical and passive recipients of stimuli from the external world. They are creative beings and try to understand the external world in their own ways.
- In this process their motivations and memories as well as values, beliefs and attitudes play an important role in giving meaning to the external world. Some of these factors are given below

Motivation

- A perceiver's needs and desires strongly influence how they perceive stimuli.
- One way to do this is to perceive objects in a picture as something that will satisfy their needs. People want to fulfill their needs and desires through various means.

Expectations or Perceptual Sets

- Our expectations about what we might perceive can influence our perception. This phenomenon of perceptual familiarisation or perceptual generalisation reflects a strong tendency to see what we except to see when the results do not accurately reflect external reality.
- For instance, if someone is accustomed to a milkman delivering milk at a particular time, they may interpret any knock at that time as the milkman, even if it is someone else.

Cognitive Styles

- Cognitive style refers to the consistent way through which individuals process their environment. There are other cognitive styles that people use in perceiving their environment. Field dependent and field independent cognitive style is the most used in studies.
- Field-dependent individuals perceive the world holistically, while field-independent individuals break down the world into smaller parts.

Cultural Background and Experiences

- Cultural settings and past experiences significantly influence how we perceive things.
- People from different cultural environments might not recognise certain objects or perceive distance in images. For example, African subjects have difficulty recognising objects in pictures, while Eskimos can distinguish various types of snow and Siberian tribes can distinguish among many skin colours of reindeer.
- These factors indicate that perception is not just a passive reception of stimuli, but a complex process shaped by personal, social and cultural influences.

4.7 Principles of Perceptual Organisation

- Our visual field is made up of different elements, such as points, lines and colours.
- However, we perceive these elements as organised wholes or complete objects. For example, we see a bicycle as a whole object, not as a collection of different parts (like saddle, wheel, handle).
- The process of organising the visual field into meaningful wholes is called form perception.
- Gestalt psychologists, including Kohler, Kofka and Wertheimer, tried to explain how we perceive the visual field as meaningful wholes. The term 'Gestalt' refers to a regular figure or form.
- According to Gestalt psychologists, we perceive stimuli not as separate elements, but as an organised whole that carries a definite form.

- They believe that the form of an object is different from the sum of its parts. For example, a flower pot with flowers is perceived as a whole. If the flowers are removed, the flower pot still remains whole. The configuration changes, but the pot remains intact.
- Gestalt psychologists suggest that our brain processes are always oriented toward the perception of a good figure, also known as 'pragnanz'.
- This is why we perceive everything in organised forms. The most basic organisation happens in the form of **figure-ground segregation**[1].
- When looking at a surface, certain aspects of it are clearly visible as separate entities, while other aspects are not.
- For example, when we see words on a page, a painting on a wall or birds flying in the sky–the words, painting or birds stand out from the background and are perceived as figures. The page, wall, or sky stays behind the figure and is perceived as the background.
- To test this experience look at the figure, given below you can see either–The white part of the figure, which looks like a vase (flower pot) or The black part, which looks like two faces.

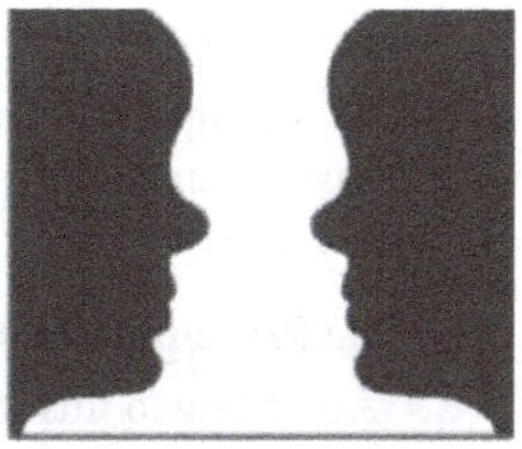

A figure can be differentiated from the ground based on the following characteristics

- The figure has a definite form, while the background is relatively formless.
- The figure is more organised compared to its background.
- The figure has a clear outline, while the background has none.
- The figure stands out from the background, while the background stays behind the figure.
- The figure appears more clear, limited and relatively closer, while the background appears unclear, unlimited and farther away.
- Gestalt psychologists provided several laws to explain how different stimuli in our visual field are organised into meaningful whole objects

1. **The Principle of Proximity**
   - Objects that are close together in space or time are perceived as belonging together or as a group.
   - For example, a pattern of dots might not look like a square, but instead as columns of dots or groups of dots in rows.

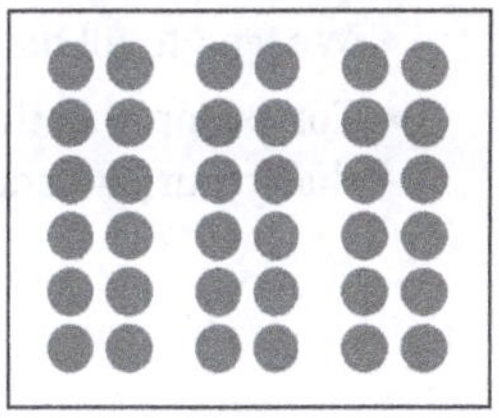

▲ *Proximity*

2. **The Principle of Similarity**
   - Objects that are similar to each other and share similar characteristics are perceived as a group.
   - For example, little circles and squares that are evenly spaced both horizontally and vertically might be seen as alternating columns of circles and squares.

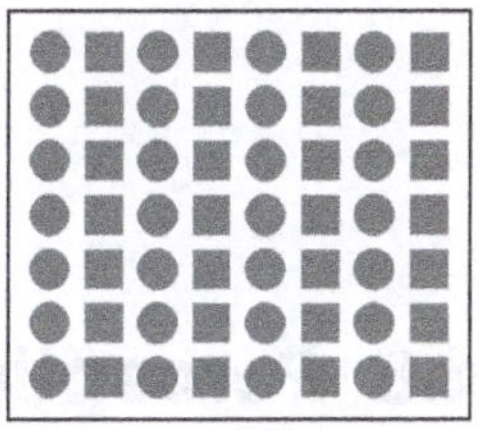

▲ *Similarity*

3. **The Principle of Continuity**
   - This principle states that we tend to perceive objects as belonging together if they appear to form a continuous pattern.
   - For example, we are more likely to identify two lines (a-b and c-d) crossing each other than to identify four lines meeting at the center (p).

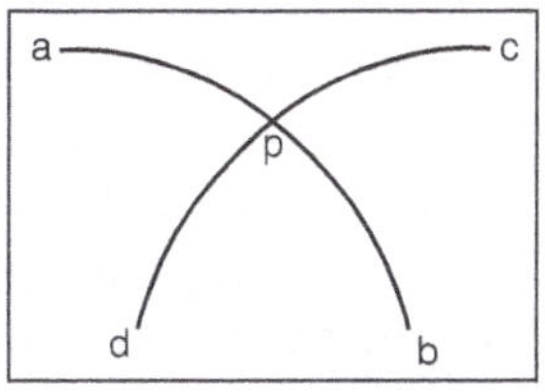

▲ *Continuity*

1 **Figure-ground Segregation** It is a type of perceptual grouping which is a vital necessity for recognising objects through vision.

4. **The Principle of Smallness**
   - According to this principle, smaller areas tend to be seen as figures against a larger background.
   - For instance, in the figure given below, we are more likely to see a black cross rather than a white cross within the circle due to this principle.

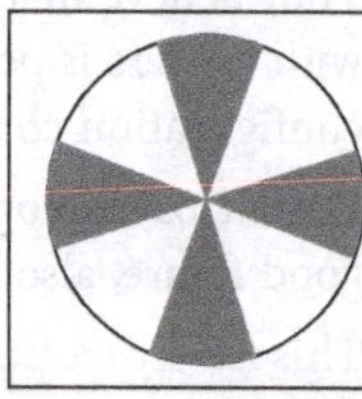

▲ *Smallness*

5. **The Principle of Symmetry**
   - This principle suggests that symmetrical areas tend to be seen as figures against asymmetrical backgrounds.
   - For example, the black areas in the figure are seen as figures because they have symmetrical properties against the white, asymmetrical background.

▲ *Symmetry*

6. **The Principle of Surroundedness**
   - According to this principle, areas surrounded by others tend to be perceived as figures.
   - For example, in the image given below, we perceive five figures against a white background rather than the word 'LIFT'.

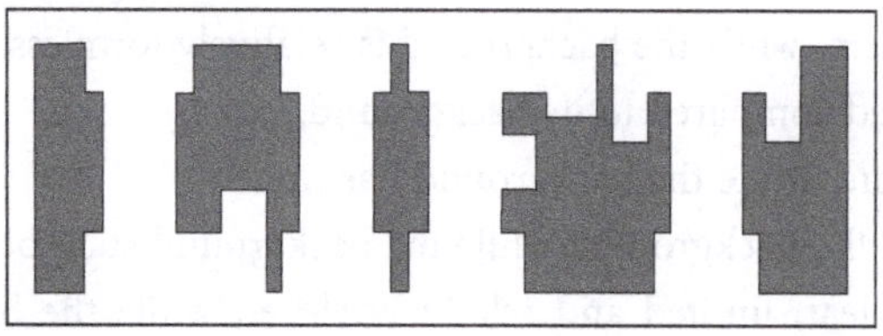

▲ *Surroundedness*

7. **The Principle of Closure**
   - We tend to fill the gaps in sensory input and perceive objects as whole rather than as separate parts.
   - For example, in the figure given below, we perceive it as a triangle instead of three different angles due to our tendency to fill in the gaps.

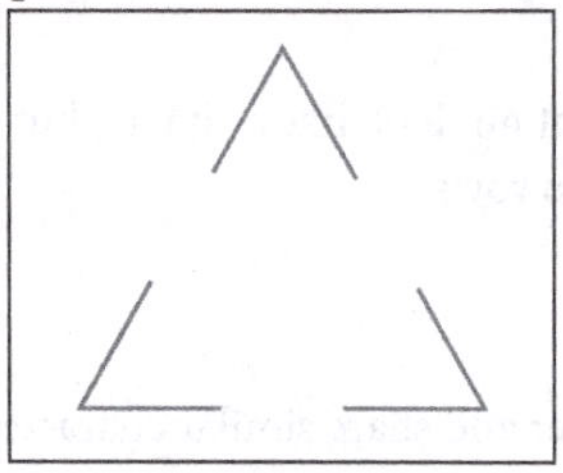

▲ *Closure*

4.8 Perception of Space, Depth and Distance

- The visual field or surface in which things exist, move or can be placed is called space.
- Space in which we live is organised in three dimensions.
- We perceive not only the spatial attributes like size, shape, and direction of different objects, but also the distance between them.
- While the images of objects projected onto our retina are flat and two-dimensional (left, right, up, down), we still perceive three dimensions in space.
- This occurs because of our ability to transfer a two-dimensional retinal vision into three-dimensional perception.

- This process of perceiving the world in three dimensions is called distance or depth perception.
- In perceiving depth, we depend on two main sources of information called cues.
  (i) **Monocular cues** These allow us to perceive depth with just one eye.
  (ii) **Binocular cues** These require both eyes.

Monocular Cues (Psychological Cues)

- Monocular cues are effective when the objects are viewed with only one eye.
- These cues are often used by artists to induce depth in two-dimensional paintings and are also called pictorial cues. Some important monocular cues include
  (i) **Relative Size** The size of the retinal image helps us to judge distance based on our past and present experiences with similar objects. The farther the object, the smaller the retinal image.
  (ii) **Interposition or Overlapping** When some portion of the object is covered by another object, the covered object is considered farther away and the object that covers it appears nearer.
  (iii) **Linear Perspective** Far objects appear to be closer together than nearer objects. For example, parallel lines like rail tracks appear to converge with increasing distance towards a vanishing point at the horizon.
  (iv) **Aerial Perspective** Distant objects appear hazy or blurry due to dust and moisture in the air. For example, distant mountains appear blue because of the scattering of blue light in the atmosphere.
  (v) **Light and Shade** Highlights and shadows provide information about an object's distance. Some parts of the object are highlighted while others become darker.
  (vi) **Relative Height** Larger objects are perceived as closer to the viewer and smaller objects as farther away. When two objects are expected to be the same size, the larger one appears closer.
  (vii) **Texture Gradient** Objects with a higher density of elements appear farther away.
  (viii) **Motion Parallax** Objects at different distances move at different relative speeds. Distant objects appear to move slowly compared to closer objects. For example, when travelling in a bus, closer objects appear to move against the direction of the bus, while further objects appear to move with it.

Binocular Cues (Physiological Cues)

Some important cues to depth perception require both eyes. Three important binocular cues are

- **Retinal or Binocular Disparity** The two eyes are separated by about 6.5 centimetres, which creates slightly different images on the retina of each eye. This difference is called retinal disparity. The brain interprets a large disparity as indicating a close object and a small disparity as indicating a distant object.
- **Convergence** When we focus on a nearby object, our eyes turn inward to bring the image on the fovea of each eye. The degree of convergence provides cues to depth perception. The more our eyes converge, the closer the object appears.
- **Accommodation** The ciliary muscles change the thickness of the lens in the eye to focus the image on the retina. If the object is closer than 2 metres, the muscles contract to make the lens thicker. The degree of contraction signals the brain about the object's distance.

4.9 Perceptual Constancies

Perceptual constancy refers to the perception of objects as relatively stable despite changes in the stimulation of sensory receptors. There are three types of perceptual constancies.

1. **Size Constancy**
   - The size of an image on our retina changes with the distance of the object from the eye. The farther the object, the smaller the image.
   - However, we perceive the object as being the same size regardless of its distance, within certain limits. For example, as you approach your friend, their size on the retina becomes larger, but you perceive their size as constant.
2. **Shape Constancy**
   - The shapes of familiar objects remain unchanged in our perception, even if the pattern of the retinal image changes due to differences in the object's orientation. It also called form constancy.
   - For example, a dinner plate looks round even when it is viewed from different angles (such as from the side, where it might appear as an ellipse or a line).
3. **Brightness Constancy**
   - Visual objects appear constant in terms of their brightness (whiteness, greyness, or blackness), even though the amount of light reflected from them may vary.
   - Our experience of brightness remains unchanged despite changes in the amount of light reflected from the object.
   - For example, a white paper looks white in both sunlight and room light and coal looks black in both settings as well.

Quick Test 3

1. What is perception?
2. Explain the difference between bottom-up and top-down processing in perception.
3. What are the main factors that influence an individual's perception?
4. Describe the principle of proximity in Gestalt psychology.
5. How cultural background and experience influence perception?
6. What is perceptual constancy?

4.10 Illusions

- Illusions are misperceptions caused by the misinterpretation of sensory information.
- These misinterpretations are typically caused by external stimuli and generate similar experiences in everyone.
- Illusions are also called primitive organisations because they occur universally.
- Psychologists mainly study illusions in the visual modality.

Universal Illusions and Personal Illusions

- Some perceptual illusions are universal and found in all individuals. These illusions are called universal illusions or permanent illusions as they do not change with experience or practice.
- Some other illusions seem to differ from individual to individual; these are called personal illusions.

Geometrical Illusions

- In the figure given below **Muller-Lyer illusion** has been shown. We perceive line A as shorter than line B, although both the lines are equal.

- This illusion is experienced even by children. There are some studies that suggest even animals experience this illusions.

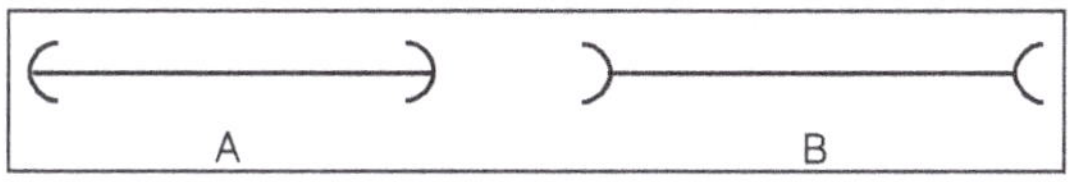

▲ *Muller-Lyer Illusion*

- In vertical-horizontal illusion, two lines of the same length appear to be different lengths, with the vertical line seeming longer than the horizontal line.

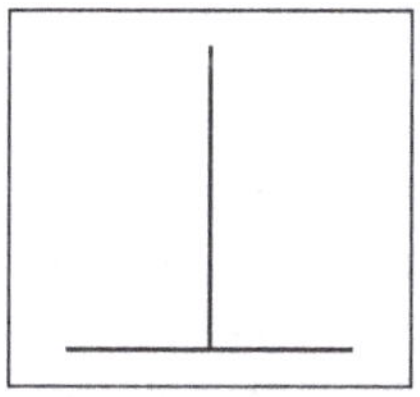

▲ *Vertical-Horizontal Illusion*

Apparent Movement Illusion

- This illusion occurs when motionless images are shown one after another at an appropriate rate. It is known as the phi phenomenon, it is seen in films and flickering lights.
- For the experience of this illusion, Wertheimer had reported the presence of appropriate level of brightness, size, spatial gap and temporal contiguity is needed for this illusion to occur.
- Without these factors, the lights will appear either stationary or will not appear to move in sequence.
- They will appear either as one point, or as different points appearing one after another, without any experience of motion.

4.11 Socio-Cultural Influences on Perception

- Psychologists believe that perception can differ based on socio-cultural contexts.
- Different cultures may have distinct ways of perceiving the world.

Studies Using Illusion Figures

- Research comparing people from different cultures (e.g. remote African villages vs. Western urban settings) shows varying susceptibility to different illusions.
- Segall, Campbell and Herskovits found that African subjects were more likely to experience the horizontal-vertical illusion, while Western subjects were more likely to experience the Muller-Lyer illusion.
- Africans, living in forested areas, had a stronger tendency to overestimate verticality due to the presence of tall trees, while Westerners, living in environments with right angles, were more prone to underestimating the length of lines with enclosures (e.g., arrowheads).

Studies Using Pictures of Objects

- Research shows that people from different cultural backgrounds interpret pictures differently.
- **Hudson's** did a seminal study in Africa and found that people unfamiliar with pictures had difficulty recognising objects and understanding depth cues like superimposition.
- **Sinha and Mishra's** study reveals that cultural experiences influence how people interpret pictures, especially actions and events. People who are not regularly exposed to pictures struggle with interpreting them accurately.

Quick Test 4

1. What are illusions?
2. Explain the difference between universal and personal illusions.
3. Describe the Muller-Lyer illusion.
4. How do socio-cultural influences affect the way people perceive illusions and interpret pictures?

NCERT Folder

1. Explain the functional limitations of sense organs.

Ans. The sense organs of human beings provide first-hand information about external or internal world. The initial experience of a stimulus or an object registered by a particular sense organ is called sensation.

Each sense organ is so specialised for dealing with a particular kind of information. However, it is important to note that our sense organs function with certain limitations. The limitations are as follows

- A stimulus has to carry a minimum value in order to get noticed.
- The Absolute Limen (AL) is not a fixed point; instead it varies considerably across individuals and situations depending on the people's organic conditions and their motivational states.
- As it is not possible to notice all stimuli, it is also not possible to differentiate between all stimuli.
- Understanding of sensation is not possible without understanding the AL and DL of different types of stimuli (for example, visual, auditory).
- Besides these, sensory processes do not depend only on the stimulus characteristics.
- Any structural or functional defect in the receptor organ and its neural pathway (the concerned brain area) may lead to a partial or complete loss of sensation.

2. Define attention. Explain its properties.

Ans. The process through which certain stimuli are selected from a group of others is generally referred to as attention.

- **Properties of Attention** Attention refers to several properties like selection, alertness, concentration and search.
- **Selection** A large number of stimuli impinge upon our sense organs simultaneously, but we do not notice all of them at the same time. Only a selected few of them are noticed.
- **Alertness** Alertness refers to an individual's readiness to deal with stimuli that appear before her/him. For example, while participating in a race in your school you might have seen the participants on the starting line in an alert state waiting for the whistle to blow in order to run.
- **Concentration** Concentration refers to focusing of awareness on certain specific objects while excluding others for the moment. For example, in the classroom, a student concentrates on the teacher's lecture and ignores all sorts of noises coming from different corners of the school.
- **Search** In search an observer looks for some specified subset of objects among a set of objects. For example, when you go to fetch your younger sister/brother from the school, you just look for him/her among innumerable boys and girls. All these activities require some kind of effort on the part of people. Attention in this sense refers to 'Effort Allocation'.

3. State the determinants of selective attention. How does selective attention differ from sustained attention?

Ans. **Selective Attention** It is concerned mainly with the selection of a limited number of stimuli or objects from a large number of stimuli. Our perceptual system has a limited capacity to receive and process information. This means that it can deal only with a few stimuli at a given moment of time.

Factors affecting Selective Attention Several factors influence selective attention. These generally relate to the characteristics of stimuli and the characteristics of individuals.

They are generally classified as external and internal factors

(i) **External Factors** These are related to the features of stimuli. The size, intensity and motion of stimuli important determinants of attention. Large, bright and moving stimuli easily catch our attention. Stimuli, which are novel and moderately complex, also easily get into our focus. Rhythmic auditory stimuli are more readily attended than verbal narrations. Sudden and intense stimuli have a wonderful capacity to draw attention.

(ii) **Internal Factors** These lie within the individuals. These may be divided into two main categories. They are motivational factors and cognitive factors.

(a) **Motivational Factors** These are related to our biological or social needs. When we are hungry, we notice even a light smell of food. A student taking an examination is likely to focus on a teacher's instructions more than other students.

(b) **Cognitive Factors** These factors include like interest, attitude and preparatory set. Objects or events, which appear interesting are readily attended by individuals. Similarly we pay quick attention to certain objects or events to which we are favourably disposed.

Difference between Selective Attention and Sustained Attention Selective attention differs from sustained attention as selective attention is mainly concerned with the selection of limited number of stimuli from a large number of stimuli. On the other hand sustained attention is concerned with concentration. It refers to our ability to maintain attention on an object or event for longer durations. It is also known as Vigilance. Sometimes people have to concentrate on a particular task for many hours.

4. What is the main proposition of Gestalt psychologists with respect to perception of the visual field?

Ans. The Gestalt psychologists have given us several laws to explain how and why different stimuli in our visual field are organised into meaningful whole objects. These are

- **The Principle of Proximity** Objects that are close together in space or time are perceived as belonging together or as a group.
- **The Principle of Similarity** Objects that are similar to one another and have similar characteristics are perceived as a group.
- **The Principle of Continuity** This principle states that we tend to perceive objects as belonging together if they appear to form a continuous pattern.
- **The Principle of Smallness** According to this principle, smaller areas tend to be seen as figures against a larger background.
- **The Principle of Symmetry** This principle suggests that symmetrical areas tend to be seen as figures against asymmetrical backgrounds.
- **The Principle of Surroundedness** As per this principle, the areas surrounded by others tend to be perceived as figures.
- **The Principle of Closure** We try to fill the gaps in stimulation and perceive the objects as whole rather than their separate parts.

5. How does perception of space take place?

Ans. The visual field or surface in which things exist, move or can be placed is called space. The space in which we live is organised in three dimensions.

We perceive not only the spatial attributes like size, shape direction of different objects, but also the distance between the objects found in this space. While the images of objects projected on to our retina are flat and two dimensional (left, right, up, down), we still perceive three dimensions in the space. It occurs because of our ability to transfer a two dimensional retinal vision into a three dimensional perception.

6. What are the monocular cues of depth perception? Explain the role of binocular cues in the perception of depth.

Ans. For answer refer to text under the heading 'Monocular Cues' and 'Binocular Cues' on page no. 97.

7. Why do illusions occur?

Ans. Our perceptions are not always truthful. Sometime we fail to interpret the sensory information correctly. This results in a mismatch between the physical stimuli and its perception.

These misperceptions resulting from misinterpretation of information received by our sensory organs are generally known as Illusions.

It results from an external stimulus situation and generate the same kind of experience in each individual. That is why illusions are also called Primitive organisations.

Although illusions can be experienced by the stimulation of any of our sense, psychologists have studied them more commonly in the visual than in other sense modalities.

Some perceptual illusions are universal and found in all individuals. For example, the rail tracks appear to be converging to all of us. These illusions are called Universal illusions or permanent illusions as they do not change with experience or practice.

Some other illusions seem to differ from individual to individual; these are called Personal illusions.

8. How do socio-cultural factors influence our perceptions?

Ans. Several psychologists have studied the processes of perception in different socio-cultural settings. Psychologists that believe ways of people in perceiving the world must be different in some respects.

Studies using Illusion Figures Psychologists have used illusion figures with several groups of people living in Europe, Africa and many other places.

Segall, Campbell and Herskovits carried out the most extensive study of illusion influence by comparing samples from remote African villages and Western urban settings.

It was found that African subjects showed greater susceptibility to horizontal-vertical illusion, whereas Western subjects showed greater susceptibility to Muller-Lyer illusion. Living in dense forests the African subjects regularly experienced verticality like long trees and developed tendency to overestimate it.

The Westerners, who lived in environment characterised by right angles, developed a tendency to underestimate the length of lines characterised by enclosure, such as arrowhead. It shows that the habits of perception are learnt differently in different cultural settings.

Studies using Pictures of Objects In some studies people living in different cultural settings have been given pictures for identification of objects and interpretation of depth or other events represented in them. Hudson did a seminal study in Africa and found that people who had never seen pictures, had great difficulty in recognising objects depicted in them and in interpreting depth cues like superimposition. It was indicated that informal instruction in home and habitual exposure to pictures were necessary to sustain the skill of pictorial depth perception.

Exam Pattern Questions

Objective Type Questions

Multiple Choice Questions (MCQs)

1. How many different stimuli we register using the seven sense organs?

(a) Ten (b) Eleven
(c) Fourteen (d) Nine

2. An example of external factor of attention is ....

(a) memory (b) forgetting
(c) competitive spirit (d) interest

3. The minimum value of a stimulus required to activate a given sensation is called ....

(a) Stimulation (b) Difference limen
(c) Sensation (d) Absolute limen

4. The perception of movement in a stationary spot is not called

(a) Hallucination (b) Phi phenomenon
(c) Apparent movement (d) Stroboscopic movement

5. Which among the following theories describes that many stimuli simultaneously enter our receptors creating a kind of 'bottleneck' situation?

(a) Filter Theory
(b) Filter-Attenuation Theory
(c) Multimode Theory
(d) None of the above

6. Which of the following factor is not sustained attention?

I. Sensory modality II. Clarify of stimuli
III. Temperal uncertainty IV. Special uncertainly

Codes

(a) Only I (b) I and II
(c) I, II and III (d) All of these

7. In rehabilitation, the patients are given .... therapy to help them become self-sufficient.

(a) occupational (b) behavioural
(c) biomedical (d) existential

8. We leave early from our house to avoid getting stuck in traffic and being late for work, this is an example of

(a) negative reinforcement
(b) positive reinforcement
(c) aversive conditioning
(d) punishment

9. Sometimes, in the therapeutic process, the client acts out her, his frustration, anger, fear and depression that she/he harboured towards that person in the past, but could not express at that time. The therapist becomes a substitute for that person in the present. This phenomenon is known as ....

(a) positive transference (b) transference neurosis
(c) negative transference (d) resistance

10. Which of the following statements are correct regarding Absolute Threshold (AL)?

I. AL refers to the minimum value of a stimulus required to activate a sensory system.
II. AL is a fixed point across individuals and situations.
III. AL varies depending on individuals' organic conditions and motivational states.
IV. AL is determined based on a single trial.

Codes

(a) I and II (b) I and III (c) II and IV (d) III and IV

11. Which of the following is true for Difference Threshold (DL)?

I. It refers to the minimum difference required between two stimuli to notice a change.
II. DL remains constant for all individuals.
III. The smallest detectable change is noticed on 50% of occasions.
IV. DL increases with increasing magnitude of the stimulus.

Codes

(a) I and III (b) II and IV (c) III and IV (d) I and IV

12. Which of the following statements are correct about Sensory Limitations?

I. Sense organs function within a limited range of stimulation.
II. Sense organs can adapt to perceive all levels of stimuli equally.
III. Structural or functional defects in sense organs can cause sensory loss.
IV. Neural pathways play no role in sensory processes.

Codes

(a) I and II (b) I and III (c) II and IV (d) III and IV

13. **Ravi observes distant mountains appearing blue and hazy. Identify the depth perception cue involved.**

I. Texture Gradient **II. Light and Shade**
III. Aerial Perspective **IV. Motion Parallax**

Codes

(a) I and III (b) II and III
(c) III and IV (d) I and II

14. **During a bus ride, nearby trees seem to move against the direction of travel, while distant mountains appear stationary. Which depth cue is illustrated?**

I. Retinal Disparity **II. Motion Parallax**
III. Texture Gradient **IV. Aerial Perspective**

Codes

(a) I and III (b) II and IV
(c) II and III (d) III and IV

Assertion-Reason Questions

Directions (Q. Nos. 15-21) In the following questions, a statement of Assertion (A) is followed by a statement of Reason (R). Mark the correct choice from the options given below.

(a) Both A and R are true and R is the correct explanation of A
(b) Both A and R are true, but R is not the correct explanation of A
(c) A is true, but R is false
(d) A is false, but R is true

15. **Assertion** (A) We have a set of seven sense organs, which are known as Sensory receptors or information gathering systems.

Reason (R) They gather information from different kinds of sources.

16. **Assertion** (A) Selective attention is concerned mainly with the selection of a limited number of stimuli or objects from a large number of stimuli.

Reason (R) Stimuli, which are novel and moderately complex, easily get into our focus.

17. **Assertion** (A) The Absolute Threshold (AL) of a stimulus is the minimum intensity required to notice a stimulus and activate a sensory system.

Reason (R) The Absolute Threshold is a fixed value for all individuals and situations and it does not vary based on a person's organic conditions or motivational states.

18. **Assertion** (A) Selective attention involves the process of filtering stimuli based on their characteristics such as size, intensity and motion.

Reason (R) External factors like the complexity of a stimulus can hinder selective attention by making it harder to focus.

19. **Assertion** (A) The principle of closure explains our tendency to perceive incomplete figures as complete objects.

Reason (R) This principle suggests that our brain actively fills in gaps, allowing us to see missing parts of an object and perceive it as a whole.

20. **Assertion** (A) Illusions result from misinterpretation of sensory information received by the sensory organs.

Reason (R) Illusions are known as Primitive organisations because they generate the same kind of experience in each individual.

21. **Assertion** (A) Socio-cultural influences significantly affect how individuals perceive illusions.

Reason (R) Studies comparing African and Western populations show that cultural settings shape susceptibility to different types of visual illusions.

Answers

1. (a) Ten
2. (c) competitive spirit
3. (d) Absolute limen
4. (a) Hallucination
5. (a) Filter Theory
6. (d) All of these
7. (a) occupational
8. (a) negative reinforcement
9. (b) transference neurosis
10. (b) I and III
11. (a) I and III
12. (b) I and III
13. (c) III and IV
14. (b) II and IV
15. (a) Both A and R are true and R is the correct explanation of A.
16. (b) Both A and R are true, but R is not the correct explanation of A.
17. (b) Both A and R are true, but R is not the correct explanation of A.
18. (c) A is true, but R is false.
19. (a) Both A and R are true and R is the correct explanation of A.
20. (a) Both A and R are true and R is the correct explanation of A.
21. (a) Both A and R are true and R is the correct explanation of A.

Subjective Questions

Very Short Answer Type Questions

1. What forms base of our knowledge?

Ans. We all have knowledge about different objects with the help of our sense organs. These organs collect information not only from the outside world, but also from our own body. This information collected by our sense organs forms the base of our knowledge.

2. Tina tells her younger sister that our body has five sense organs and with the help of these we live our life intelligently. What are these sense organs?

Ans. Human body has five sense organs namely eyes, ears, nose, tongue and skin. With the help of these organs we collect information from outside world.

Eyes are responsible for vision, ears for hearing, nose for smell, tongue for taste and skin is responsible for the experiences of touch, warmth, cold and pain.

3. Define sensation.

Ans. The initial experience of a stimulus or an object registered by a particular sense organ is called sensation. It refers to a process through which we detect and encode a variety of physical stimuli.

4. Difference between focus and fringe of attention.

Ans. Attention has a focus as well as a fringe (outer part of an area). When the field of awareness is centered on a particular object or event, it is called focus or the focal point of attention.

On the other hand, when the objects or events are away from the center of awareness and one is not very clear of them, they are said to be at the fringe of attention.

5. What do you mean by vigilance?

Ans. Vigilance refers to our ability to maintain attention on an object or event for longer durations. It is also known as sustained attention.

6. Define illusion.

Ans. Misperceptions resulting from misinterpretation of information received by our sensory organs are generally known as illusions.

7. Why are sense organs called sense modalities?

Ans. Each sense organ is highly specialised for dealing with a particular kind of information. Hence, each one of them is known as a sense modality.

8. Differentiate between divided and selective attention.

Ans. When we can attend two different things at the same time, it is called divided attention. Whereas, selective attention is concerned mainly with the selection of a limited number of stimuli or objects from a large number of stimuli.

9. What is the difference between field dependent and field independent people?

Ans. Field dependent people perceive the external world in its totality i.e. in a global or holistic manner. On the other hand, field independent people perceive the external world by breaking it into smaller units i.e. in an analytic or differentiated manner.

Short Answer Type Questions

1. Explain Filter-attenuation theory.

Ans. Filter-attenuation theory was developed by Triesman in 1962 by modifying Broadbent's theory. As per this theory, stimuli is not getting access to the selective filter at a given moment of time are not completely blocked. The filter only attenuates (weakens) their strength.

Thus, some stimuli manage to escape through the selective filter to reach higher levels of processing.

It is indicated that personally relevant stimuli like one's name in a collective dinner can be noticed even at a very low level of sound. Such stimuli, even though fairly weak, may also generate response occasionally by slipping through the selective filter.

2. Discuss about the size constancy.

Ans. The size of an image on our retina changes with the change in the distance of the object from the eye. The further away it is, the smaller is the image. On the other hand, our experience shows that within limits, the object appears to be about the same size irrespective of its distance.

The tendency for the perceived size of objects to remain relatively unchanged with changes in their distance from the observer and the size of the retinal image is called size constancy.

3. Differentiate between top-down and bottom-up approaches.

Ans. **Bottom-up Processing Approach** The idea that recognition process starts from the parts, and form as the basis for the recognition of the whole is known as bottom-up processing. The bottom-up approach lays importance on the features of stimuli in perception and considers perception as a process of mental construction.

Top-down Processing Approach The notion that recognition process begins from the whole, and leads to identification of its various parts is known as top-down processing. The top-down approach lays importance on the perceiver and considers perception as a process of recognition or identification of stimuli.

4. What is the significance of the study of Sinha and Mishra? What kind of instruction is necessary to have skill of pictorial depth perception?

Ans. Sinha and Mishra have carried out several studies on pictorial perception using a variety of pictures with people from diverse cultural settings, such as hunters and gatherers living in forests, agriculturists living in villages and people employed and living in cities.

It was indicated that informal instruction in home and habitual exposure to pictures were necessary to sustain the skill of pictorial depth perception.

5. Explain about 'phi-phenomenon' in detail.

Ans. Apparent movement illusion is experienced when some motionless pictures are projected one after another at an appropriate rate. This illusion is referred to as phi-phenomenon.

For the experience of this illusion, Wertheimer had reported the presence of appropriate level of brightness, size, spatial gap and temporal contiguity (two stimuli are experienced close together in time) of different lights to be important.

In the absence of these, the light points will not appear as moving. They will appear either as one point, or as different points appearing one after another, without any experience of motion.

6. Explain absolute limen.

Ans. A stimulus has to have a minimum value or weight in order to get noticed. The minimum value of a stimulus required to activate a given sensory system is called absolute threshold or Absolute Limen (AL).

For example, one or two granules of sugar will not bring sweetness in a glass of water, but there will be some minimum amount of sugar with which a glass of water becomes sweet. This minimum quantity will be the AL of sweetness. Here, AL is not a fixed point it differs for different individuals and situations depending on the people's organic conditions and their motivational states.

So, it can be estimated based on a number of trials. The number of sugar granules that might produce the experience of sweetness in water on 50 per cent of occasions will be called the AL of sweetness. If you add more number of sugar granules, the chances are greater that the water will be reported more often as sweet than plain.

7. Discuss about difference limen.

Ans. It is not possible for us to observe all stimuli, and it is also not possible to differentiate between all stimuli. There should be some minimum difference between the two stimuli, in order to notice the difference.

The smallest difference in the value of the two stimuli that is necessary to tell them that they are different is called difference threshold or difference limen (DL). If we take same sugar glass experiment, now if we want to experience sweetness different from the previous sweetness, we need to add a minimum amount of sugar granules.

The number of sugar granules added to water to generate an experience of sweetness that is different from the previous sweetness on 50 per cent of the occasions will be called the DL of sweetness.

Thus, difference threshold is the minimum amount of change in a physical stimulus that is capable of producing a sensation difference on 50 per cent of the trials.

8. Air traffic controllers and radar readers have to constantly watch or monitor signals on screens. The occurrence of signals in certain situations is unpredictable and error in detecting signals may be fatal. Hence, a great vigilance is required. What type of attention is followed by the traffic controllers and write their factors affecting that attention.

Ans. The type of attention followed by the Air traffic controller is Sustained Attention.

(i) **Sensory Modality** Performance is found to be superior when the stimuli are auditory than when they are visual.

(ii) **Clarity of Stimuli** Intense and long lasting stimuli facilitate sustained attention and result in better performance.

(iii) **Temporal Uncertainty** When stimuli appear at regular intervals of time they are attended better than when they appear at irregular intervals.

(iv) **Spatial Uncertainty** Stimuli that appear at a fixed place are readily attended, whereas those that appear at random locations are difficult to attend.

9. During a parent-teacher meeting with a psychologist, she/he explains about Attention Deficit Hyperactivity Disorder (ADHD) to parents in order to diagnose the symptoms and provide timely proper treatment to the affected children. Discuss about ADHD.

Ans. ADHD is a very common behavioural disorder found among children of the primary school age. It is characterised by impulsivity, excessive motor activity and an inability to attend. The disorder is more common among boys than girls. If not managed properly, the attention difficulties may continue into adolescence or adult years.

Difficulty in maintaining attention is the main feature of this disorder, which gets reflected in several other domains of the child. For example, such children are highly distractible, they do not follow instructions, have difficulty in getting along with parents and are negatively viewed by their peers.

They do poorly in school, and show difficulties in reading or learning basic subjects in schools in spite of the fact that there is no deficit in their intelligence.

10. What do you understand by binocular disparity?

Ans. Some important cues to depth perception in three dimensional space are provided by both the eyes. Three of them have particularly been found to be interesting.

These are

(i) **Retinal or Binocular Disparity** Retinal disparity occurs because the two eyes have different locations in our head. They are separated from each other horizontally by a distance of about 6.5 centimeters.

(ii) **Convergence** When we see a nearby object, our eyes converge inward in order to bring the image on the fovea of each eye. A group of muscles send message to brain regarding the degree to which eyes are turning inward and these messages are interpreted as cues to the perception of depth. The degree of convergence decreases as the object moves further away from the observer.

(iii) **Accommodation** It refers to a process by which we focus the image on the retina with the help of ciliary muscle. These muscles change the thickness of the lens of the eye.

11. Discuss about the studies conducted by psychologists using Muller-lyer and horizontal-vertical illusions.

***Or* Explain in detail about the seminal studies conducted by Hudson in Africas and also by Sinha and Mishra.**

Ans. Psychologists have conducted studies using the Muller-Lyer illusion and Horizontal-vertical illusion to explore the influence of socio-cultural factors on perception.

(i) **Muller-Lyer Illusion** This illusion involves two lines of equal length, where one appears longer due to arrow-like ends. Studies show that Western subjects are more susceptible to this illusion, likely due to their environment, which is characterised by right angles and enclosed spaces, such as buildings and furniture.

(ii) **Horizontal-Vertical Illusion** This illusion involves perceiving a vertical line as longer than a horizontal one, even though both are of equal length. Studies have found that African subjects from remote villages show greater susceptibility to this illusion.

12. How do we distinguish figure as per Gestalt psychologists?

Ans. The Gestalt psychologists indicate that our cerebral processes are always oriented towards the perception of a good figure or pragnanz. The most primitive organisation takes place in the form of figure ground segregation.

Any figure can be differentiated from the ground on the basis of the following characteristics

- Figure has a definite form while the background is relatively formless.
- Figure is more organised as compared to its background.
- Figure has a clear outline while the background has none.
- Figure stands out from the background while the background stays behind the figure.
- Figure appears more clear, limited and relatively nearer while the background appears relatively unclear, unlimited and away from us.

Long Answer Type Questions

1. What is selective attention? Explain different theories proposed for selective attention.

Ans. Selective attention refers to the process of focusing on a limited number of stimuli from a large pool of stimuli, as our perceptual system has a limited capacity to process information. It allows us to concentrate on a few stimuli at a given moment.

Some of the theories of selective attention are

- **Filter Theory (Broadbent, 1956)** This theory suggests that multiple stimuli enter our receptors simultaneously, creating a 'bottleneck'. A selective filter allows only one stimulus to pass through for further processing, while others are ignored.
- **Filter-Attenuation Theory (Triesman, 1962)** In this modified version of Broadbent's theory, stimuli that don't pass through the selective filter are not

completely blocked but attenuated (weakened). Some stimuli may still reach higher processing levels if they are personally relevant, like hearing one's name.

- **Multimode Theory (Johnston and Heinz, 1978)** This theory proposes that attention is flexible and can select stimuli at three stages
- Sensory representation (visual images)
- Semantic representation (meanings of words)
- Consciousness (combination of sensory and semantic).

  More processing requires more mental effort and early-stage selection requires less effort than late-stage selection.

2. How can we form a stable perception of an object seen from any position and in any intensity of light? Justify.

Ans. Perception of the objects as relatively stable in spite of changes in the stimulation of the sensory receptors is called perceptual constancy. There are three types of perceptual constancies

(i) **Size Constancy** The size of an image on our retina changes with the change in the distance of the object from the eye. The further away it is, the smaller is the image. On the other hand, our experience shows that within limits, the object appears to be about the same size irrespective of its distance.

The tendency for the perceived size of objects to remain relatively unchanged with changes in their distance from the observer and the size of the retinal image is called size constancy.

(ii) **Shape Constancy** In our perceptions, the shapes of familiar objects remain unchanged despite changes in the pattern of retinal image resulting from differences in their orientation. It is also called form constancy.

(iii) **Brightness Constancy** Visual objects appear constant in their degree of whiteness, greyness or blackness even though the amount of physical energy reflected from them changes considerably. The tendency to maintain apparent brightness constant under different amount of illumination is called brightness constancy. For example, surface of paper which appears white in the sunlight is still perceived as white in the room light.

Case Based Questions

1. Read the case and answer the questions that follow.

Ravi is a sensory researcher studying how human beings perceive various stimuli through their sense organs. His research focuses on the sensitivity and limitations of the sense organs, such as vision, hearing and taste. Ravi conducts an experiment where he adds sugar granules to a glass of water and asks participants to identify when the water tastes sweet. Initially, they do not notice the sweetness until enough sugar is added. Ravi explains that the minimum number of sugar granules required to trigger the sensation of sweetness is called the Absolute Threshold (AL). He further adds that when comparing different sweetness levels, participants can detect a change in sweetness after a certain number of sugar granules are added. This difference in sweetness perception is called the Difference Threshold (DL). Ravi's findings show that individuals have varying AL and DL based on their organic conditions and motivational states.

(i) In the given case, what does Ravi's experiment focus on? What is the Absolute Threshold (AL) as described in the case?

(ii) How does Ravi differentiate between Absolute Threshold (AL) and Difference Threshold (DL)?

Ans. (i) Ravi's experiment focuses on understanding how people perceive sweetness in water through the addition of sugar granules. The Absolute Threshold (AL) is the minimum number of sugar granules required to trigger the sensation of sweetness, i.e., the point at which individuals can notice the sweetness of the water.

(ii) In the case of sweetness AL is the point where sweetness is first noticed and DL is the point where the sweetness level is perceived to be different from the previous level.

2. Read the case and answer the questions that follow.

In the study of perception, researchers have noted how cultural background and experiences can influence an individual's perception. For instance, in a study, Hudson examined how African subjects perceived pictures. Many of them had difficulty recognising objects like an antelope or a spear and also had trouble perceiving distance in pictures. This was largely due to the differences in cultural learning and experiences. Similarly, Eskimos have been found to make fine distinctions among different types of snow, something we might not be able to do. These studies show that a perceiver's cultural background plays an important role in how they process and interpret stimuli. Perception is not just a mechanical process but is shaped by individual experiences and environmental factors.

(i) According to the case, what is one factor that affects an individual's perception?

(ii) How does the perception of Eskimos differ from that of others, according to the case?

Ans. (i) According to the case, cultural background and experiences significantly affect an individual's perception. For example, African subjects had difficulty recognising certain objects due to differences in cultural experiences.

(ii) Eskimos are able to make fine distinctions among different types of snow, a skill that others, especially those not exposed to such an environment, might not be able to do. This is a result of their unique cultural background and experiences with snow.

3. Read the case and answer the questions that follow.

Besides the Muller-Lyer illusion, several other visual illusions are experienced by human beings, birds and animals. In the image below, we can see the illusion of vertical and horizontal lines. Although both the lines are equal, we perceive the vertical line as longer than the horizontal line.

Ravi is a student studying psychology and is keen on learning about illusions and how they work. He has recently read about the Muller-Lyer illusion and other similar visual illusions. One day, Ravi notices a picture showing two lines–one vertical and the other horizontal–which appear to be of different lengths, although they are actually the same. Ravi recalls that this is an example of a visual illusion. While discussing it with his classmates, he realises that these kinds of illusions are not unique to humans; they are also experienced by birds and animals in a similar way.

(i) What is the type of illusion Ravi experiences in the given case?

(ii) What can be inferred about the nature of illusions from Ravi's experience?

Ans. (i) Ravi experiences a geometrical illusion where two lines, one vertical and the other horizontal, appear to be different lengths although they are the same. This is an example of a perceptual illusion.

(ii) The illusion Ravi experiences is a universal illusion, meaning it is perceived similarly by humans, birds, and animals. This suggests that illusions like the one Ravi saw are consistent and experienced similarly across species.

SELF ASSESSMENT TEST

Objective Type Questions

1. One's ability to distinguish find details is called
(a) Sensation (b) Perception
(c) Visual acuity (d) Apperception

2. .... is a very common behavioural disorder found among children of the primary school age.
(a) ADHD (b) Perception
(c) IDHD (d) None of these

3. Which among the following is a monocular cue?
(a) Retinal disparity (b) Motion parallax
(c) Convergence (d) Accommodation

4. The minimum value of a stimulus required to activate a given sensation is called
(a) Stimulation (b) Difference Limen
(c) Sensation (d) Absolute Limen

Very Short Answer Type Questions

1. Define attention.

2. What do you mean by 'bottom-up processing'?

3. What do you mean by cognitive styles?

4. Name primary colours.

Short Answer Type Questions

1. Discuss in brief 'Attention Deficit Hyperactivity Disorder' (ADHD).

2. What are the functional limitations of sense organs?

3. Explain the role of binocular cues in the perception of depth.

Long Answer Type Questions

1. Discuss monocular cues of perception.

2. Discuss socio-cultural influences on perception.

Case Based Questions

Read the case and answer the questions that follow.

In print advertising, you have approximately two seconds to create a visual appeal. Your design should be simple, bold and with a streamlined message that is memorable. Viewers are exposed to several messages and advertisements simultaneously but, they only focus on one of them at a time. In general, the image and the headline draw attention, although colour contrast can also impact the viewer's attention. Images of people can attract attention and increase empathy. For company's brand building the name and logo might be appropriate targets.

(i) What are external factors related to selective attention? Which external factors are highlighted in the above case that influence the selective attention?

(ii) Viewers are exposed to several messages and advertisements simultaneously. But they only focus on one of them at a time. Relate this statement with the bottleneck theory of attention.

05

CHAPTER

Learning

Learning may be defined as "any relatively permanent change in behaviour or behavioural potential produced by experience".

YOUR STUDY GOALS

YOUR PRACTICE GOAL

- Objective Type Questions (19 Qs ; MCQs, A-R)
- Subjective Questions (23 VSAs, 12 SAs, 3 LAs, 3 Case Based)

5.1 Introduction

- As the child grows and matures, she/he becomes capable of making diverse types of responses. These responses include identifying the images of persons like mother, father or grandfather.
- The child learns to use a spoon while eating food and learns how to identify alphabets, write and combine them into words.
- The child also observes others doing things in specific environmental conditions and imitates them.
- Learning names of objects such as a book, orange, mango, cow, boy and girl, and retaining them is another important task.
- Each individual manages their life and solves various problems because of the capacity to learn and adapt.

5.2 Meaning and Nature of Learning

- Learning is a psychological process that gradually develops in a human being.
- Due to learning, a person becomes hardworking, socially knowledgeable, skilled and professionally competent.
- It refers to a range of changes that take place as a result of one's experience.
- Relatively permanent changes, which occur due to practice and experience, are examples of learning.

Features of Learning

1. Learning by Experience

- Learning always involves some kinds of experience. We experience an event occurring in a certain sequence during different occasions.
- If an event happens, it may be followed by other events. For example, students learn that if the bell rings in the hostel in the evening, it implies that dinner is ready to be served.
- If an action is repeatedly done in a specified manner and it gives satisfaction, this experience leads to the formation of a habit.
- For example, if a child strikes a matchstick on the side of a matchbox and burns their finger, they become more careful while handling the matchbox in the future.

2. Temporary Behavioural Changes

- In the process of learning, behavioural changes that occur due to learning are relatively permanent.
- It is important to distinguish these from behavioural changes that are neither permanent nor learned.
- Sometimes, behavioural changes happen due to continuous exposure to stimuli, called **habituation**, which is not due to learning. For example, the sound of a loudspeaker might distract us from whatever we are doing.
- Gradually, we make some orienting reflexes and become habituated to this sound.
- Behavioural changes can also occur due to fatigue, habituation or drugs. For example, if a girl is reading a textbook or trying to learn how to drive a motor car, she may eventually feel tired and stop reading or driving. This type of change is not considered learning.

3. Learning Involves Sequence of Psychological Events

Psychologists suggest that the learning process always involves the following sequences

(i) A pre-test is done to know how much the person knows before learning.
(ii) A list of words is presented to be remembered for a fixed time.
(iii) During this time, the list of words is processed towards acquiring new knowledge.
(iv) After processing is complete, new knowledge is acquired and learning is completed.
(v) After some time, the processed information is recalled by the person.

4. Learning as an Inferred Process but Different from Performance

- When a student recites a poem, the student is performing.
- By observing the student's performance, the teacher infers that the student has learned the poem, which they did not know previously.
- The teacher can compare the number of words the student now knows compared to what they knew earlier to infer that learning took place.
- Learning is an inferred process and differs from performance.
- Performance refers to a person's observed behaviour, response or action.

5.3 Paradigms of Learning

- In psychology, learning occurs in various ways using different methods.
- Some methods are used for acquiring simple responses, while others are used for acquiring complex responses.
- Conditioning is the simplest kind of learning. Conditioning is the process of training a person or animal to do something or behave in a certain way in a specific situation.
- There are two types of conditioning–classical conditioning and operant instrumental conditioning.
- Besides these, there are observational learning, cognitive learning, verbal learning, concept learning, and skill learning.

5.4 Classical Conditioning

- Classical conditioning is also known as **respondent conditioning**.
- It is a learning procedure where a biological agent like food is paired with a neutral agent like a bell. In this, a new behaviour is learned through the process of association.
- After classical conditioning, the response given to the neutral agent (bell) will be the same as the response given to the biological agent (food).

Experiment of Pavlov

- Ivan P. Pavlov was the first to experiment with this type of learning.
- Pavlov conducted an experiment with dogs to understand the process of classical conditioning.
- He observed that dogs secreted saliva whenever they saw the plate in which they were served food.
- Saliva secretion is a reflexive response to food or something in the mouth.
- Pavlov designed an experiment using dogs, where a tube was inserted in the dog's jaw to measure the amount of saliva secreted.
- In the first phase the dog was kept hungry and placed in a box and harness, with one end of the tube in its jaw and the other end in a glass jar.
- A bell was rung and immediately after the bell, food (meat powder) was served to the dog.

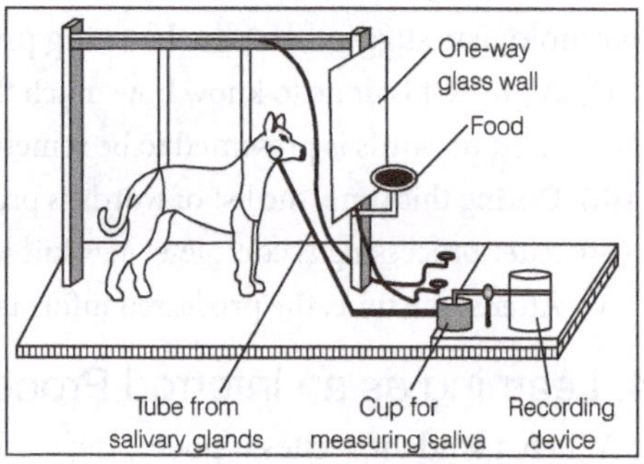

▲ *A Dog in Pavlovian Harness for Conditioning*

- This routine was repeated for several days, with food being given immediately after the bell.
- After several trials, a test trial was conducted where everything was repeated except food was not served after ringing the bell.
- The dog still secreted saliva upon hearing the bell, expecting food, because it associated the bell with food.
- This connection between the bell and food resulted in a new response–salivating at the sound of the bell.
- This is called Conditioning.

Components of Conditioning in Pavlov's Experiment

- Food is an Unconditioned Stimulus (US) because it naturally triggers a response (salivation).
- The secretion of saliva after food is called an Unconditioned Response (UR).
- After conditioning, the bell becomes a **Conditioned Stimulus**[1] (CS) and salivation becomes a **Conditioned Response**[2] (CR).
- Classical conditioning is a process of S-S learning, meaning one stimulus (like the sound of the bell) becomes a signal for another stimulus (like food).
- Many daily life examples of classical conditioning occur, such as
  - After eating lunch, seeing a sweet dish on the table can trigger salivation, which is a conditioned response.
  - In childhood, a loud noise from a bursting balloon might cause fear and the sight of the balloon will trigger the same fear in the future due to its association with the noise.

Determinants of Classical Conditioning

The main determinants of classical conditioning include

(i) Time relations between stimuli
(ii) Types of unconditioned stimuli
(iii) Intensity of conditioned stimuli

Time Relations Between Stimuli

There are four types of classical conditioning procedures

(i) **Simultaneous Conditioning** When the conditioned response and unconditioned response start at the same time.

(ii) **Delayed Conditioning** When the conditioned response starts before the unconditioned response and ends before the unconditioned response ends.

(iii) **Trace Conditioning** When the conditioned response starts and ends before the unconditioned response starts, with a time gap between the two.

(iv) **Backward Conditioning** When the unconditioned response comes before the conditioned response.

Type of Unconditioned Stimuli

There are two types of Unconditioned Stimuli (US) used in classical conditioning

(i) **Appetitive Stimuli**
  - These stimuli automatically elicit approach responses such as eating, drinking, caressing, etc.
  - These events make us feel good and we enjoy participating in them.
  - They lead to satisfaction and pleasure.
  - Appetitive classical conditioning is generally slower and requires a large number of acceptance trials.

(ii) **Aversive Stimuli**
  - These stimuli, such as noise, bitter taste, electric shock and painful injections, are harmful and elicit avoidance and escape responses.
  - Aversive classical conditioning can be established in one, two or three trials, depending on the intensity of the aversive stimulus.

---

1 **Conditioned Stimulus** It's something that used to be normal but now triggers a specific response because it was paired with something else.

2 **Conditioned Response** It's a simple reaction that happens automatically when seen or experience something common.

Intensity of Conditioned Stimuli

- The intensity of the conditioned stimulus influences the direction of both appetitive and aversive classical conditioning.
- More intense conditioned stimuli are more effective in accelerating the acceptance of conditioned responses.
- The more intense the conditioned stimulus, the fewer the number of acquisition trials needed for conditioning.

Stages of Conditioning	Nature of Stimulus	Nature of Response
Before Conditioning	Food (US), Sound of the Bell	Salivation (UR), Alertness (No specific response)
During Conditioning	Sound of the Bell (CS) + Food (US)	Salivation (UR)
After Conditioning	Sound of the Bell (CS)	Salivation (CR)

5.5 Operant/Instrumental Conditioning

- It is a learning process where the strength of behaviour is modified by rewards or punishments.
- BF Skinner was the first to conduct research on this type of conditioning.
- The term 'operant' refers to behaviours that the organism performs in the environment. Conditioning of these behaviours is called operant conditioning.

Experiment by Skinner

- Skinner conducted experiments on rats and pigeons using specially designed boxes called skinner Box.
- A hungry rat was placed inside the box and could only move around inside it.
- A lever connected to a food container was placed in the chamber.
- While exploring the box, the rat accidentally pressed the lever and food was dispensed.
- Over successive trials, the rat learned to press the lever to receive food, reducing the time taken to do so.
- The behaviour of pressing the lever became an operant response and getting food became its consequence. This process is called **instrumental conditioning.**
- Children learn to find a hidden jar of sweets when their mother is not around.

▲ *Skinner Box*

- Children learn to say 'please' to get favours from parents.
- People learn to operate mechanical gadgets like radios, cameras and TVs through instrumental conditioning.
- Humans often learn shortcuts to achieve desired goals through instrumental conditioning.

Determinants of Operant Conditioning

- Operant conditioning is influenced by the consequences of behaviour, called Reinforcers.
- Reinforcers are stimuli or events that increase the probability of a behaviour.

Features of reinforcers that affect conditioning

(i) **Positive or Negative** Reinforcers can either add something pleasant (positive) or remove something unpleasant (negative).

(ii) **Number or Frequency** The number of reinforcements matters.

(iii) **Quality** Reinforcers can be superior or inferior.

(iv) **Schedule** Reinforcement can be continuous or partial.

- The nature of the behaviour being conditioned and the time interval between the response and reinforcement also affect conditioning.

Differences Between Classical and Operant Conditioning

(i) **Control of Responses** In classical conditioning, responses are controlled by a stimulus, as they are reflexes automatically triggered by certain stimuli. These stimuli are called Unconditioned Stimuli (US), and the responses elicited by them are **Unconditioned Responses**[3] (UR). This is often called respondent conditioning (Pavlovian conditioning). In operant conditioning, responses are under the control of the organism and are voluntary (called 'operants'). The organism actively engages in the process to receive reinforcement.

(ii) **Role of CS and US** In classical conditioning, the Conditioned Stimulus (CS) and **Unconditioned Stimulus**[4] (US) are clearly defined. In operant conditioning, the Conditioned Stimulus (CS) is not clearly defined. It can be inferred but is not directly known.

(iii) **Control of Reinforcement** In classical conditioning, the experimenter controls when the Unconditioned Stimulus (US) occurs. In operant conditioning, the occurrence of reinforcement is under the control of the organism. The organism's actions determine when reinforcement happens. Thus, in classical conditioning, the organism is passive, while in operant conditioning, the organism is active.

(iv) **Technical Terms and Functions** The technical terms in both types of conditioning differ. In operant conditioning, the term reinforcer is used, while in classical conditioning, the term US (Unconditioned Stimulus) is used. The US has two roles in classical conditioning *i.e.,* it elicits a response and it reinforces the response that will later be triggered by the Conditioned Stimulus (CS).

Key Learning Processes

Different processes that are involved in learning through either classical or operant conditioning are

- Reinforcement
- **Extinction**[5] (non-occurrence of learned responses)
- Generalisation and Discrimination
- Spontaneous Recovery

Reinforcement

- It involves the use of reinforcers by the experimenter to increase the likelihood of a behaviour.
- Reinforcers increase the probability of the responses that precede them.
- There are two types of reinforcement

(i) **Positive Reinforcement** Involves stimuli that have pleasant consequences, such as food, praise or money. These reinforcers strengthen the behaviour.

(ii) **Negative Reinforcement** Involves stimuli that are unpleasant or painful. It strengthens the behaviour that helps an organism avoid or escape the unpleasant stimuli. For example, Learning to wear woollen clothes or use heaters to avoid cold weather, moving away from dangerous situations to avoid harm.

Punishment vs. Negative Reinforcement

- Negative reinforcement is different from punishment.
- Punishment suppresses a response, while negative reinforcement increases the probability of a behaviour by helping the organism to avoid or escape pain.
- Mild or delayed punishment may have no effect.

---

3 **Unconditioned Responses** It is an unlearned response that occurs naturally in reaction to the unconditioned stimulus.

4 **Unconditioned Stimulus** It refers to one that unconditionaly, naturally and automatically triggers a response.

5 **Extinction** This means that if you stop rewarding a behaviour, people will eventualy stop doing it.

- Stronger punishment has a more lasting effect but may not permanently suppress behaviour.
- Punished individuals may develop dislike for the punisher or the person administering the punishment.

Number of Reinforcement

- Number of reinforcement refers to how many times an organism is reinforced or rewarded.
- Amount of reinforcement refers to how much of the reinforcing stimulus (food, water, intensity of pain-causing agent) an organism receives in each trial.
- Quality of reinforcement refers to the type of reinforcer given.
- The process of operant conditioning usually becomes faster as the number, amount and quality of reinforcement increases.

Schedules of Reinforcement

- The schedule refers to how reinforcement is delivered during conditioning trials.
- Each schedule influences how conditioned responses develop in different ways.

The organism may be reinforced every time, or sometimes, reinforcement may be given in some trials and omitted in others. Reinforcement can be

- **Continuous Reinforcement** Reinforcement is given every time the desired response occurs.
- **Intermittent Reinforcement (also called Partial Reinforcement)** Sometimes the response is reinforced and sometimes it is not. This produces greater resistance to extinction than continuous reinforcement.

Delayed Reinforcement

- If there is a delay in giving reinforcement, the level of performance decreases.
- Children tend to prefer smaller, immediate rewards rather than a bigger reward after a long delay.

Other Types of Reinforcement

- **Primary Reinforcers** These are biologically important reinforcers, such as food for a hungry organism.
- **Secondary Reinforcers** These are reinforcers that gain value through experience, such as money, praise, and grades.

Extinction

- Extinction is the disappearance of a learned response when reinforcement is no longer provided.
- If a Conditioned Stimulus (CS) or behaviour like lever pressing is no longer followed by a reward (such as food pellets in a Skinner box), the learned behaviour weakens and eventually stops.
- Even without reinforcement, learned responses can continue for a while, showing resistance to extinction.

Resistance to extinction depends on factors such as

- Increasing number of reinforced trials, resistance to extinction also increases.
- It increases with the increasing number of reinforcements during acquisition trials.
- Delayed reinforcement during acquisition trials increases resistance.
- Continuous reinforcement makes the response less resistant to extinction, while partial reinforcement makes it more resistant.

Generalisation and Discrimination

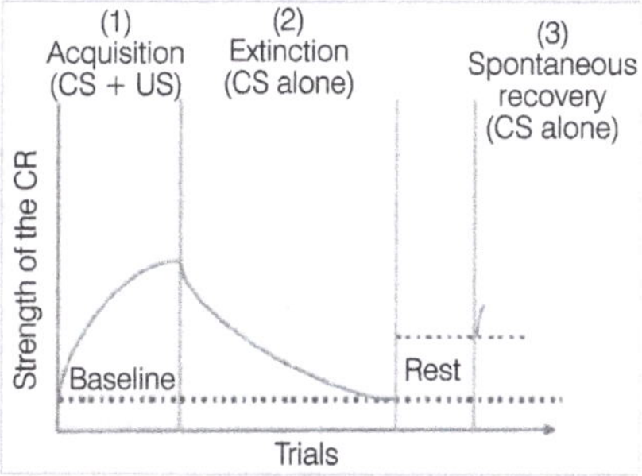

▲ *Phenomenon of Spontaneous Recovery*

- **Generalisation** The tendency to respond to similar stimuli in the same way. For example, a child who learns where the sweets are kept can find them in a jar of similar shape and size.
- **Discrimination** Learning to respond differently to different stimuli. For example, a child conditioned to fear a person with a long moustache and black clothes will show fear when meeting another person with similar features but not when meeting a person who is clean-shaven and wears grey clothes.

Spontaneous Recovery

- Spontaneous recovery happens when a learned response reappears after extinction has occurred.
- After a period of time, the learned response may recover and occur when the conditioned stimulus is presented again.
- The strength of spontaneous recovery depends on how long the extinction period lasted. The longer the time between extinction and the presentation of the stimulus, the stronger the recovery.

Learned Helplessness

Learned helplessness occurs when people or animals feel unable to avoid negative situations. It is considered one of the causes of depression. Seligman and Maier conducted experiments on dogs to demonstrate this phenomenon. The dogs were exposed to a sound (CS) and an electric shock (US) using classical conditioning. The dogs had no way to escape or avoid the shock. This process was repeated several times. The dog could escape the shock by pressing its head against the wall, but it did not attempt to do so. This behaviour of the dog, where it stopped trying to escape, was called learned helplessness. When humans experience continuous failures in tasks, they also show learned helplessness. Learned helplessness in humans is measured by their ability and persistence in completing tasks. Continuous failure leads to low persistence and poor performance. Studies show that persistent depression is often caused by learned helplessness.

Quick Test 1

1. Name two types of learning.
2. Name determinants of classical conditioning.
3. What did Pavlov's experiment show about learning?
4. What is classical conditioning is simple words?
5. What is reinforcement?
6. What does the term 'learning' mean in psychology?

5.6 Observational Learning

- Learning happens by observing others. It is also known as lmitation.
- In this kind of learning, human beings learn social behaviours, it is called social learning.
- In observational learning, individuals try to copy the behaviour of others in various situations, which is called modelling.

Experimental Study by Bandura

- Bandura conducted an experiment where children watched a five-minute film showing a large room with toys, including a Bobo doll.
- In the film, a grown-up boy enters the room and shows aggressive behaviour towards the toys, such as hitting and throwing the Bobo doll. Three versions of the film were shown to the children

(i) In the first version the boy (model) was rewarded for being aggressive.
(ii) In the second version the boy was punished for being aggressive.
(iii) In the third version the boy was neither rewarded nor punished.

- After viewing a specific version of the film, the children were then placed in a experimental room with similar toys. The children who saw the boy being rewarded for aggression behaved in the most aggressive manner. The children who saw the boy being punished for aggression behaved in the least aggressive manner.
- The performance of the observer is influenced by whether the model's behaviour was rewarded or punished.
- Children acquire many social behaviours like aggression, pro-social behaviour, courtesy and diligence by observing and imitating adults.

5.7 Cognitive Learning

- Cognitive learning refers to learning that involves a behavioural change based on the information the learner acquires about the environment.
- This type of learning results in a change in what the learner knows, not just what they do.
- Cognitive learning can be seen in insight learning and latent learning.

Insight Learning

- In insight learning, the solution to a problem suddenly becomes clear.
- Kohler conducted experiments with chimpanzees to demonstrate this. He placed chimpanzees in an enclosed play area where food was placed outside their reach.
- Tools such as poles and boxes were kept there the chimpanzees learned how to use boxes and poles to reach the food.
- They did not use trial-and-error method; instead, they had a sudden realisation of how to solve the problem (insight).
- Once the solution was found, it could be repeated when the problem occurred again.

Latent Learning

- Latent learning occurs when new behaviour is learned but is not shown until reinforcement is provided.
- Tolman conducted experiments with rats in a maze. One group of rats was rewarded with food at the end of the maze and learned to navigate it quickly.
- The second group of rats was not rewarded and showed no sign of learning.
- However, when the second group was later rewarded, they ran through the maze just as efficiently as the first group.
- The rats developed a cognitive map, which is a mental representation of the maze and the key locations needed to reach their goal.

5.8 Verbal Learning

- Verbal learning is a type of learning that is unique to humans, where knowledge is acquired using words.
- Psychologists have developed various methods to study verbal learning, using verbal materials such as nonsense syllables, familiar words, unfamiliar words, sentences and paragraphs.

Methods Used in Studying Verbal Learning

There are various methods used to study verbal learning, including paired-associates learning, serial learning, free recall and skill learning.

1. Paired-Associates Learning

- This method is used in learning a foreign language equivalent to mother tongue words.
- It is similar to S-S conditioning and S-R learning.
- In this method, a list of paired associates is prepared, where the first word of each pair is the stimulus and the second word is the response.
- The learner is shown both the stimulus-response pairs together and is instructed to remember and recall the response after each stimulus.
- A learning trial begins when the stimulus word is presented and the participant tries to recall the correct response.

2. Serial Learning

- This method studies how participants learn a list of words in a specific order.
- Verbal items are prepared for the experiment, which may include nonsense syllables, familiar or unfamiliar words, and interrelated words.
- The participant is given the list and asked to recall the items in the same order as presented. This process is called the Serial Anticipation Method. Learning trials continue until the participant can correctly recall all items in the given order.

3. Free Recall

- In this method, participants are presented with a list of words, each shown for a fixed amount of time.
- Afterward, the participants are asked to recall all the words in any order.
- The words in the list can be interrelated or unrelated, and more than ten words are included.
- The order of presentation varies across trials.
- This method helps study how participants arrange words for storage in memory.
- Studies show that the items placed in the begining or end of the list are easier to remember compared to those in the middle.

Determinants of Verbal Learning

- There are several factors influence the course of verbal learning, such as the length of the list and the meaningfulness of the material.
- The meaningfulness of material is measured in different ways, including
  (i) Number of associations made in a fixed time
  (ii) Familiarity of the material, frequency of usage
  (iii) Relationships among words in the list
  (iv) Sequential dependence of each word of the list on the preceeding words.

- On the basis of research findings the following generalisations have been made
- Learning time increases with the length of the list. More time is required to learn a larger amount of material and longer learning times result in stronger learning.
- If participants are allowed free recall, verbal learning becomes organisational. For example, participants will recall words in a new sequence or order compared to the original list.
- Bousfield conducted an experiment with a list of 60 words from different categories, such as names, animals, professions, and vegetables. When presented in random order, participants recalled words by categorising them, a process called Category Clustering.
- Verbal learning can be both intentional and incidental, meaning people may learn some features of words unintentionally or incidentally.

5.9 Skill Learning

- Skill learning involves performing tasks with accuracy, speed, and efficiency after significant practice.
- A skill is the ability to perform difficult tasks smoothly, such as driving, piloting an aeroplane or shorthand writing. These skills are learned through practice and exercise.

Phases of Skill Learning

- Skill learning progresses through various phases. With each attempt, the level of skill improves and becomes smoother and more automatic.
- The transition from one phase to the next may involve a performance plateau, where performance remains constant before improving.
- Fitts identified three phases of skill learning
  - (i) **Cognitive Phase** The learner must understand and memorise the instructions, while keeping every signal, instructional demand and response in consciousness.
  - (ii) **Associative Phase** In this phase, sensory inputs (such as hearing and seeing) are linked with appropriate responses. With practice, errors decrease, performance improves and the time taken to complete the task is reduced.
  - (iii) **Autonomous Phase** In this phase, attention to sensory inputs decreases and external interference reduces. Skilled performance becomes automatic, with minimal conscious effort.

Practice in Skill Learning

- Practice is essential for skill learning. As practice increases, performance improves and the process becomes more efficient.
- Automaticity in errorless performance becomes an important feature of skill learning.

Quick Test 2

1. How many versions of films did Bandura show to children in his experiment?
2. In which type of learning is a new behaviour learned but not shown until reinforcement is provided for displaying it?
3. The example of chimpanzees using boxes and poles to get food without trial and error demonstrates which type of learning?
4. What type of learning do activities such as driving, aeroplane piloting and ship navigating represent?
5. In which phase of skill acquisition does the learner have to understand and memorise the instructions?

5.10 Factors Facilitating Learning

The following are the key factors that help in facilitating learning

Schedule of Reinforcement Delivery

- In learning experiments, reinforcement can be delivered based on a particular schedule.
- Two main schedules of reinforcement are– continuous and partial reinforcement.

Continuous Reinforcement

- It is the reinforcement given after every correct response.
- This schedule leads to a high rate of response. However, when reinforcement is stopped, the response rate decreases quickly and can eventually stop.

Partial Reinforcement

- In partial reinforcement or intermittent reinforcement, reinforcement is not given after every response, meaning some responses go without reinforcement.
- This schedule generally results in very high response rates, especially when responses are reinforced based on a ratio.
- It is harder to determine when reinforcement is completely stopped or just delayed in this schedule.
- This makes it more difficult to notice when reinforcement has stopped, which affects extinction.
- Responses learned under partial reinforcement are harder to extinguish, and this is known as the Partial reinforcement effect.

Motivation

- Motivation is a mental and physiological state that drives an organism to act in order to fulfill a need or goal.
- The act will continue until the goal is achieved and the need is satisfied.
- Motivation is necessary for learning. It can come from two sources
  (i) **Intrinsic Motivation** When we learn something because we enjoy it.
  (ii) **Extrinsic Motivation** When we learn something because it helps to achieve another goal.

Preparedness for Learning

- Different species have different sensory capacities and response abilities, which affect their ability to learn.
- The processes required for establishing associations, like S-S (Stimulus-Stimulus) or S-R (Stimulus-Response), are also different for various species.
- The genetic makeup of a species influences what associations it can easily learn.
- Preparedness for learning refers to an organism's readiness to learn certain associations based on its genetics.

Understanding Preparedness

- Preparedness can be understood as a **continuum**, meaning it is a continuous range where tasks or associations are easier for some species and harder for others.
- On one end, we have tasks that are easy for a species to learn and on the other end, tasks that they cannot learn at all.
- Tasks that can be learned with effort and practice fall in the middle of this continuum.

5.11 Learning Disabilities

- Learning disabilities refer to a group of disorders that make it difficult for an individual to acquire skills like learning, reading, writing, speaking, reasoning and doing mathematical activities.
- These disabilities are inherent in the child and originate from issues with the functioning of the Central Nervous System (CNS).
- These disorders can occur with or without other physical or sensory impairments and intellectual disabilities.

Symptoms of Learning Disabilities

Some common symptoms of learning disabilities are

- Difficulty writing letters, words, phrases, reading, speaking and listening, even when there are no auditory problems.
- Difficulty in focusing, getting distracted easily and being hyperactive with poor attention spans.
- Poor space orientation and inadequate sense of time, such as getting lost, being confused about directions, and misjudging time.
- Poor motor coordination and manual dexterity, like difficulty walking, running, or doing tasks with hands.
- Struggling to understand and follow oral instructions.
- Misjudging social cues, like who is friendly or not, and difficult in understanding body language.
- Perceptual disorders, including visual, auditory, or kinesthetic misperception (e.g., confusing a call-bell with a telephone ring).
- In dyslexia, children fail to copy letters and words correctly and mix up letters like p and q or words like was and saw.

Treatment for Learning Disabilities

- Learning disabilities are not incurable.
- Remedial teaching methods can help children with learning disabilities by overcoming these difficulties and improve their learning.
- Educational psychologists have developed several techniques to address the symptoms of learning disabilities.

Quick Test 3

1. What are the factors that facilitate learning?
2. What is the partial reinforcement effect?
3. What are the names of the two types of motivation that facilitate learning?
4. How does preparedness for learning vary across species?
5. What are some common symptoms of learning disabilities?

NCERT Folder

1. What is learning? What are its distinguishing features?

Ans. Learning may be defined as "any relatively permanent change in behaviour or behavioural potential produced by experience". It refers to a range of changes that take place as a result of one's experience. There are different features for the process of learning. These are discussed as follows

(i) **Learning by Experience** We experience an event occurring in a certain sequence during different occasions. If an event happens then it might be followed by some other events. If some action is repeatedly done and if it gives satisfaction, this experience will lead to the formation of habit.

Sometimes a single experience can lead to learning. For example, when a child strikes a matchstick on the side of a matchbox and gets her/his fingers burnt, she/he will learn that matchbox should be carefully handled.

(ii) **Temporary Behavioural Changes** In the process of learning, behavioural changes that occur due to learning are relatively permanent. Changes in behaviour might occur due to the effects of tiredness, repeated monotonous work and drugs.

(iii) **Learning Involves Sequence of Psychological Events** Psychologists suggest that learning process always needs a series of psychological events on consecutive sequences, *viz.* a pre-test to know the extent of learning, list of words to be remembered, after processing information is to be recalled etc.

(iv) **Learning is an Inferred Process and is Different from Performance** When a student recites a poem, he gives his performance. By seeing his performance the teacher infers that now learning took place which was not done by the student previously.

2. How does classical conditioning demonstrate learning by association?

Ans. Classical conditioning is also known as respondent conditioning. It is a learning procedure in which a biological agent like food is paired with a neutral agent like bell. After classical conditioning the response given to the neutral agent like bell will be same as the response given to the biological agent like food. Learning by association can be understood through the following experiment of Pavlov

Experiment of Pavlov

- Pavlov designed an experiment using dog to understand this process. He observed that dogs secreted saliva whenever they saw the plate in which they were served food.
- In the first part of the experiment, a dog was kept in the box to conduct experiment.
- A simple surgery was conducted, and one end of a tube was inserted in the dog's jaw and the other end of tube was put in a measuring glass. This was used to measure the amount of saliva dog secreted.
- In the second part of the experiment, the dog was kept hungry and placed in harness.
- A bell was rang and immediately after the sound, food (meat powder) was served to dog. The dog was allowed to eat it.
- This routine was continued for next few days i.e immediately after ringing the bell, food was given to the dog.
- After a number of such trials, a test trail was conducted in which, everything was repeated except that food was not served to dog after ringing the bell.
- The dog still secreted saliva after listening to the sound of the bell, expecting its food to be served, because dog thought bell and food were connected.
- This connection between bell and food resulted in obtaining a new response by the dog, i.e secreting saliva to the sound of bell. This has been called conditioning.

3. Define operant conditioning. Discuss the factors that influence the course of operant conditioning.

Ans. Operant conditioning is a learning process through which strength of the behaviour is modified by reward or punishment. The factors that influence the course of operant conditioning are

(i) **Types of Reinforcement** Reinforcement may be positive or negative. Positive reinforcement has agents that have pleasant consequences and thus strengthen and maintain the responses. Food, water, medals, praise, money, status, information, etc. are positive reinforcers which satisfy needs. Negative reinforcers has unpleasant and painful agents. Thus, negative reinforcement leads to learning of avoidance and escape responses.

(ii) **Number of Reinforcement and Other Features** It refers to the number of trials after which an organism is reinforced or rewarded. Amount of reinforcement means how much food or water or intensity of pain causing agent is used as reinforcing stimulus or agent for each trial. Reinforcers like chickpeas or pieces of bread compared to raisins or pieces of cake are inferior in quality. This refers to quality of reinforcement. The course of operant conditioning is accelerated such that number, amount and quality of reinforcement increases.

(iii) **Schedules of Reinforcement** It refers to the arrangement of the delivery of reinforcement during conditioning trials. Reinforcement given in every trial or in some trials i.e. it may be continuous or intermittent (partial). In continuous reinforcement, desire response is reinforced every time and in partial reinforcement, responses may or may not get reinforced. Partial reinforcement produces greater resistance to extinction. Here extinction means end of occurrence of a behaviour.

(iv) **Delayed Reinforcement** Delay in the delivery of reinforcement leads to decrease in the level of performance.

4. A good role model is very important for a growing up child. Discuss the kind of learning that supports it.

Ans. A good role model is very important for a growing up child and that good role model can be anyone, be it father, mother or some great people from the society like Abdul Kalam, Mother Teresa, etc. It is important because a child will try to observe and imitate their behaviour. This kind of learning is helped by observational learning.

In this type, learning happens by observing others. It was earlier called imitation. Bandura and his colleagues studied observational learning in detail. It is also called Social learning because humans learn social behaviour through this. Individuals try to emulate the behaviour of others in many situations and this is called Modelling.

5. Explain the procedures for studying verbal learning.

Ans. The procedures for studying verbal learning include several methods to examine how individuals acquire and recall verbal material

(i) **Paired-Associates Learning** A list of paired words (stimulus-response) is presented. The learner first memorises the pairs and is then tested by showing the stimulus word and asking for the corresponding response.

(ii) **Serial Learning** Participants learn a list of words in a specific order and must recall them in the same sequence. The serial anticipation method is used, where participants are tested repeatedly until they recall the items in the correct order.

(iii) **Free Recall** A list of words is presented to participants, who must recall all the words in any order. The method helps study how words are stored in memory and organised during recall. Typically, words at the start and end are easier to remember than those in the middle.

6. What is a skill? What are the stages through which skill learning develops?

Ans. A skill is the ability to perform a task accurately, quickly, and efficiently after extensive practice. Examples of skills include driving, piloting an aeroplane and shorthand writing.

The stages through which skill learning develops are

(i) **Cognitive Phase** The learner understands and memorises instructions and learns how to perform the task. This phase requires conscious attention to every step and response.

(ii) **Associative Phase** Sensory inputs (e.g., hearing, seeing) are linked with appropriate responses. With more practice, errors decrease, performance improves and the time taken to complete the task reduces. The learner remains attentive and focused on the task.

(iii) **Autonomous Phase** The task becomes automatic, with minimal attention required. External interference decreases and the performance reaches error-free automaticity, demanding less conscious effort.

7. How can you distinguish between generalisation and discrimination?

Ans. **Generalisation** The phenomenon of responding similarly to similar stimuli is known as Generalisation. For example, a child finding the hidden jar in the kitchen to get sweets is a learned operant. Now mother keeps the sweets in an another jar of a different size and shape and at a different location in the kitchen. If child locates this new jar in the absence of the mother, this refers to the generalisation, i.e. when a learned response occurs by a new stimulus (agent), it is called Generalisation.

Discrimination Discrimination is a response due to difference. If a child is conditioned to fear a person wearing black clothes and long beard, then whenever child sees a person with same features she/he will fear that person. This fear of child is generalised. But now, if a child sees a stranger who wears white clothes and clean shaven, then she/he doesn't show fear response. This is called Discrimination. Discriminative response depends on the discrimination capacity or discrimination learning of the organism.

8. Why is motivation a prerequisite for learning?

Ans. Motivation is considered a prerequisite and acts as a main facilitator of learning in following ways

(i) Motivation is a mental and physiological (bodily part functions) state, which excites an organism to act for fulfilling the present need.

(ii) Motivation energises an organism to act with high energy for attaining some goal. These acts will continue until the goal is achieved and the need is satisfied. That is why motivation is required as a prior condition for learning.

For example, students who secure good marks or grades in examination are more motivated and thus work hard for learning.

(iii) Motivation for learning comes from two sources. One is we learn something because we enjoy it, this is called **intrinsic** motivation, e.g. learning cricket. The other source of learning helps to achieve goal is called Extrinsic Motivation.

9. What does the notion of preparedness for learning mean?

Ans. Preparedness is a reference to the fact that organism are better able to associate certain combination of stimuli, responses and reinforces than others. It can be explained in the following ways

- The member of different species are very different from one another in their sensor capacities and response abilities.
- Species have biological constrains on their learning capacities. The kinds of S-S or S-R learning an organism can easily acquire depends on the associative mechanism it is genetically endowed with or prepared for.
- A particular kind of associative learning is easy for apes and human beings, but may be extremely difficult for another species like cats or rats.
- It implies that one can learn only those associations for which one is genetically prepared.

10. Explain the different forms of cognitive learning?

Ans. The different forms of cognitive learning are

(i) **Insight Learning** This is when a solution to a problem suddenly becomes clear. It is not learned through trial and error but through a cognitive understanding of the relationship between means and end. Once the solution is found, it can be repeated when the problem arises again. Kohler's experiment with chimpanzees demonstrated this type of learning.

(ii) **Latent Learning** In this form of learning, new behaviour is acquired but not displayed until reinforcement is provided. Tolman's experiment with rats in a maze showed that rats learned a cognitive map of the maze, but their learning was only demonstrated when they were rewarded with food.

11. How can we identify students with learning disabilities?

Ans. Following are some of the problems faced by students with learning disabilities

- Difficulties in writing letters, words and phrases, reading out text and speaking. Many times they have listening problems though they may not have any auditory problems. These children are very different from others in developing learning strategies and plans.
- Disorders of attention, i.e. they get easily distracted and cannot pay attention on one point for long. This lack of attention leads to hyperactivity i.e. they are always moving, doing different things and trying to control things without interruption.
- Poor body postures, inadequate knowledge about one's own space and inadequate sense of time are common symptoms. Such children do not get easily adapt to new surroundings and get lost.
- Poor motor coordination i.e. poor ability to walk, run, hold objects, etc and poor manual dexterity i.e. poor skill in doing tasks with hands. This we can see in children with their lack of balance, inability to sharpen pencil, handle doorknobs, unable to learn ride bicycle, etc.
- Fail to understand and follow oral directions for doing things.
- Misjudge relationships as to which classmates are friendly and who are not. They fail to learn and understand body language.
- Perceptual disorders i.e. unable to interpret things. It may be visual, auditory, sense of touch, and kinaesthetic (movement of body parts) misperception. They can not differentiate between call bell and telephone ring. They do not have any problem in their sensory organs but they just can not use it in performance.
- Dyslexia i.e. children usually fail to copy letters and words. They fail to differentiate between p and q, P and 9, was and saw, unclear, and nuclear etc. i.e. fail to organise verbal materials.

Exam Pattern Questions

Objective Type Questions

Multiple Choice Questions (MCQs)

1. Every human baby at the time of birth has ability to make

(a) innumerable responses
(b) limited number of responses
(c) no responses
(d) None of the above

2. Learning is a

(a) physical process (b) chemical process
(c) mechanical process (d) psychological process

3. Making some orienting reflexes i.e. getting accustomed to the event is involved in following phenomenon

(a) Habituation (b) Reinforcement
(c) Extinction (d) Transfer effect

4. The phenomenon of responding similarly to similar stimuli is known as

(a) Discrimination (b) Generic process
(c) Generalisation (d) Spontaneous recovery

5. Reasons for dropouts in schools is/are

(a) Sensory impairment (b) Learning disability
(c) Emotional disturbance (d) All of these

6. Which one of the following is true?

(a) Repeated experience of satisfaction after doing something in a specified manner leads to the formation of habit.
(b) Learning always involves some kinds of experience.
(c) Behavioural changes that occur due to learning are relatively permanent.
(d) All of the above

7. Classical conditioning type of learning was first investigated by ……… .

(a) BF Skinner (b) Sham Arnold
(c) Ivan P Pavlov (d) B Bandura

8. Which of the following is/are true about reinforcement?

I. Negative reinforcement occurs when behaviour is accompanied by the removal of an unfavourable consequence.
II. Positive reinforcement occurs when behaviour is followed by a favourable consequence that encourages the repetition of that behaviour.
III. Punishment occurs when the administration of an unfavourable consequence discourages certain behaviour.
IV. Extinction occurs when the target behaviour decreases because the reinforcement follows it.

Codes

(a) I and II (b) II and III (c) III and IV (d) All of these

9. In free recall method participants are given list of words of four semantic categories like names, animals, professions and vegetables. These are given to participants one by one in random order. The participants recall the words of each category together, which is known as ……… .

(a) Category clustering (b) Modelling
(c) Dyslexia (d) Biofeedback

10. Which of the following is true about Pavlov's experiment on classical conditioning?

I. Food was considered an Unconditioned Stimulus (US).
II. Salivation to the bell after conditioning was called a Conditioned Response (CR).
III. The dog's initial salivation upon seeing food was termed a Conditioned Response (CR).
IV. Delayed conditioning is the least effective form of classical conditioning.

Codes

(a) I and II (b) II and III (c) III and IV (d) I and IV

11. Identify the accurate statements about unconditioned stimuli in classical conditioning.

I. Appetitive stimuli include things like food and water.
II. Aversive stimuli require many trials for conditioning.
III. Appetitive stimuli lead to slower classical conditioning than aversive stimuli.
IV. Aversive stimuli involve responses like escape or avoidance.

Codes

(a) I and II (b) I and III (c) II and IV (d) I and IV

12. Which type of reinforcement best explains wearing seat belts to avoid fines or injury?

I. Positive reinforcement
II. Negative reinforcement
III. Appetitive reinforcement
IV. Aversive reinforcement

Codes

(a) I and II (b) II and III (c) II and IV (d) I and IV

13. **Which learning method involves linking foreign and native language words?**

I. Free recall

II. Serial learning

III. Paired-associates learning

IV. Trace conditioning

Codes

(a) I and II (b) II and III

(c) III and IV (d) I and III

Assertion-Reason Questions

Directions (Q. Nos. 14-19) In the following questions, a statement of Assertion (A) is followed by a statement of Reason (R). Mark the correct choice from the options given below.

(a) Both A and R are true and R is the correct explanation of A.

(b) Both A and R are true, but R is not the correct explanation of A.

(c) A is true, but R is false.

(d) A is false, but R is true.

14. **Assertion** (A) Learning is a psychological process which gradually develops in human being.

Reason (R) Learning can be defined as any relatively permanent change in behaviour or behavioural potential produced by experience.

15. **Assertion** (A) Instrumental conditioning is also known as respondent conditioning.

Reason (R) Conditioning is the process of training a person or animal to do something or to behave in a certain way in a particular situation.

16. **Assertion** (A) Operant conditioning relies on the use of rewards or punishments to modify behaviour.

Reason (R) In operant conditioning, the organism remains passive while learning, with reinforcers controlled by the experimenter.

17. **Assertion** (A) Appetitive classical conditioning is established slower than aversive classical conditioning due to the need for more acceptance trials.

Reason (R) Aversive stimuli, such as pain or loud noise, result in a more immediate response due to their intense nature.

18. **Assertion** (A) Intrinsic motivation is the type of motivation that arises when an individual learns something because they enjoy the activity itself.

Reason (R) Extrinsic motivation is when individuals learn something to achieve a specific goal or reward.

19. **Assertion** (A) Learning disabilities can affect children with average to superior intelligence and adequate sensory-motor systems.

Reason (R) Learning disabilities are a result of problems in the Central Nervous System (CNS) and often occur alongside physical handicaps.

Answers

1. (b) limited number of responses
2. (d) psychological process
3. (a) Habituation
4. (c) Generalisation
5. (d) All of these
6. (d) All of the above
7. (c) Ivan P Pavlov
8. (d) All of these
9. (a) Category clustering
10. (a) I and II
11. (d) I and IV
12. (c) II and IV
13. (c) III and IV
14. (b) Both A and R are true, but R is not the correct explanation of A.
15. (d) A is false, but R is true.
16. (c) A is true, but R is false.
17. (a) Both A and R are true and R is the correct explanation of A.
18. (a) Both A and R are true and R is the correct explanation of A.
19. (b) Both A and R are true, but R is not the correct explanation of A.

Subjective Questions

Very Short Answer Type Questions

1. Give an example of learning by experience.

Ans. When a child strikes a matchstick on the side of a matchbox and gets her/his fingers burnt, she/he will learn that matchbox should be carefully handled. This is learning by experience.

2. Give an example of temporary behavioural change.

Ans. If you are reading your textbook of psychology for sometime or trying to learn how to drive a motor car, after some time you will feel tired. Then you will stop reading or driving. This is a behavioural change due to tiredness which is temporary.

3. What is habituation?

Ans. Habituation is a case of change in one's behaviour. The change is because of the continuous exposure to agents that arouse some activity or action. This phenomenon is called habituation.

4. Define the term operants.

Ans. Operants are those behaviours or responses which are shown by animals and humans voluntarily and are under their control.

5. What is conditioning?

Ans. Conditioning is the process of training a person or animal to do something or to behave in a certain way in a particular situation.

6. What is conditioned stimulus and conditioned response?

Ans. Conditioned stimulus is a previously neutral stimulus, that triggers same response in an organism after being associated through classical conditioning. Conditioned response is an automatic response established by training to an ordinary neutral stimulus.

7. Define unconditioned stimulus and unconditioned response.

Ans. Unconditioned stimulus refers to one that unconditionally, naturally and automatically triggers a response.

Unconditioned response is an unlearned response that occurs naturally in reaction to the unconditioned stimulus.

8. What is positive reinforcement?

Ans. Positive reinforcement has agents that have pleasant consequences and thus strengthen and maintain the responses. Food, water, medals, praise, money, status, information, etc. are positive reinforcers which satisfy needs.

9. What is negative reinforcement?

Ans. Negative reinforcers has unpleasant and painful agents. Thus, negative reinforcement leads to learning of avoidance and escape responses.

10. What is extinction?

Ans. Extinction means disappearance of a learned response due to removal of reinforcement from the situation in which the response used to occur.

11. What is cognitive learning?

Ans. Cognitive learning defines learning as a behavioural change based on the information obtained about the environment. In cognitive learning, there is a change in what the learner knows rather than what she/he does.

12. Define the term free recall.

Ans. Free recall is one of the methods used in studying verbal learning. In this method, participants are presented with a list of words which they speak and read out. Each word is shown for a fixed amount of time.

Immediately after the presentation of the list, the participants are required to recall the words in any order they can. This method is used to study how participants organise words for storage in memory.

13. What is a feature?

Ans. A feature is any characteristic or quality of an object or event or living organism that is observed in them and can be considered similar to some features observed or discriminated in other objects.

14. What is skill and skill learning?

Ans. A skill is defined as the ability to perform some difficult task smoothly and efficiently.

The learning of a task to give accuracy, speed and performance after a high amount of practice is called skill learning.

15. What is perceptual modality?

Ans. They are biologically-based reactions to the physical environment. It refers to the preferences of persons through which they take in information like auditory, visual, smell, kinaesthetic (awareness of the position and movement of the parts of the body by using sense organs) and tactile (sense of touch).

16. Give the meanings of learning disabilities.

Ans. Learning disability is a diverse group of disorders which are visible in terms of difficulty in the acquisition of learning, reading, writing, speaking, reasoning and mathematical activities.

17. What is systematic desensitisation?

Ans. Systematic desensitisation is a technique to help people suffering from excessive anxieties (feeling of worry or nervousness) and fears.

18. What is motivation?

Ans. Motivation is a mental and physiological state, which excites or provokes an organism to act to fulfill the present need or future goal.

19. Distinguish between primary and secondary reinforcer.

Ans. **Primary reinforcer** is biologically important because it is needed for the survival of organism (e.g. food).

Secondary reinforcer has got characteristics of a reinforcer because of the organism's experience with environment. Reinforcers like money, praise and grades are called as Secondary reinforcers.

20. Distinguish between continuous reinforcement and partial reinforcement?

Ans. In continuous reinforcement, participant is given reinforcement after every target response. This produces a high rate of responding. On the other hand, in schedules, where reinforcement is not continuous, some responses are not reinforced, they are called Partial or Intermittent reinforcement.

21. Mention the importance of aversion operant.

Ans. Aversion therapy is used to eliminate habits that are undesirable and injurious to health and happiness.

In this treatment, an arrangement of things made in such a way that the occurrence of maladjustive habits creates painful experiences and to avoid them clients learn to give them up.

22. How are classical and operant conditioning used in child rearing?

Ans. Classical conditioning procedure is used to make children learn necessary signs of danger and safety. Operant conditioning is used to change the behaviour of the children.

23. Harsh is a student of Class VI. He fails to copy words properly from the blackboard and can not distinguish between b and d, p and q, p and I and so on. What disability he has? Competency Based Que.

Ans. Harsh is a child who has dyslexia. This learning disability order prevents him to learn his subjects properly. But he can be cured by remedial teaching method and become like other students.

Short Answer Type Questions

1. Discuss about types of unconditioned stimuli in studying classical conditioning.

Ans. There are two types of unconditioned stimuli used in studying classical conditioning. They are

(i) **Appetitive** This stimuli automatically draws out approach responses like eating, drinking, caressing, etc. It means these kind of events will make us feel good and we would love to participate in such events.

These kind of responses give satisfaction and pleasure. Appetitive classical conditioning is slower and it requires large number of acceptance trials.

(ii) **Aversive** This stimuli like noise, bitter taste, electric shock, painful injections, etc are painful, harmful and draws out avoidance and escape responses. Aversive classical conditioning is established in one, two or three trials depending on the intensity of the aversive Unconditioned Stimulus (US).

2. List different scenarios that affect the resistance to extinction.

Ans. Different scenarios affecting resistance to extinction are

- Resistance to extinction increases and learned response reaches its highest level and performance gets stabilised, when number of reinforced trials are increased. Hereafter, response strength is not affected by number of trials.
- Resistance to extinction increases when number of reinforcements are increased during acquisition trials. After a point, if we increase number of reinforcements, the resistance to extinction decreases.
- Resistance to extinction increases if reinforcement is delayed during acquisition trials. Continuous reinforcement makes the learned response to be less resistant to extinction and more in case of partial reinforcement.

3. Discuss about learned helplessness.

Ans. Learned helplessness occurs when people or animals feel helpless to avoid negative situations. It is one of the causes for depression. Seligman and Maier conducted experiments on dogs to demonstrate this phenomenon.

In first part, dogs were subjected to sound (conditioned stimulus) and electric shock (unconditioned stimulus) using classical conditioning procedure. There was no scope for dogs to escape shock.

After repeated trials, they were subjected to shock in an operant conditioning procedure, in which dogs could escape shock by pressing their head against wall. But dog just suffered the shock and did not attempt to escape. This behaviour of dog was called learned helplessness.

4. List the differences between classical and operant conditioning.

Ans. Differences between classical and operant conditioning are as follows

Classical	Operant
Responses are under control of some stimulus because they are automatically given by the appropriate stimuli.	Responses are under control of the organism and are voluntary responses or operants.
Conditioned Stimulus (CS) and Unconditioned Stimulus (US) are well defined.	CS is not defined. It can be just inferred, not directly known.
Experimenter controls the occurrence of US. Organism remains passive.	The occurrence of the reinforcer is under the control of the organism i.e. learning. Subject is active in order to be reinforced.

5. Rahul wants to be a good dancer. To acquire the skill, he has to pass through several phases of learning process. What are the different process according to Fitts?

Competency Based Que.

Ans. According to Fitts, skill learning process passes through three phases, *viz.* cognitive, associative and autonomous. Rahul should pass through all these three stages.

In cognitive phase he has to understand and memorise the instructions of his teacher, and also understand how the task to be performed. In the associative phase different sensory inputs or stimuli are linked with appropriate responses.

As he increases his practice, his performance will improve and errors decreases. Finally, Rahul attains skill and performs automatically with minimal demand on conscious effort.

6. Discuss about how psychologists conduct learning experiments to know how a list of words is learned.

Ans. Learning involves a series of psychological events. This can be understood using a learning experiment. Suppose psychologists wanted to know about how a list of words is learned. They will conduct a series of experiments in the following consequences

- Do a pre-test to know how much the person knows before learning.
- Present the list of words to be remembered for a fixed time.
- The list of words is processed towards acquiring new knowledge.
- After processing is complete, new knowledge is acquired and information is recalled by the persons.

Now psychologists will compare the number of words which a person has newly learnt compared to what she/he knows before the test. By doing this, they will infer that learning did take place.

7. Discuss about the classical conditioning procedures based on time relations between stimuli.

Ans. There are basically four types of classical conditioning procedures. They are based on the time relations between the beginning of Conditioned Stimulus (CS) and Unconditioned Stimulus (US).

The first three are called Forward conditioning procedures, and the fourth one is called Backward conditioning procedure. Following are the basic experimental arrangements of these procedures

- When the CS and US are started together, it is called simultaneous conditioning.
- When CS is started first before the start of US and CS ends first before the end of US, it is called Delayed conditioning.
- When CS starts and ends before the start of US, and if there is a time gap between the two, it is called trace conditioning.
- When US comes before the start of CS, it is called Backward conditioning.

8. Explain Skinner experiment with respect to operant conditioning.

Ans. Skinner conducted his studies on rats and pigeons in specially made boxes called Skinner Box. One hungry rat is placed inside the box such that it could not come out but just move inside the box as shown in the figure.

A lever which was connected to a food container was kept at the top of the chamber. While moving around which is called exploratory behaviour, the rat accidentally presses the lever and a food pellet drops on the plate and the hungry rat eats it. In next trial, after a while the exploratory behaviour again starts and this continues.

As number of trials increases, the time taken to press the lever by the rat for the food decreases. Conditioning is complete when rat presses the lever immediately after it is kept in the chamber. In this scenario, lever pressing is an operant response and getting food is its consequence. As the response is instrumental in getting the food, this type of learning is called Instrumental conditioning.

9. Explain the experiment conducted by the Bandura to understand observational learning.

Ans. Bandura conducted an experiment to study observational learning using a five-minute film. The film showed a large room with toys, including a Bobo doll. A grown-up boy entered the room and displayed aggressive behaviour towards the toys, including hitting and kicking the Bobo doll. There were three versions of the film shown to children

(i) The boy was rewarded for being aggressive.
(ii) The boy was punished for being aggressive.
(iii) The boy was neither rewarded nor punished.

After watching the film, the children were placed in a similar room with toys. The results showed that children who saw the boy being rewarded behaved more aggressively, while those who saw the boy being punished exhibited the least aggressive behaviour. This experiment demonstrated that observational learning occurs by watching others and the behaviour is influenced by whether the model's actions are rewarded or punished.

10. Discuss about Bousfield experiment.

Ans. Bousfield did an experiment using list of 60 words which had 15 words each drawn from different categories like names, animals, professions and vegetables. When these words were presented to participants in random order, participants recalled words by organising them in categorywise.

He called this category clustering. Free recall is always organised subjectively i.e. participants organise words or items in their individual ways and recall accordingly.

Verbal learning is usually intentional but a person may learn some features of the words incidentally. Participants notice features like two or more words rhyming, starting with identical letters, having same vowels, etc. Thus, verbal learning is both intentional and incidental (happens as a result of an activity).

11. Pooja is studying seriously, she is a student of science stream. Explain what is her motivation for study. Competency Based Que.

Ans. Pooja is studying seriously, as she wants to pass with good marks or grades in her final examination. She is a motivated student and does hard work for learning. Her motivation for learning arises from two sources. She learns her subjects because she enjoys them. It is her intrinsic motivation. Again she learns subjects for attaining some other goal. It is her extrinsic motivation. May be she wants to become an engineer or doctor. This motivation makes her to study seriously.

12. "Many of the children join schools but dropout because some of them find the demands of educational process very difficult." Justify the statement. Competency Based Que.

Ans.
- We have heard, observed or read that thousands of children get enrolled for education in schools. Some of them however, find the demands of educational process too difficult to meet and they dropout such students are called 'Dropouts'.
- There are many reasons for this drop-out like sensory impairment, intellectual disability, social and emotional disturbance, poor economic conditions of the family, cultural beliefs and norms or other environmental influences.
- Other than these reasons there is another important source of problem in the path of education, that is called learning disabilities.
- It makes school learning i.e. obtaining knowledge and skill very difficult.
- Such children also fail to move forward in their learning activities.
- Sometimes students with learning disabilities also cannot continue their study in schools. Often they get easily distracted and cannot pay attention. They fail to understand and follow oral directions for doing things.
- Students with dyslexia quite often fail to copy letters and words. For all these reasons students dropout from the school.

Long Answer Type Questions

1. "Learning is a psychological process." What is learning? Elaborate about different features of the process of learning.

Ans. Learning is a psychological process that leads to relatively permanent changes in behaviour or behavioural potential through experience. It involves the acquisition of knowledge, skills and competencies, resulting from practice or exposure to various stimuli and experiences.

Features of the process of learning

- **Learning by Experience** Learning involves experience, where repeated exposure to events leads to the formation of habits or new knowledge. For example, a student learns that the bell ringing signifies dinner time.
- **Temporary Behavioural Changes** Not all behavioural changes are permanent. Temporary changes, like those caused by fatigue or habituation (e.g., getting used to the sound of a loudspeaker), are not considered learning.
- **Learning Involves Sequence of Psychological Events** Learning follows a structured process: pre-test, presentation of information, processing, acquisition of knowledge and recall. These steps reflect the progression from initial exposure to learned behaviour.
- **Learning is an Inferred Process, Different from Performance** Learning is inferred through changes in behaviour or knowledge. It differs from performance, which is the observed expression of what has been learned (e.g., reciting a poem).

2. Discuss about different key processes of learning.

Ans. Learning is a psychological process which gradually develops in human being.

Different processes that are involved in learning through either classical or operant conditioning are

Reinforcement It is the activity of managing a reinforcer by the experimenter. Reinforcers are agents that increase the rate of the responses that come ahead. Reinforced responses increase in rate and non-reinforced responses decrease in rate.

A positive reinforcer increases the rate of response that comes before its presentation and negative reinforcer increases the rate of response that comes before their removal. Reinforcers may be primary or secondary. Primary reinforcer is biologically important because it is needed for the organism survival (e.g. food). Secondary reinforcer has got characteristics of a reinforcer because of the organism's experience with environment. Reinforcers like money, praise and grades are called as secondary reinforcers.

Extinction

It means disappearance of a learned response due to removal of reinforcement from the situation in which the response used to occur. Learning shows resistance to extinction, it means even if learned response is not reinforced, it would continue for sometime. There are number of factors that influence the time period for which a learned response shows resistance to extinction.

- Resistance to extinction increases and learned response reaches its highest level and performance gets stabilised, when number of reinforced trials are increased.
- Resistance to extinction increases when number of reinforcements are increased during acquisition trials.
- Resistance to extinction increases if reinforcement is delayed during acquisition trials. Continuous reinforcement makes the learned response to be less resistant to extinction and more in case of partial reinforcement.

Generalisation and Discrimination

The phenomenon of responding similarly to similar stimuli is known as generalisation. Discrimination is a response due to difference. Discriminative response depends on the discrimination capacity or discrimination learning of the organism.

Spontaneous Recovery

It occurs after a learned response has ended. It has been shown that after lapse of considerable time, the learned or conditioned response recovers and occurs to the conditioned stimulus.

The amount of spontaneous recovery depends on the duration of the time lapsed after the extinction session. Recovery of the learned response is stronger if the duration of time lapse is longer and such a recovery occurs spontaneously.

3. Elaborately discuss about the different factors that facilitate learning.

Ans. The following are the factors that facilitate learning

(i) **Schedule of Reinforcement Delivery** Reinforcement delivery plays a crucial role in learning. There are two types of reinforcement schedules

(a) **Continuous Reinforcement** Reinforcement is given after every target response. This results in a high rate of response, but when reinforcement is stopped, responses decrease quickly.

(b) **Partial Reinforcement** Reinforcement is delivered intermittently, which results in higher response rates. This type of schedule is more resistant to extinction, meaning responses acquired under partial reinforcement are less likely to disappear when reinforcement is stopped. This phenomenon is known as the Partial reinforcement effect.

(ii) **Motivation** Motivation is a mental and physiological state that drives an organism to act in order to fulfill its needs or achieve a goal. Motivation is crucial for learning and can be intrinsic (learning because of enjoyment) or extrinsic (learning to achieve an external goal). Both types of motivation are essential to initiate and sustain the learning process.

(iii) **Preparedness for Learning** Different species have different sensory capacities and response abilities, which influence their learning capabilities. The ability to form certain associations, like Stimulus-Stimulus (S-S) or Stimulus-Response (S-R), depends on an organism's biological makeup. Some species are biologically prepared to learn certain associations more easily than others. The concept of **preparedness** refers to a continuum, where tasks range from easy to difficult based on the species' genetic predisposition.

Case Based Questions

1. Read the case and answer the questions that follow.

In his experiment, Pavlov observed that dogs would naturally salivate when they were presented with food. This is known as an Unconditioned Response (UR) triggered by an Unconditioned Stimulus (US), which in this case is food. Pavlov then paired the sound of a bell (a neutral stimulus) with the presentation of food several times. After a number of trials, the dogs started salivating just by hearing the bell, even when no food was presented. This phenomenon is known as classical conditioning, where the neutral stimulus (bell) becomes a Conditioned Stimulus (CS) and the salivation in response to it becomes a Conditioned Response (CR). Pavlov's experiment showed that the dog learned to associate the bell with food, which caused the conditioned response to occur.

(i) **In the given case, what is the Unconditioned Stimulus (US) and the Unconditioned Response (UR)?**

(ii) **What is the Conditioned Stimulus (CS) and the Conditioned Response (CR) in Pavlov's experiment?**

Ans. (i) The Unconditioned Stimulus (US) is food and the Unconditioned Response (UR) is salivation in response to food.

(ii) The Conditioned Stimulus (CS) is the bell (which was originally neutral) and the Conditioned Response (CR) is salivation triggered by the sound of the bell.

2. Read the case and answer the questions that follow.

Bandura conducted an experimental study in which he showed a movie of five minutes duration to children. The film depicted a large room filled with toys, including a large-sized Bobo doll. In the video, a grown-up boy enters the room and shows aggressive behaviour towards the toys, hitting the Bobo doll, throwing it on the floor, kicking it and sitting on it. There were three versions of the film shown to the children

(i) The boy (model) was rewarded for being aggressive.

(ii) The boy was punished for being aggressive.

(iii) The boy was neither punished nor rewarded.

Afterward, when the children were kept in a similar room with toys, they behaved differently. The children who saw the boy being rewarded acted in a very aggressive manner, while those who saw the boy being punished acted the least aggressively.

(i) **In the given case, how did the children react after watching the film?**

(ii) **What does this case illustrate about observational learning?**

Ans. (i) The children who saw the boy being rewarded for aggression acted most aggressively, while the children who saw the boy being punished for aggression behaved the least aggressively.

(ii) This case illustrates that in observational learning, observers learn by watching the behaviour of others. The children imitated the model's aggressive behaviour, but their actions were influenced by whether the model was rewarded or punished for the behaviour, highlighting the role of reinforcement in social learning.

3. Read the case and answer the questions that follow.

Ravi is a 10-year-old boy who is facing difficulties in his learning process. He struggles with reading, writing and understanding instructions despite being of average intelligence and receiving adequate learning opportunities. His teachers have observed that he often gets distracted and has trouble concentrating on tasks for long periods. Additionally, Ravi has difficulty organising his thoughts and writing, often confusing letters like 'p' and 'q' or words like 'was' and 'saw'. His motor coordination is also poor, as he finds it hard to hold a pencil or walk in a straight line. Despite these challenges, Ravi does not have any physical or sensory impairments and his vision and hearing are normal. His parents are concerned and are considering seeking remedial teaching methods to help improve his learning process.

(i) **In the given case, what type of difficulties does Ravi face?**

(ii) **What are some common symptoms of learning disabilities based on the case?**

Ans. (i) Ravi faces difficulties related to learning disabilities. These difficulties include issues with reading, writing, attention, motor coordination and organising thoughts.

(ii) Based on the case, some common symptoms of learning disabilities include

- Difficulty in reading, writing and understanding instructions.
- Getting easily distracted and having trouble concentrating.
- Misjudging letters and words (e.g., confusing 'p' and 'q', 'was' and 'saw').
- Poor motor coordination and manual dexterity (e.g., difficulty holding a pencil).

SELF ASSESSMENT TEST

Objective Type Questions

1. Making some orienting reflexes i.e getting accustomed to the event is involved in following phenomenon.

(a) Habituation (b) Reinforcement

(c) Extinction (d) Transfer effect

2. The phenomenon of responding similarly to similar stimuli is known as

(a) Discrimination (b) Generic process

(c) Generalisation (d) Spontaneous recovery

Very Short Answer Type Questions

1. Who are Pavlov and Skinner?

2. Define the term learned helplessness.

3. Define perceptual modality.

4. Give the meaning of biofeedback.

5. What is assertive learning used for?

Short Answer Type Questions

1. List the differences between Classical and Operant conditioning.

2. Discuss about Bandura's experiment on observational learning.

3. Briefly describe generic and specific transfer.

4. Mention the different phases of skill acquisition.

Long Answer Type Questions

1. What are the symptoms of learning disabilities?

2. State the differences between classical and operant conditioning differences.

Case Based Questions

Read the case and answer the questions that follow.

Two friends, Arjun and Puneet were attacked by a white Pomeranian dog. Since then, Puneet developed fear for all dogs and would escape any encounter with them. Arjun only developed fear of Pomeranian dogs and was comfortable with other breeds.

(i) Explain the two different learning processes displayed by them in this situation.

(ii) "Verbal Learning is different from conditioning and is limited to human beings." Explain any two procedures for studying verbal learning.

06

CHAPTER

The first systematic study on memory was conducted by German psychologist Hermann Ebbinghaus in 1885. Ebbinghaus observed that we do not forget learned material at a steady rate; initially, memory loss is fast but later becomes stable. Fredrick Bartlett (1932) noted that memory is an active, constructive process, meaning that our memories can change over time.

▼ **YOUR STUDY GOALS**

▼ **YOUR PRACTICE GOAL**

- Objective Type Questions (21 Qs ; MCQs, A-R)
- Subjective Questions (22 VSAs, 13 SAs, 3 LAs, 4 Case Based)

Human Memory

6.1 Nature of Memory

Memory is the ability to store and recall information over a period of time, depending on the mental task.

Memory is conceptualised as a process consisting of three independent but interrelated stage. These are

(i) **Encoding** This is the first stage where information is recorded so it can be used. When a stimulus affects our senses, it generates a neural impulse, which is then processed in the brain. In encoding, some meaning is derived from incoming information.

(ii) **Storage** The second stage where information is stored for future use. It refers to the process through which information is retained and held over a period of time.

(iii) **Retrieval** The final stage where stored information is brought to awareness for tasks like problem-solving. Failure to recall may happen if encoding or storage was weak, making retrieval difficult.

6.2 Information Processing Approach

- Initially, memory was seen as a vast storehouse for information gained through learning and experience.
- With advent of computers, human memory was compared to how a computer registers, stores and manipulates information.
- Computers have temporary (RAM) and permanent (hard disk) memory, following commands to perform tasks.
- Similarly, human memory too registers, information, stores and processes information as needed, like recalling maths operations to solve a mathematical problem.
- This led to the Stage Model of memory by Atkinson and Shiffrin in 1968.

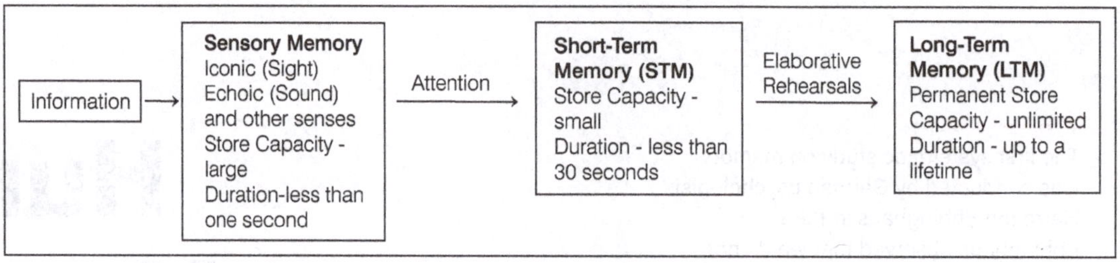

▲ *The Stage Model of Memory*

6.3 Memory Systems

According to the Stage Model, there are three memory systems; the sensory memory, the short-term memory and the long-term memory. Each of these systems have different features and perform different functions with respect to the sensory inputs.

Sensory Memory

- The first memory system where information enters and lasts for less than a second.
- Sensory memory has a large capacity and registers information from all senses accurately, as exact copies.
- Experiencing visuals after images or reverberations of sound when the sound has ceased are the examples of Iconic (visual) or Echoic (auditory) sensory registers.

Short-Term Memory (STM)

- Information that receives attention moves into STM, holding a small amount of information, for around 30 seconds or less.
- Atkinson and Shiffrin proposed that STM encodes information acoustically (through sound) and if not practiced, it can be lost within 30 seconds.
- STM is more durable than sensory registers but can still decay quickly without rehearsal.

Long-Term Memory (LTM)

- Information that surpasses the capacity and time limits of Short-Term Memory (STM) moves into Long-Term Memory (LTM).
- LTM acts as a permanent storage for information, whether it's from recent events or distant memories from years ago.
- This durability is due to encoding that is logical or meaningful, as information is stored based on its meaning.

Control Processes

- Atkinson and Shiffrin introduced the concept of **control processes**[1] to manage the movement of information through various memory stores.
- Not all sensory information is registered in memory; only information that receives attention moves from sensory registers to STM.
- Selective Attention is the first control process, determining which sensory inputs advance to STM while the rest fade quickly.
- **Maintenance Rehearsal** is the another control process that helps to retain information in STM for as long as needed through continuous repetition. When repetition stops, information is lost.
- **Chunking** is another control through which it is possible to expands STM's capacity by grouping information. For example, to remember '194719492004', it can be chunked into '1947, 1949, 2004' to make it easier to retain.

Elaborative Rehearsals

- From the STM information enters to LTM through **elaborative rehearsals**[2], which link new information to existing knowledge in LTM.
- Creating connections between new information and already stored information enhances memory retention.
- For instance, learning the meaning of the word 'humanity' may be easier if concepts like 'compassion', 'truth', and 'benevolence' are already understood.
- The more associations made with the new information, it is likely to be remembered for a long-term.
- Elaborative rehearsals analyse the information based on the various connections it creates.

Experimental Evidence on the Stage Model

- Experiments to test the stage model have shown mixed results; while some support separate STM and LTM memory stores, other findings raise doubts.
- Initially, STM was thought to encode information acoustically, while LTM used semantic encoding. Later experiments revealed that STM can also use semantic encoding, whereas LTM can use acoustic encoding.
- Arrangement of incoming information in multiple ways aids in memory retention.

Case Study of 'KF'

- In 1970, researchers Shallice and Warrington studied a patient called 'KF' who had brain damage in the left cerebral hemisphere from an accident.
- KF's LTM remained unaffected, but his STM was significantly impaired.
- The stage model implies that information enters LTM via STM, yet KF's case showed normal LTM despite STM issues, challenging the model.
- Other studies have also shown that memory processes might be similar regardless of the retention period, questioning the need for distinct memory stores.
- These findings led to alternative conceptualisations of memory beyond the stage model.

---

1 **Control Processes** They function to monitor the flow of information through various memory stores.

2 **Elaborative Rehearsals** It is a memory technique that involves thinking about the meaning of the term to be remembered, as opposed to simply repeating the word to yourself over and over.

Working Memory

The concept of Working Memory was introduced by Baddeley in 1986. He proposed that Short-Term Memory (STM) is not just a passive storehouse but rather functions as a workbench. This workbench holds various memory materials that are actively handled, manipulated and transformed as people perform cognitive tasks. This active memory workbench is referred to as Working Memory.

Working Memory has three main components

(i) **Phonological Loop** This component is related to speech sounds. It holds a limited number of sounds. If not rehearsed, these sounds decay within 2 seconds.

(ii) **Visuospatial Sketchpad** This component is responsible for storing visual and spatial information. It helps in the visual perception of spatial relations. Similar to the phonological loop, the capacity of the visuospatial sketchpad is also limited.

(iii) **Central Executive** The central executive organises information from both the phonological loop and the visuospatial sketchpad, as well as from Long-Term Memory (LTM). It functions like an executive by allocating attentional resources to manage different types of information. The central executive also monitors, plans and controls behaviour during cognitive operations.

6.4 Levels of Processing

In 1972, Craik and Lockhart introduced the concept of levels of processing in memory. This theory suggests that deeper levels of analysis result in more elaborate, long-lasting and stronger memory traces than shallow levels. These levels are described as given below

1. **Shallow Level**
   - At this level, information is processed based on its physical or structural features.
   - For example, focusing only on the shape of letters in a word (e.g., 'cat') without paying attention to details like uppercase or lowercase letters or ink colour.
   - This is the first and shallowest level of processing.
2. **Intermediate Level**
   - At this level, attention is given to the phonetic (pronunciation) sounds associated with the letters.
   - Structural features of words are transformed into at least one meaningful word.
   - For example, recognising that 'cat has three specific letters and a particular sound.
   - Information processed at this level tends to be weak and decays quickly.
3. **Deepest Level**
   - The deepest level involves processing information based on its meaning.
   - Information retained at this level lasts longer.
   - For example, imagining a cat as an animal with four legs, fur, a tail and connecting this image with personal experiences.
   - This level, known as Semantic encoding, results in stronger memory that resists forgetting.

- Analysing information by its structural or phonetic features leads to shallow processing, while encoding it based on its meaning leads to the deepest level of processing.
- Recognising that memory formation depends on how information is initially encoded is essential for effective learning.
- This approach highlights that while learning a new lesson, one should focus on understanding and elaborating the meaning of the content rather than relying on rote memorisation.
- Long-term Retention is the meaning of information and relating it to other facts, concepts and life experiences helps with long-term memory retention.

6.5 Types of Long-Term Memory (LTM)

- Long-term memory is not a single unit; it contains different types of information.
- Psychologists classify long-term memory into declarative and procedural memories.

Declarative Memory

- Contains all information related to facts, names and dates.
- Information stored in declarative memory is verbal and can be classified as episodic or semantic
  - (i) Episodic Memory It includes biographical details of personal life experiences. It is often emotional in nature because it holds memories related to personal life events.
  - (ii) Semantic Memory It holds general awareness and knowledge, including concepts, ideas and rules. It is neutral in nature and less prone to forgetting because it relates to facts and ideas.

Procedural Memory

- It stores memories related to procedures for completing tasks and skills.
- The examples include skills like riding a bicycle or playing a sport.
- The procedural memory is hard to explain verbally; for instance, describing the act of riding a bicycle can be challenging.

Additional Types and Features of Long-Term Memory

Flashbulb Memories

- These are vivid memories tied to surprising or significant events.
- Such memories appear as if 'frozen' in time and are linked to specific dates, places and times.
- Creating flashbulb memories involves more detailed processing, enhancing memory retrieval.

Autobiographical Memory

- Personal memories that are unevenly distributed across different life periods.
- For example, childhood amnesia it is lack of memory from early childhood up to 4-5 years of age.
- Memory frequency increases after early adulthood, especially in the twenties, possibly due to the emotional importance of events.
- In old age, recent years are often better remembered, although memory decline begins around 30 years of age for certain types.

Implicit Memory

- Memory that a person is not consciously aware of. It Retrieved automatically and influences behavior without the person realising it.
- Observed in individuals with brain injuries; for instance, patients who could not recall specific words when asked directly were still able to recall them when prompted with initial letters.
- Implicit memory also exists in people without brain injuries.

Methods of Measuring Memory

Memory is assessed through various experimental methods, tailored to different types of memories. Here are the main methods used

(i) **Free Recall and Recognition**

- **Free Recall** Participants are given a list of words to memorise and later asked to recall them in any order. The number of words recalled indicates the strength of their memory.
- **Recognition** Participants are shown the words they memorised along with unfamiliar words (distractors). They must identify the words they learned. The higher the recognition of memorised words, the stronger the memory.

(ii) **Sentence Verification Task** This method measures **semantic memory.** Participants are given sentences and asked to confirm whether they are true or false. Faster responses indicate better retention of the knowledge needed to verify these sentences.

(iii) **Priming** Used to measure memory that cannot be verbally reported. Participants first see a list of words (e.g., garden, playground, house). Later, they are shown word fragments (e.g., 'gar', 'pla', 'ho') along with other unseen fragments. Participants typically identify the seen words faster, even if they feel they are only guessing.

Quick Test 1

1. What are the three stages of memory?
2. How does selective attention affect memory processing?
3. Mention one difference between sensory memory and short-term memory.
4. Explain the concept of elaborative rehearsal.
5. What is episodic memory?
6. Mention one difference between procedural memory and declarative memory.

6.6 Forgetting: Nature and Causes

- Forgetting is a common experience that happens frequently for everyone.
- Hermann Ebbinghaus was the first to try and understand forgetting.
- He memorised lists of nonsense syllables and then measured how many trials it took to relearn them at different time intervals.
- Ebbinghaus used a graph to show the pattern of forgetting.
- The graph showed that the rate of forgetting is highest in the first nine hours, especially within the first hour.

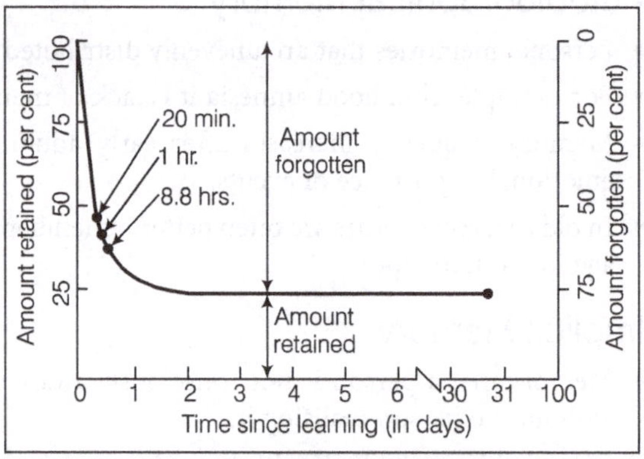

▲ *Ebbinghaus's Curve of Forgetting*

- After the initial drop, the rate of forgetting slows down, and not much is forgotten after many days.
- Ebbinghaus's experiments were early but influenced memory research significantly.
- It is now accepted that memory decreases sharply initially and then declines slowly.

Forgetting Due to Trace Decay

- Trace decay is also called the Disuse theory, the earliest theory on forgetting.
- It suggests that when memories are not used for a long time, they fade and become unavailable.
- This theory claims that memory modifies the brain's central nervous system, creating memory traces.
- However, the limitations of theory are
  - (i) If memory traces decay due to disuse, people who sleep after memorising should forget more than those who stay awake.
  - (ii) But the opposite is true–people who stay awake forget more than those who sleep.

Forgetting Due to Interference

- The interference theory suggests that forgetting happens because different pieces of information in memory interfere with each other.
- Learning and memorising form associations between items and these associations remain intact in memory.
- Interference occurs during retrieval, when these associations compete with each other for access.
- For example, if someone learns two lists of nonsense syllables (List A and List B) one after another and later tries to recall List A, interference from List B might occur.

Types of Interference

- **Proactive Interference** (Forward-moving) means what you have learned earlier interferes with recalling new information. For example, if someone knows English and finds it difficult to learn French, this is due to proactive interference.
- **Retroactive Interference** (Backward-moving) means new learning interferes with recalling past information. For example, if someone struggles to remember English equivalents of French words they are learning, this is retroactive interference.

Experimental Designs for Retroactive and Proactive Interference

	Phase 1	Phase 2	Testing Phase
Retroactive Interference			
Experimental Participant/group	Learns A	Learns B	Recalls A
Control participant/group	Learns A	Rests	Recalls A
Proactive Interference			
Experimental participant/group	Learns A	Learns B	Recalls B
Control participant/group	Rests	Learns B	Recalls B

Forgetting Due to Retrieval Failure

- Forgetting can also happen because of failure in retrieving memory.
- Retrieval failure occurs when the right retrieval cues are either absent or unsuitable.
- Retrieval cues are aids that help us to retrieve stored memories.
- Tulving and his associates showed in experiments that memories can become inaccessible if the right cues are not available or appropriate during recall.

Repressed Memories

Traumatic Experiences and Memory A Traumatic experiences emotionally hurt a person deeply. Sigmund Freud suggested that such experiences are repressed (pushed into the unconscious) and are not accessible for retrieval from memory. Repression is when painful, threatening or embarrassing memories are kept out of conscious awareness.

Psychological Amnesia Traumatic experiences can cause psychological amnesia in some individuals. Amnesia refers to the selective ignoring of events or actions that are not useful or favourable to one's purpose or position. When individuals face a crisis, they may be unable to cope and might mentally block out harsh realities. This can lead to a highly generalised form of amnesia.

Fugue State A result of mental escape or flight is the development of a fugue state[3]. In a fugue state, individuals assume a new identity, including a new name and address. People in a fugue state have two personalities: one personality knows nothing about the other.

Forgetfulness under Stress Forgetfulness due to stress and anxiety is common. Many ambitious students aim to score high and study long hours. However, when they receive the exam question paper, extreme nervousness can cause them to forget everything they have prepared.

6.6 Enhancing Memory

- There are various strategies called mnemonics[4] to improve memory.
- Some mnemonics involves use of images, while others focus on organising learned information.

Mnemonics Using Images

It suggests to create images which are interacting and bring out powerful feelings and clarity in mind, around the material or information a person wish to remember. The two famous mnemonic devices, which make interesting use of images are

1. Keyword Method

- A keyword is associated with the information to be remembered.
- For example, to remember the Spanish word for 'duck' (Pato), the English word 'pot' can be used as a keyword.
- Visualise the keyword (pot) and target word (duck) interacting, like imagining a duck in a pot.
- This method is more effective than rote memorization, especially for learning foreign languages.

2. Method of Loci

- Items to be remembered are imagined as objects placed in specific physical locations.
- For example, to remember bread, eggs, tomatoes and soap, visualise them placed around your house (bread in the kitchen, eggs on a table, soap in the bathroom).
- To recall the items, mentally walk through these locations in a specific order.
- This method is useful for remembering items in a specific sequence.

Mnemonics Using Organisation

- Organising refers to imposing certain order on the material a person want to remember. Memories of this kind are helpful. Some of the methods are
  - **Chunking** Chunking involves grouping smaller units of information together to form larger, more manageable chunks. This method increases the capacity of short-term memory and helps with easy retrieval of information.

---

3 **Fugue State** Persons who become victims of such a state which assumes a new identity, name, address, etc. They have two personalities and one known nothing about the other.

4 **Mnemonics** It is a memory technique to help your brain to better encode and recall important information.

- **First Letter Technique** The first letter of each word to be remembered is taken and arranged to form a word or sentence. For example, 'VIBGYOR' helps remember the colours of the rainbow (Violet, Indigo, Blue, Green, Yellow, Orange and Red).

Other Approaches to Memory Improvement

- Mnemonic strategies underestimate complexities of memory tasks and difficulties people experience while memorising.
- Therefore more comprehensive approach to memory improvement has been suggested by many psychologists which focuses on applying knowledge about memory processes to improve memory. Such approach are as follows

Deep Level Processing

- According to Craik and Lockhart, processing information based on its meaning improves memory.
- Deep processing involves asking questions about the information, its meaning and its relationship to what you already know.
- This makes new information part of your existing knowledge, increasing the chance it will be remembered.

Minimise Interference

- Interference is a major cause of forgetting.
- Maximum interference occurs when similar materials are learned together. To reduce interference, study different subjects at different times.

Enough Retrieval Cues

- Use retrieval cues to help remember study material.
- Cues are easier to remember than the entire material.
- Creating links between the material and retrieval cues will help in recalling information.
- PQRST Method, developed by Thomas and Robinson is the strategy to help students in remembering. It stands for preview, question read, self-recitation and test.
  - **Preview** Quickly look through the chapter to get an idea of its content.
  - **Question** Raise questions and seek answers from the lesson.
  - **Read** Read and look for answers to your questions.
  - **Self-recitation** Try to rewrite what you have read in your own words.
  - **Test** Test yourself on what you've learned to see how much you understand.

Conclusion

- There is no one-size-fits-all method to improve memory.
- Memory can be improved by considering factors like health, interest, motivation and familiarity with the subject.
- Learning and using effective strategies are key to improving memory.

Quick Test 2

1. Give an example of the first letter method.
2. Explain two limitations of trace decay.
3. What is the role of retrieval failure in forgetting?
4. What is chunking?
5. Explain the PQRST method.

NCERT Folder

1. What is the meaning of the terms 'encoding', 'storage' and 'retrieval'?

Ans. Encoding It refers to a process by which information is recorded and registered for the first time so that it becomes usable by our memory system. Whenever an external stimulus impacts on our sensory organs, it generates neural impulse i.e the way nerve cells communicate with one another. These are received in different areas of our brain for further processing. In this stage, incoming information is received and some meaning is derived. Then, it represented in a way so that it can be processed further.

Storage It is a process through which information is retained and held over a period of time.

Retrieval It refers to bringing the stored information to her/his awareness so that it can be used for performing various cognitive tasks like problem-solving and decision-making.

2. How is information processed through sensory, short-term and long-term memory systems?

Ans. Sensory Memory It has large capacity but for very short duration i.e. less than a second. The incoming information first enters sensory memory. It registers information from each of the senses with reasonable accuracy.

This system is referred as sensory memories or sensory registers, because informations from all the senses are registered here as exact copy of the stimulus. For example, seeing visual after-images i.e. the trial of light that stays after the bulb is switched off and hearing reverberations of a sound after the sound has stopped. These are iconic (visual) or echoic (auditory) sensory registers.

Short-Term Memory Information to which attention is payed enters the second memory store called the Short-Term Memory (STM). It holds small amount of information for a brief period of time (usually for 30 seconds or less). Atkinson and Shiffrin proposed that information in STM is usually encoded in terms of sound and unless practised continuously, it may get lost from the STM in less than 30 seconds.

Long-Term Memory Information that survive the capacity and duration limitations of STM finally enter the Long-Term Memory (LTM). It is a permanent storehouse of all informations that may be very recent incidents or very distant events that might happened 10 years back. It has been shown that once any information enters LTM, it is never forgotten. The reason for this is that information gets encoded logically or meaningfully i.e. in terms of the meaning that any information carries.

3. How are maintenance rehearsals different from elaborative rehearsals?

Ans. Maintenance Rehearsals

These are part of short-term memory control process for retaining information for as much time as required.

These kinds of rehearsals simply maintain information through repetition and when such repetitions discontinue, the information is lost.

Elaborative Rehearsals

From the short-term memory, information enters long term memory through elaborative rehearsals. In this rehearsal, it attempts to connect the 'to be retained information' to the already existing information in long-term memory.

In elaborative rehearsals, one tries to analyse the information in terms of various associations it arouses. It involves arrangement of the incoming information in as many ways as possible.

4. Differentiate between declarative and procedural memories.

Ans. Differences between declarative and procedural memories are as follows

Declarative Memories	Procedural Memory
All information related to facts, names, dates, like Sun rises in East, cricket player's names, birth dates of your friends, 15th August, 1947 the day India got independent, etc. are part of declarative memory.	It refers to memories relating to procedures for achieving different tasks and skills like how to ride a bicycle, play football, etc.
Facts stored in the declarative memory can described using verbal descriptions.	Contents of procedural memory cannot be described easily. For instance, we can describe how a game of cricket is played but if someone asks how do you ride a bicycle, it is difficult to describe.

5. Why does forgetting take place?

Ans. Forgetting is a common problem among all of us which we experience very frequently. It was observed that forgetting takes place due to a sharp drop in the memory. There are many reasons of forgetting which can be understood through the following theories

For answer see text under the headings 'Forgetting Due to Trace Decay', 'Forgetting Due to Interference' and 'Forgetting Due to Retrieval Failure' on page no. 141.

6. How is retrieval related forgetting different from forgetting due to interference?

Ans. **Forgetting Due to Retrieval Failure** Forgetting can also occur because at the time of recall, either the retrieval cues are absent or they are not suitable. Retrieval cues are aids which help us in recovering information stored in the memory.

Tulving and his associates carried out several experiments to show that contents of memory may become inaccessible either due to absence or unsuitability of retrieval cues that are available/employed at the time of recall.

Forgetting Due to Interference Interference theory has been the most influential theory which suggests that forgetting is due to interference between different informations that the memory store contains. It is assumed that learning and memorising involve forming associations between items.

Once associations are formed, they remain intact in the memory. People get many number of such associations and each stays independently without any mutual conflict. Interference comes during the time of retrieval, when these different sets of associations compete with one another for retrieval.

7. Define mnemonics. Suggest a plan to improve your own memory.

Ans. There are a number of strategies and methods for improving memory called Mnemonics. Some of them involve using images and other lay importance of organisation or arranging learned information by oneself.

Mnemonics Using Images It suggests to create images which are interacting and bring out powerful feelings and clarity in mind, around the material or information which is wish to remember.

The two famous mnemonic devices, which make interesting use of images are

(i) **The Keyword Method** In this method, we associate a keyword with the information we need to remember. For instance, if we want to learn words of any foreign language an English word that sounds similar to the word of a foreign language is identified. This English word will act as a keyword. This method of learning words of a foreign language is much superior compared to any kind of rote memorisation.

(ii) **The Method of Loci** In this method, items we want to remember are kept as objects arranged in a physical space in the form of visual images. This method is useful in remembering items in a serial order. In this method, we first visualise objects/places in a specific sequence and imagine the objects we want to remember and pair them one by one to the physical locations.

Mnemonics using Organisation Organisation is like arranging material which you want to remember in a particular order. Some of the methods of organisation are

- **Chunking** It refers to mainly grouping together. This method helps in increasing capacity of STM. In chunking, smaller units are combined to form large chunks. Some organisation/arranging principles should be identified in linking smaller units. This will help to retrieve the information very easily.
- **First Letter Technique** In this method, you need to pick up first letter of each word you want to remember and arrange them to form another word or a sentence. For example, VIBGYOR (Violet, Indigo, Blue, Green, Yellow, Orange and Red) which are colours of a rainbow are remembered using this method.

Exam Pattern Questions

Objective Type Questions

Multiple Choice Questions (MCQs)

1. Iconic (sight), Echoic (sound) and other senses are related to which stage of memory model?

(a) Short-term memory (b) Sensory memory
(c) Long-term memory (d) None of these

2. Short-term memory can hold information for how much time?

(a) Less than 2 seconds (b) For 30 seconds or less
(c) For more than a minute (d) For 20 seconds or less

3. Which process function to monitor the flow of information through various memory stores?

(a) Control process (b) Priming
(c) Encoding (d) Phonological loop

4. Memory as per Bartlett is which process?

(a) Destructive (b) Static
(c) Constructive (d) Complex

5. The capacity of short-term memory can be increased using

(a) Amnesia (b) Chunking
(c) Meditation (d) Method of Loci

6. Which of the following components, Baddeley calls the chief executive of working memory?

(a) Second (b) First
(c) Third (d) Fourth

7. Memory of riding bicycle or playing violin is measured using

(a) Priming (b) Free recall
(c) Flashbulb (d) Schema

8. Which of the following is/are true about memory?

I. Memory is made up of a sensory processor, short term memory and long term memory.
II. Short term memory is a limited recollection of perceived stimuli. While long term. memory is a permanent store of memories.
III. Sensory memory holds information, derived from the senses.
IV. Three types of sensory memories exist i.e. conic memory, echoic memory and haptic memory.

Codes

(a) Only I is true (b) I and II is true
(c) I, II and III is true (d) All of these

9. Which of the following is true about flashbulb memories?

I. They are memories of surprising or interesting events.
II. They are associated with personal emotional experiences.
III. They are evenly distributed throughout a person's life.
IV. They often involve detailed processing and cues for retrieval.

Codes

(a) I and II (b) I and IV (c) II and III (d) III and IV

10. Which one of the following statements is correct about implicit memory?

I. It is a type of memory that is retrieved automatically.
II. It does not influence behaviour in any way.
III. It can operate outside the boundaries of awareness.
IV. It is primarily associated with autobiographical experiences.

Codes

(a) I and II (b) I and III (c) II and IV (d) III and IV

11. Identify the correct statements about Ebbinghaus's forgetting curve.

I. The rate of forgetting is maximum during the first nine hours.
II. The decline in memory becomes gradual after the first hour.
III. Sleep accelerates the process of forgetting.
IV. The pattern of forgetting remains the same across all individuals.

Codes

(a) I and II (b) II and III (c) III and IV (d) I and IV

12. If a person uses the keyword method to remember foreign words, what type of memory technique are they using?

I. Mnemonics using images
II. Mnemonics using organisation
III. Implicit memory recall
IV. Explicit memory retrieval

Codes

(a) I and III (b) II and IV (c) I and IV (d) III and IV

13. The Method of Loci is best described as

I. A technique that involves grouping smaller units into larger chunks.
II. A memory aid that pairs items to physical locations in a sequence.
III. A method of recalling items by mentally walking through a sequence.
IV. A memory retrieval process independent of conscious organisation.

Codes

(a) I and II (b) II and III (c) I and IV (d) III and IV

14. Which of the following best describes the concept of chunking?

I. It involves arranging items in a specific serial order.
II. It helps increase the capacity of short-term memory.
III. It is a form of mnemonics using visual imagery.
IV. It groups smaller units of information into larger units.

Codes

(a) I and III (b) II and IV (c) I and IV (d) II and III

Assertion-Reason Questions

Directions (Q. Nos. 15-21) In the following questions, a statement of Assertion A is followed by a statement of Reason R. Mark the correct choice from the options given below.

(a) Both A and R are true and R is the correct explanation of A
(b) Both A and R are true, but R is not the correct explanation of A
(c) A is true, but R is false
(d) A is false, but R is true

15. **Assertion** (A) Long-term memory too is not unitary.

Reason (R) It contains a wide variety of information.

16. **Assertion** (A) Episodic memory contains biographical details of our lives.

Reason (R) Episodic memory contains general awareness and knowledge.

17. **Assertion** (A) According to the Stage Model, once information enters Long-Term Memory (LTM), it is never forgotten.

Reason (R) Information in LTM is stored semantically and meaningfully, which contributes to its permanence.

18. **Assertion** (A) In the Working Memory Model, the Central Executive allocates attentional resources to various types of information.

Reason (R) The phonological loop is responsible for holding visual and spatial information, whereas the visuospatial sketchpad handles auditory tasks.

19. **Assertion** (A) Flashbulb memories are particularly vivid and emotional, and are associated with surprising or significant events.

Reason (R) Flashbulb memories are formed because they undergo shallow levels of processing, which makes them easier to recall.

20. **Assertion** (A) Repressed memories are traumatic experiences that are not accessible to conscious recall.

Reason (R) Freud suggested that traumatic memories are deliberately suppressed due to their emotional pain, making them inaccessible to conscious awareness.

21. **Assertion** (A) The method of Loci involves using physical locations and visual images to improve memory.

Reason (R) This method is particularly effective for remembering items in a serial order by associating them with specific places.

Answers

1. (b) Sensory memory
2. (b) For 30 Seconds or less
3. (a) Control process
4. (c) Constructive
5. (b) Chunking
6. (c) Third
7. (d) Schema
8. (d) All of these
9. (b) I and IV
10. (b) I and III
11. (a) I and II
12. (c) I and IV
13. (b) II and III
14. (b) II and IV
15. (a) Both A and R are true and R is the correct explanation of A.
16. (c) A is true, but R is false.
17. (b) Both A and R are true, but R is not the correct explanation of A.
18. (c) A is true, but R is false.
19. (c) A is true, but R is false.
20. (a) Both A and R are true and R is the correct explanation of A.
21. (a) Both A and R are true and R is the correct explanation of A.

Subjective Questions

Very Short Answer Type Questions

1. Who conducted the first systematic research on memory?

Ans. The first systematic research on memory was done by a German psychologist of later nineteenth century (1885) Hermann Ebbinghaus. He carried out many experiments on himself and found that we do not forget the learned material at an even pace or completely. In the beginning the rate of memory loss is fast but later it stabilises.

2. Define memory.

Ans. Memory is a very interesting phenomenon which engages human power. It functions to save our sense of identity, maintains our interpersonal relationships and helps us in solving problems and taking decisions.

3. List different stages of memory.

Ans. Memory is conceptualised as a process consisting of three independent but interrelated stages. They are encoding, storage and retrieval.

4. Name different memory systems present in stage model.

Ans. As per stage model, there are three memory systems. They are the sensory memory, the short-term memory and the long-term memory.

5. Give the significance long-term memory.

Ans. Information that survive the capacity and duration limitations of short-term memory finally enter the long-term memory. It is a permanent storehouse of all informations that may be very recent incidents or very distant events that might happened 10 years back.

6. What do you know about control process?

Ans. Atkinson and Shiffrin proposed the idea of control processes which function to monitor the flow of information through various memory stores.

7. What do you understand by chunking?

Ans. Chunking refers to mainly grouping together. In chunking, smaller units are combined to form large chunks. Chunking is used to expand the capacity of STM.

8. Define working memory.

Ans. According to Baddeley, the short-term memory is not a passive storehouse but rather a work bench that holds a wide variety of memory materials that are constantly handled, manipulated and transformed as people perform various cognitive tasks. This work bench is called the Working memory.

9. Which component of working memory is called Executive and why?

Ans. Baddeley calls the third component of working memory as Central Executive. It organises information from phonological loop, visuos- patial sketchpad and long-term memory. Like a true executive, it allocates attentional resources to be distributed to various informations needed to perform a given cognitive operation and monitors, plans and controls behaviour.

10. Who proposed the idea of levels of processing?

Ans. In 1972, Craik and Lockhart proposed the idea of levels of processing. This theory says that the deeper levels of analysis produce more elaborate, long-lasting and stronger memory traces than shallow level analysis.

11. What does episodic memory contain?

Ans. Episodic memory contains biographical details of our lives. Memories related to our personal life experiences are part of the episodic memory and thats why, its contents are generally emotional in nature.

12. Define implicit memory? Give an example.

Ans. Implicit memory is a kind of memory that a person is not aware of it. It is a memory that is retrieved automatically. Implicit memories lie outside the boundaries of awareness i.e. we are not aware of the fact that a memory or record of a given experience exists.

13. Give the significance of sentence verification task.

Ans. It is used for measuring semantic memory. The participants are asked to indicate whether the given sentences are true or false. Faster the participants respond, the better the information needed to verify those sentences is retained.

14. What is priming used for?

Ans. Priming is used for measuring information we cannot report verbally. In this method, participants are shown a list of words, such as garden, playground, house, etc. After that they are shown parts of these words like gar, pla, ho, along with parts of other words they had not seen. Participants complete parts of seen words more quickly than parts of words they had not seen. When asked, they are often unaware of this and report that they have only guessed.

15. Riya of Class XI prepared well for her exams but forgot everything after looking at the question paper. What would be the possible reason for forgetting?

Ans. Stress and high anxiety are main reasons for forgetting or loss of memory. When students go to examination hall and look at the question paper, they become very nervous and forget everything they had prepared well.

16. What is the first letter technique? Give an example.

Ans. In this method, you need to pick up first letter of each word you want to remember and arrange them to form another word or a sentence. For example, VIBGYOR (Violet, Indigo, Blue, Green, Yellow, Orange and Red) which are colours of a rainbow are remembered using this method.

17. How do you counter interference and enhance memory?

Ans. If you can arrange your study in a manner that, you do not learn similar subjects one after the other, then you will be able to counter interference and enhance memory. For example, after practising maths, study social science. If this is not possible, you can distribute your learning/practice, i.e. giving yourself small rest periods while studying to minimise interference.

18. Who developed the PQRST method?

Ans. Thomas and Robinson have developed a method called PQRST to help students remembering more. It stands for Preview, Question, Read, Self-recitation and Test.

19. What should be done to retain information for a longer period?

Ans. If information is processed at deepest level then it is retained for a longer period which describes that the information should be understood in terms of its meaning.

20. How do you measure memory using free recall method?

Ans. In free recall method, participants are given some words and are asked to memorise and recall them in any order. The more they are able to recall, the better their memory becomes.

21. Mention the difference between proactive and retroactive interference?

Ans. In proactive interference, past learning interferes with the recall of newer learning while in retroactive interference, the newer learning interferes with the recall of past learning.

22. The first component of the working memory is the phonological loop which holds a limited number of sounds and if we do not rehearse they decay within two seconds. Which type of memory is discussed here? Name the other two components of it.

Ans. Short-term memory is discussed here. The other two components of STM are *Visuospatial sketchpad* which gives visual and spatial information and *control executive* which organised information from phonological loop, visuospatial sketchpad and long-term memory.

Short Answer Type Questions

1. Explain encoding in detail.

Ans. Encoding refers to a process by which information is recorded and registered for the first time so that it becomes usable by our memory system. Whenever an external stimulus impacts on our sensory organs, it generates neural impulse i.e. the way nerve cells communicate with one another.

These are received in different areas of our brain for further processing. In this stage, incoming information is received and some meaning is derived.

Then, it represented in a way so that it can be processed further.

2. Discuss in detail about Sensory Memory.

Ans. The incoming information first enters sensory memory. It has large capacity but is of very short duration i.e. less than a second. It registers information from each of the senses with reasonable accuracy.

This system is referred as sensory memories or sensory registers, because informations from all the senses are registered here as exact copy of the stimulus.

For example, seeing visual after-images i.e. the trial of light that stays after the bulb is switched off and hearing reverberations of a sound after the sound has stopped. These are iconic (visual) or echoic (auditory) sensory registers.

3. Describe Shallice and Warrington's case study.

Ans. In the year 1970, Shallice and Warrington had referred the case of a man known as KF who damaged a portion of the left side of his cerebral hemisphere due to an accident.

This case questioned the stage model assumption that informations are committed to LTM *via.* STM. Because if KF's STM was affected, how could his LTM be normal.

But other studies have shown that memory processes are similar, irrespective of whether any information is retained for a few seconds or for many years and that memory can be sufficiently understood without putting them in separate memory stores. These evidences led to the development of another model of memory.

4. Discuss about deepest level of processing.

Ans Craik and Lockhart proposed the idea of levels of processing. The third level in this model is deepest and if information is processed here, it is retained for a longer period. In order to retain information for longer period, information should be understood in terms of its meaning.

For example, if we imagine cat as an animal with four legs, fur, a tail and invoke an image of a cat and connect that image with our experiences, then word cat will be retained for longer period of time.

It implies that, analysing information in terms of its structural and phonetic features will be regarded as shallower processing while encoding in terms of meaning it carries is the deepest processing level that leads to memory that resists forgetting largely.

5. What is trace decay? What are the shortcomings of this theory?

Ans. Trace decay is also called Disuse theory, which is the earliest theory on forgetting. It is assumed that memory leads to modification in the central nervous system, which is similar to physical changes in the brain called Memory traces.

When we do not use these memory traces for long time, they simply fade away and become unavailable.

This theory is inadequate on many grounds. If this theory is true, then people who go to sleep after memorising should forget more than those who remain awake, because memory traces decay due to disuse. But results, show just the opposite i.e. people who remain awake after memorising show greater forgetting than those who sleep.

6. What is the role of traumatic experiences in developing fugue state in a person?

Ans. Traumatic experiences may cause psychological amnesia in some persons. Amnesia means the selective overlooking or ignoring events or acts that are not favourable or useful to one's purpose or position. When some individual experience crisis in life, they are completely incapable of coping with such events. They just close their eyes, ears and mind to such harsh realities of life and take mental flight (i.e. instance of running away) from them. It results in highly generalised amnesia.

One of the results of such flights is the emergence of a disorder known as 'fugue state'. Persons who become victims of such a state assume a new identity, name, address etc. They have two personalities and one knows nothing about the other.

7. Explain the method of Loci in detail.

Ans. In method of Loci, items we want to remember are kept as objects arranged in a physical space in the form of visual images. This method is useful in remembering items in a serial order.

In this method, we first visualise objects/places in a specific sequence and imagine the objects we want to remember and then pair them one by one to the physical locations.

For example, if we want to remember bread, eggs, tomatoes and soap for shopping, we just have to visualise bread and eggs in kitchen, tomatoes in fridge and soap in bathroom. When we go to market, all we have to do is, take a mental walk from kitchen to bathroom recalling all the items in your shopping list in a sequence.

8. Whenever Pooja sees the pictures of the celebration of her 10th Birthday, she can remember everything in minute detail. Explain the type of memory Pooja has.

Competency Based Que.

Ans. This type of memory of Pooja is known as *Flashbulb Memories*. These memories are very detailed. They are like a photo taken with an advanced model camera. Flashbulb memories are like images frozen in memory and tied to particular places, dates and times. People put in greater effort in the formation of these memories.

Here flashbulb memories are frozen in Pooja's mind with the particular place of the celebrations, timings of it and the friends who attended the party etc. in detail.

Thus, whenever she sees the picture, after one minute the recreation of the scene starts in her mind.

9. Explain in detail about working memory and its components.

Ans. A multi-component view of STM was proposed by Baddeley (1986) who suggested that the STM is not a passive storehouse but rather a work bench that holds a variety of memory materials that are constantly handled, manipulated and transformed as people perform various cognitive tasks. This work bench is called Working memory. The various components of working memory are

- First component is the phonological (related to speech sounds) loop which holds a limited number of sounds and unless rehearsed they decay within 2 seconds.
- Second component is visuospatial (visual perception of spatial relations) sketchpad which stores visual and spatial information and like phonological loop the capacity of the sketchpad too is limited.
- Third component which Baddeley calls the Central Executive, organises information from phonological loop, visuospatial sketchpad as well as from the LTM. Like a true executive, it allocates attentional resources to be distributed to various informations needed to perform a given cognitive operation and monitors, plans and controls behaviour.

10. Explain how information from short-term memory enters into long-term memory.

Ans. From the short-term memory, information enters long-term memory through elaborative rehearsals. In this rehearsal, it attempts to connect the 'to be retained information' to the already existing information in long-term memory.

For example, the task of remembering the meaning of the word humanity will be easier if the meanings of concepts such as compassion, truth and benevolence are already in place. The number of associations we can create around the new information will determine its permanence.

In elaborative rehearsals, one tries to analyse the information in terms of various associations it arouses. It involves arrangement of the incoming information in as many ways as possible. We can expand the information in some kind of logical framework and link it to similar memories or we could create a mental image.

11. Yash is student of Class 12th. He adopts the method of PQRST for his preparation. Explain the method in detail.

Competency Based Que.

Ans. Yash adopts the method PQRST which helps him to remember easily. This method stands for preview, question, read, self-recitation and test.

- Preview refers to having quick look at the chapter and knowing about its contents. First Yash follows this step.

- Question means raising questions and seeking answers from the lesson. Yash seeks the probable answers from the lesson.
- He himseft read and look for answers of question that he has raised.
- Self-recitation means try to rewrite what Yash has already read.
- At the end Yash tests himself how much he has understood the chapter.

12. "The most important unit of representation of knowledge in long-term memory is a concept." Explain this. Competency Based Que.

Ans. Concepts are mental categories for objects and events, which are similar to each other in one or in more than one way. Concepts once formed get organised in categories. A category itself is a concept but it also functions to organise similarities among other concepts based on common features.

For example, the word mango is a category as different varieties of mango can be subsumed within it and it is also a concept within the category of fruit. Concept may also get organised in schema. They are mental frameworks which represents our knowledge and assumptions about the world. So we examine the concept as the basic level at which knowledge is represented in the long-term memory and the notions of category and schema as the first level at which concepts are organised.

13. "Some individuals undergo experiences that are traumatic." Explain. Competency Based Que.

Ans. A traumatic experience emotionally hurts a person. Sigmund Freud believed that such experiences are repressed into the unconscious and are not available for retrieval from memory. It is a kind of repression i.e. painful, threatening and embarrassing memories which are held out of consciousness.

In some persons, traumatic experiences may give rise to psychological amnesia. Some individual experiences crisis and are utterly incapable of coping with such events. They close their eyes, ears and minds to such harsh reality of life, and make mental flight from them. It results in highly generalised amnesia. One of the results of such flight is emerging of a disorder known as Fugue state. Persons who become victims of such a state have two personalities and one knows nothing about the other.

Long Answer Type Questions

1. A child was asked to describe a bird. He/She generated an image in his/her mind. Explain How do mental models help in this process?

Ans. Information can be coded in a perceptual format or in terms of images. An image is a definite form of representation which directly communicates perceptual attributes (things that can be interpreted) of an object. For example, when we see word 'school', it will generate an image of our own school. Almost all definite objects and concepts generate images and the knowledge related to them is encoded both verbally and visually. This is called Dual coding hypothesis. This was originally proposed by Paivio.

According to this hypothesis, information related to definite objects are encoded and stored in the form of images and information related to abstract concepts are in the form of verbal and a descriptive code.

For example, when we are asked to describe a bird, the image of a bird is generated in our mind and we describe accordingly. But when we are asked to describe concepts like truth or honesty, no such images will be generated. Thus, any information which can be encoded verbally and in the form of image can be recalled with greater ease.

Information which has been encoded and stored in the form of images leads to the development of mental models. Mental models are required by many routine tasks.

For example, following a road direction, preparing to cook an attractive dish, following the instructions given in a cookery book requires that spatial mental models are created from verbal descriptions.

Mental models, thus refer to our belief about the manner in which our environment is structured and such beliefs are formed with the help of definite images as well as verbal descriptions.

2. Explain Hermann Ebbinghaus's curve of forgetting and also interference theory on forgetting?

Ans. **Hermann Ebbinghaus' Curve of Forgetting** The first proper attempt to understand the nature of forgetting was made by Hermann Ebbinghaus, who memorised lists of nonsense syllables and then measured the number of trials he took to relearn the same list at different time intervals.

He used a graph to show the pattern of forgetting which is given below

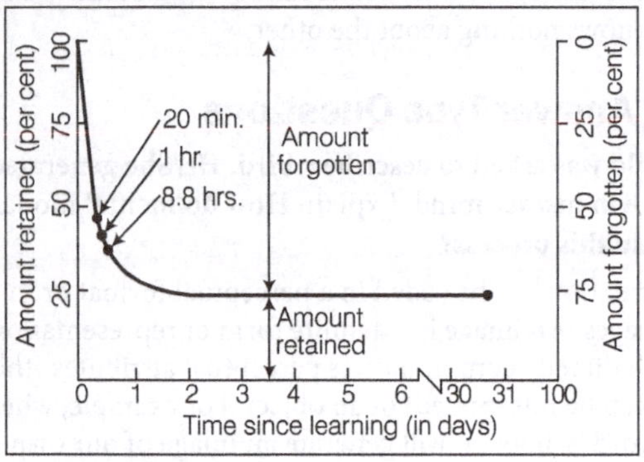

In the above graph, one can observe that the rate of forgetting is maximum in the first 9 hours in general and first 1 hour in particular.

Later, the rate slows down and not much is forgotten even after many days.

Though this research was very simple, it influenced memory research. As of now, it is accepted by all that memory drops sharply and thereafter the decline is gradual.

Forgetting due to Interference

Interference theory has been the most influential theory which suggests that forgetting is due to interference between different informations that the memory store contains. It is assumed that learning and memorising involve forming associations between items.

Once associations are formed, they remain intact in the memory. People get many number of such associations and each stays independently without any mutual conflict.

Interference comes during the time of retrieval, when these different sets of associations compete with one another for retrieval.

3. "Mnemonic strategies for memory improvement are too simple and sometimes underestimate complexities of memory tasks and difficulties people experience while memorising." Discuss other methods of memory improvement which are more effective.

Competency Based Que.

Ans. While mnemonic strategies are simple, they may overlook the complexities of memory tasks. More effective methods for memory improvement include

(i) **Deep Level Processing** According to Craik and Lockhart, processing information by focusing on its meaning leads to better memory. This involves asking questions about the information, understanding its relationships to existing knowledge, and integrating it into a broader knowledge framework.

(ii) **Minimise Interference** Interference, particularly when learning similar material consecutively, can hinder memory. To minimise interference, it is helpful to study different subjects or materials at different times rather than studying similar topics back to back.

(iii) **Enough Retrieval Cues** Linking study material to retrieval cues can make recalling information easier. By associating parts of the content with specific cues, students can more easily access the information when needed. The PQRST method (Preview, Question, Read, Self-recitation, and Test) helps by encouraging active engagement with the material and regular self-testing.

Case Based Questions

1. Read the case and answer the questions that follow.

A film clipping of an event (a car accident) was shown to the participants. This was followed by some questions. One of the questions was "how fast were the cars going when they smashed into each other". In another question the verb smashed was replaced with the verb contacted. Those who were asked the first question (which included the word 'smashed') estimated the speed of the cars as 40.8 mph. Those who were given the second question (i.e. with the word 'contacted') estimated that the speed of the cars was only 31.8 mph.

(i) Identify the kind of memory being reinforced in above case. What are repressed memories?

(ii) Mention any two methods for enhancing memory.

Ans. (i) The kind of memory being reinforced in the above case is eyewitness memory.

Repressed memories are held out of consciousness. A traumatic (deeply disturbing) experience emotionally hurts a person. Sigmund Freud put forward his view that such experiences are repressed (restrained or oppressed) into the unconscious and are not available for retrieval from memory. It is a kind of repression–painful, threatening and embarrassing (ashamed) memories.

(ii) Two methods for enhancing memory are

(a) **The Keyword Method** In this method, we associate a keyword with the information we need to remember. In the keyword method, an English word that sounds similar to the word of a foreign language is identified.

(b) **The Method of Loci** In this method, items we want to remember are kept as objects arranged in a physical space in the form of visual images.

2. Read the case and answer the questions that follow.

Shallice and Warrington (1970) suggested that a man known as 'KF' met with an accident and damaged a portion of the left side of his cerebral hemisphere. It was found that his long-term memory was intact, but the short-term memory was seriously affected.

(i) **In the given case, how did the damage to 'KF' affect his memory?**

(ii) **What does this case suggest about the relationship between short-term and long-term memory?**

Ans. (i) The damage to 'KF' affected his short-term memory severely, but his long-term memory remained intact. This suggests that short-term and long-term memories can be independently affected.

(ii) This case suggests that short-term memory and long-term memory are not entirely dependent on each other. Despite the damage to his short-term memory, 'KF' was able to retain information in his long-term memory, indicating that they may involve distinct processes or systems.

3. Read the case and answer the questions that follow.

Forgetting can occur because at the time of recall, either the retrieval cues are absent or they are not suitable. Retrieval cues are aids/cues which help us in recovering information stored in the memory. Tulving and his associates carried out several experiments to show that contents of memory may become inaccessible either due to absence or unsuitability of retrieval cues that are available/employed at the time of recall.

(i) **In the given case, what causes forgetting according to the content? What is the role of retrieval cues in memory recall?**

(ii) **How can we relate the concept of retrieval failure to real-life situations?**

Ans. (i) Forgetting occurs due to the absence or unsuitability of retrieval cues. Retrieval cues help in recovering information stored in the memory. If these cues are unavailable or inappropriate at the time of recall, the memory may become inaccessible.

(ii) Retrieval failure can happen in situations like forgetting a friend's name or a fact during an exam. This occurs when the right cues to trigger the memory are missing or not fitting with the stored information. For example, forgetting a name despite knowing the person well can be due to an absent or incorrect retrieval cue.

4. Read the case and answer the questions that follow.

Karan is a student who is preparing for his final exams and has been struggling with memorising important concepts and information. He often finds himself forgetting crucial facts during his study sessions. One day, his friend suggests using mnemonic devices to enhance memory. Karan tries the Keyword Method, where he associates an English word with a foreign language word he needs to remember. For example, he remembers the Spanish word for 'duck' (Pato) by associating it with the word 'pot' and visualising a duck in a pot of water. This makes it easier for Karan to recall the word during his study sessions.

In addition to this, Karan uses the Method of Loci, where he arranges the items he needs to remember in a mental walk through his house, placing items in various locations. This technique helps him remember a list of groceries, like bread, eggs and soap, by imagining them in different places in his home.

(i) **Which mnemonic methods does Karan use to enhance his memory?**

(ii) **How does the Keyword Method help Karan improve his memory?**

Ans. (i) Karan uses the following mnemonic methods

- **Keyword Method** He associates an English word with a foreign language word to remember it better.
- **Method of Loci** He mentally arranges items he needs to remember in different locations to improve recall.

(ii) The Keyword Method helps Karan improve his memory by associating a familiar English word with a foreign language word. Visualising the interaction between these two words creates a strong mental image that makes it easier to remember and recall the target information, as seen with the Spanish word for 'duck' (Pato) by associating it with the word 'pot'. This method offers a more effective alternative to rote memorisation.

SELF ASSESSMENT TEST

Objective Type Questions

1. Which of the following is defined as overlapping or disturbance of different memory traces on each other?

(a) Forgetting (b) Conditioning
(c) Interference (d) Recall

2. What is defined as the temporary or long-term loss of material that was learnt earlier?

(a) Forgetting (b) Memory
(c) Perception (d) None of these

3. A kind of memory that a person is not aware of is called

(a) Childhood amnesia (b) Implicit memory
(c) Declarative memory (d) Semantic memory

Very Short Answer Type Questions

1. Define memory. List its stages.

2. Who gave stage model? List different memory systems present in stage model.

3. Define chunking with an example.

4. Why is third component of working memory called Executive?

5. Define implicit memory with an example.

6. What do you mean by cognitive economy?

7. What are proactive and retroactive interferences?

Short Answer Type Questions

1. Discuss briefly about sensory memory.

2. Write about deepest level of processing.

3. What is fugue state? How does it develop?

4. Describle the functioning of PQRST method.

5. How is semantic memory different from episodic memory?

Long Answer Type Questions

1. What are the three levels of processing memories?

2. Discuss various methods of memory improvement which are more effective than mnemonics in detail.

Case Based Questions

Read the case and answer the questions that follow.

The history of psychological research on memory spans over 100 years. The first systematic exploration of memory is credited to Herman Ebbinghaus, a German psychologist of the late 19th century (1885). He carried out many experiments on himself and found that we do not forget long material at an even pace or completely. Initially, the rate of forgetting is faster but eventually stabilizes. There are other psychologists who have influenced memory research in a major way.

(i) "Memory is conceptualised as a process consisting of three independent but interrelated stages." Explain.

(ii) Explain the nature and causes of forgetting.

07

CHAPTER

Thinking is the foundation of all mental (cognitive) activities or processes. It is unique to human beings. It involves manipulating and analysing information received from the environment.

Thinking

YOUR STUDY GOALS

YOUR PRACTICE GOAL

- Objective Type Questions (19 Qs ; MCQs, A-R)
- Subjective Questions (18 VSAs, 11 SAs, 5 LAs, 5 Case Based)

7.1 Nature of Thinking

- Thinking is a higher mental process where we manipulate and analyse acquired or existing information.
- Thinking is done through methods like abstracting, reasoning, imagining, problem-solving, judging and decision-making.
- Thinking is mainly organised and goal-directed. To reach the goal, you plan, recall previous steps if the task is familiar or infer new strategies if the task is unfamiliar.
- Thinking is an internal mental process that can be inferred from external behaviour.
- For example, a chess player thinking for a long time before making a move cannot be directly observed, but you can infer their thought process from their next move.

Building Blocks of Thought

- Thinking depends on knowledge we already have, which is represented in either images or words (concepts). People usually think through mental images or words.
- For example, when travelling by road to a place visited long ago, you use the mental image of streets and other places.
- Another example, when deciding to buy a storybook, your choice depends on your knowledge of different authors and themes. Here, thinking is based on words or concepts.

Mental Images

- A mental image is a representation of a sensory experience that helps in thinking about things, places or events.
- For example, if asked to imagine a cat sitting on a tree with its tail raised and curved, you form a visual image of the situation.
- Another example, when asked to imagine standing in front of the Taj Mahal and describe what you see, you form a visual image of the event.
- The process of imagining is similar to how you read a map and later locate the places on a physical map.

Concepts

- A concept is a **mental representation**[1] of a category and refers to a class of objects, ideas or events that share common properties.
- When we encounter an object or event, familiar or unfamiliar, we identify it by its characteristics.
- We match it with an existing category, and if it fits, we categorise it.
- For example, an apple is categorised as a fruit, a table as furniture and a dog as an animal.
- While walking on the road, if you encounter a small quadruped (an animal with four feet), you might identify it as a dog, even if it's a new breed, because it shares the characteristics of a dog (tail-wagging, barking).
- A concept is thus, a mental representation of a category that groups objects, ideas or events with similar properties.

Concept Formation

- Concept formation helps in organising knowledge, making it easier to access quickly and efficiently.
- For example, children who are organised keep their books, bags and other items in specific places, making it easy to find them later.
- Similarly, by forming concepts and categorising objects and events, our thought process becomes faster and more efficient.

Culture and Thinking

Our thinking is influenced by our beliefs, values and social practices. A study showed that American and Asian students had different ways of thinking when shown pictures of fish swimming underwater. American students focused on the biggest, brightest and most unique features, like the largest fish. Asian students focused more on the background, such as the rocky bottom and green water. Researchers concluded that Americans use analytical thinking, where they analyse objects separately. On the other hand, Asians use holistic thinking, where they consider the relationships between objects and their surroundings.

7.2 The Process of Thinking: Problem Solving

- Problem solving is an orderly process in which thinking is directed towards the solution of a specific problem.
- Most day-to-day activities aim to reach a specific goal.
- Problems are not always obstacles but can be simple activities performed to achieve a goal.
- For example, preparing a quick snack for a friend who has just arrived at your place, is a form of problem solving.
- Problem solving involves two states–the initial state (problem) and the end state (goal).

1 **Mental Representation** Cognitive process of creating and storing mental images or concepts of external events, past events or imaginary events in the mind.

- These two states are connected by mental operations through several steps
  - Identify the problem
  - Represent the problem
  - Plan the solution (Set sub-goals)
  - Evaluate all solutions
  - Select one solution and execute it
  - Evaluate the outcomes
  - Rethink and redefine problems and solutions
- The two major obstacles to solve problem are mental set and lack of motivation.

1. Mental Set

- A tendency to solve problems by using previously tried methods.
- Mental set can lead to mental rigidity, making it hard to adapt to new methods.
- This obstructs the problem solver from thinking of new strategies.
- For example, in maths problems, once you find a solution method, you may keep using the same steps even when they fail.

2. Lack of Motivation

- If people are not motivated, their skills and talents are of no use.
- Lack of motivation can lead people to give up easily when facing problems or failure.
- Continuous effort is needed to find solutions.

7.3 Reasoning

- Reasoning is the process of gathering and analysing information to arrive at conclusions.
- It is also a form of problem-solving.
- For example, if you see a person running on a railway platform, you can make different conclusions about why they are running, such as catching a train, saying goodbye or he has left his bag in the train.
- There are two types of reasoning *i.e.*, deductive and inductive reasoning.

1. Deductive Reasoning

- Deductive Reasoning a psychological process that people use to make decisions and solve problems. It is a cognitive process that involves using general ideas to reach a specific conclusion.
- For example, you assume that people run on the platform because they are late for the train and then conclude the person running is late.
- One mistake people make in deductive reasoning is assuming the basic statement is true without verifying it.

2. Inductive Reasoning

- Inductive reasoning is a form of reasoning that takes specific knowledge, through observation and experience and then creates a general conclusion.
- For example, by observing the person entering the train and returning with a bag, you conclude that they left their bag on the train.
- One mistake in inductive reasoning is drawing conclusions without knowing all the facts.
- Most scientific reasoning is inductive, where general rules are drawn from specific observations.

Analogy

- Analogy is a form of reasoning that compares relationships between two pairs of things.
- For example, water is to fish as air is to humans or white is to snow as black is to coal.
- Analogies help in solving problems by identifying and visualising the key properties of an object or event.

Quick Test 1

1. Name three levels of concepts.
2. What is thinking?
3. Explain the concept of mental images.
4. What are concepts?
5. Mention two differences between analytical thinking and holistic thinking.
6. What is problem-solving?
7. What is Decision-making?

7.4 Decision-Making

- Inductive and deductive reasoning help in making judgements and decisions.
- Judgement involves drawing conclusions, forming opinions and evaluating events or objects based on knowledge and available evidences.
- For example, a man who is talkative and likes interacting with others may be judged suitable for a salesperson's job.
- Judgements are sometimes made automatically, like applying brakes when seeing a red light.
- Evaluating something new, like a novel or a painting, requires referencing past knowledge and personal preferences.
- Judgements are influenced by beliefs and attitudes and can change with new information.
- For example, Initially, students may judge a new teacher as strict but may change their opinion after interacting with the teacher and realising they are student-friendly.

Choosing Options

- Decision-making involves choosing one option from several alternatives.
- Sometimes decisions are based on personal preferences.
- Judgement and decision-making are interrelated processes.
- In decision-making, we evaluate the cost and benefit of each alternative.
- For example, choosing between psychology and economics as subjects in Class XI involves considering factors like interest, future prospects, availability of books and teacher efficiency.
- Decision-making is different from problem solving, as the solutions (choices) are already known in decision-making.
- For example, choosing between practising badminton or studying for exams involves evaluating the outcomes of each choice.
- People make different decisions based on their priorities and real-life decisions are often made quickly, without evaluating every outcome in detail.

7.5 Nature and Process of Creative Thinking

- Creative thinking involves generating new and original ideas or solutions to problems.
- For examples of creativity include art forms like music, painting, and poetry.
- Creative thinkers can solve problems in new ways, like AD Karve, who developed a smokeless 'chullah' using dry sugarcane leaves or Ashish Panwar, who built a robot at the International Robotics Olympiad.
- Creativity does not always need to be expressed in extraordinary ways; everyone has the potential to think creatively.

- Creative thinking can be applied to various areas like writing, teaching, cooking, problem-solving and conflict resolution.
- 'Everyday Creativity' is different from 'special talent creativity', which leads to exceptional achievements.

Nature of Creative Thinking

- Creative thinking is characterised by novelty and originality.
- For example, new models of household appliances, cars or other products are not considered original unless unique features are added.
- Creative thinking involves producing original ideas or solutions that did not exist before.
- According to Burner, creative thinking leads to an 'effective surprise', meaning people are often shocked or surprised by new, unusual ideas or products.
- Creative thinking is not purposeless. Simply thinking in a non-conformist way or having bizarre ideas without context is not creative.
- For thinking to be considered creative, it must be reality-oriented, appropriate, constructive and socially desirable.

Types of Creative Thinking

Convergent thinking and divergent thinking are two main types of creative thinking proposed by JP Guilford.

1. Convergent Thinking

- Convergent thinking focuses on solving problems with only one correct answer.
- The mind converges on the right solution. For example,
  - **Question** 3, 6, 9... What comes next?
  - **Answer** 12 (This has only one correct answer).

2. Divergent Thinking

- Divergent thinking is open-ended, where there are multiple answers to a problem based on personal experiences.
- It is important for producing novel and original ideas. Divergent thinking includes the following abilities
  - **Fluency** The ability to generate many ideas for a given task or problem. More ideas a person produces the higher his fluency ability will be. For example, more the number of uses of a paper cup, more would be the fluency.
  - **Flexibility** The ability to think in different ways or from various perspectives. For example, a paper cup can be used as a container, a pencil holder or a drawing tool.
  - **Originality** The ability to produce rare or unusual ideas by seeing new relationships or combining old ideas with new ones. For example, combining food production with desert farming to extract protein from weeds is an original idea.
  - **Elaboration** The ability to expand on ideas, going into details and exploring their implications. For example, enhancing food production could involve using better seeds, fertilisers, irrigation and other creative solutions.

Importance of Both Thinking Styles

- **Divergent thinking** helps to generate a wide range of ideas.
- **Convergent thinking** helps to identify the most useful or appropriate idea.
- Both types are important for creative thinking, with divergent thinking generating ideas and convergent thinking narrowing them down to the best one.

Lateral Thinking

Edward de Bono introduced the term 'lateral thinking' to replace 'divergent thinking' given by Guilford. He differentiates between vertical thinking and lateral thinking. Vertical thinking involves mental operations that move in a straight line between lower and higher-level concepts. While lateral thinking involves looking for alternative ways to define and interpret problems. De Bono suggests that lateral thinking helps to make mental leaps and creates many ways of thinking. He developed the 'Six Thinking Hats' technique to generate different models of thinking.

These are

(i) **White Hat** Involves gathering information, facts, figures and filling gaps in information.
(ii) **Red Hat** Involves expressing feelings and emotions on the subject.
(iii) **Black Hat** Represents judgement, caution and logic.
(iv) **Yellow Hat** Focuses on thinking about what will work and why it will be beneficial.
(v) **Green Hat** Involves creativity, alternatives and changes.
(vi) **Blue Hat** Focuses on thinking about the process rather than the ideas themselves.

The 'Six Thinking Hats' represent different viewpoints from which an issue or problem can be viewed. This technique can be used both individually or in groups.

Process of Creative Thinking

- The starting point in the creative process is the need to think or bring out something new, which sparks the effort.
- The need for new ideas and solutions arises from recognising problems and gaps in information.

The process of creative thinking includes several stages

1. **Preparation Stage**
   - Creative thinking begins with understanding the task or problem at hand, analysing it and becoming aware of the background facts and related information.
   - This stage raises curiosity and excitement, leading the person to think in various directions.
   - Divergent thinking abilities play an important role in this stage.
2. **Incubation Stage**
   - In this stage, when a person is trying to develop alternative ideas and viewing the problem from unusual viewpoints, they may feel stuck or frustrated.
   - The individual may leave the problem for some time, leading to a period of **incubation**[2].
   - Research shows that creative ideas may not come immediately during incubation, but rather when the individual is not consciously thinking about the problem, such as while sleeping, waking up, taking a bath or walking.
3. **Illumination Stage**
   - This stage is associated with the emergence of creative ideas.
   - A person feels excitement and satisfaction when they find a creative idea.
4. **Verification Stage**
   - This is the final stage where the worth or suitability of the ideas or solutions is tested and judged.
   - Convergent thinking plays a role in selecting the appropriate idea or solution that works.

2 **Incubation** It is a stage in the creative or problem solving process in which attention (consciousness) is diverted from the task at hand and focuses on something else.

Quick Test 2

1 Mention one difference between judgement and decision-making?
2 Explain the role of creative thinking in problem-solving.
3 What is the significance of convergent thinking in the creative process?
4 Describe the stages of creative thinking.
5 What is lateral thinking?
6 Who proposed two types of creative thinking?

Strategies for Creative Thinking

Researchers have proven that certain attitudes, dispositions and skills in creative people help to facilitate their creative thinking. Some strategies to improve creative thinking abilities and skills are

Cultivate Different Activities

- Become more aware and sensitive to your surroundings to notice and respond to feelings, sights, sounds, textures and other elements around you.
- Spot problems, missing information, anomalies (things that are different from the standard), gaps and deficiencies.
- Try to notice contradictions and incompleteness in situations that others may not notice.
- Cultivate the habit of wider reading, exposure to a variety of information and develop the art of asking questions.
- Ponder over the mysteries of situations and objects to improve creative thinking.

Develop New Attitudes

- Generate ideas, responses, solutions or suggestions for a given task or situation to increase your flow of thoughts.
- Intentionally look for multiple angles of a task or situation to increase flexibility in your thinking.
- For example
  - Think of alternative arrangements of furniture in a room to create more space.
  - Explore different ways of conversing with people.
  - Look for costs and benefits of a course of study or career.
  - Explore ways of helping others.

Using Various Techniques

- Osborn's Brainstorming Technique can be used to increase fluency and flexibility of ideas for open-ended situations.
- Brainstorming is based on the principle that, generating ideas should be kept separate from evaluating their worth.
- The basic assumption is to allow the mind to think freely and judgement about the worth of ideas should be postponed until all ideas are exhausted.
- Brainstorming can be practised by playing brainstorming games with family and friends, keeping these principles in mind.
- For examples of brainstorming questions include
  - What other changes could be made?
  - In how many ways could it be done?
  - What could be the other uses of this object?

7.6 Thought and Language

- The relationship between language and thought can be explained through three different aspects
  - (i) Language determines thought.
  - (ii) Thought determines language.
  - (iii) Language has different origins.

Language as Determinant of Thought

- In Hindi and other Indian languages, there are many different words for various kinship relationships (e.g., different terms for mother's brother, father's elder brother, etc.).
- In English, the term 'uncle' is used for all these kinship relationships.
- Some tribal languages have only two or four colour terms, while English has many words for colours.
- Benjamin Lee Whorf proposed the linguistic relativity hypothesis, suggesting that language determines the contents of thought.
- According to linguistic determinism, an individual's thinking is determined by the language and linguistic categories they use.
- Experimental evidence suggests that the quality and level of thought can be similar in all languages, depending on the availability of linguistic categories and structures. Some thoughts may be easier in one language than another.

Thought as Determinant of Language

- Jean Piaget, a Swiss psychologist, suggested that thought not only determines language but also precedes it. He also argued that children form internal representations of the world through thinking.
- For example, when children see something and later copy it (a process called imitation), thinking happens, but it does not involve language. A child's observation of others' behaviour and imitation of that behaviour involves thinking, but not language.
- Language is just one means of thinking.
- As actions become internalised, language may affect a child's range of symbolic thinking but is not necessary for the origins of thought.
- Piaget believed that though language can be taught to children, it is important to understand words, which require knowledge of the concepts (thinking).
- Thus, thought is basic and necessary for understanding language.

Different Origins of Language and Thought

- Lev Vyogotsky, a Russian psychologist, proposed that thoughts and language develop separately in a child until about two years of age. Before this age, thought occurs prior to the development of speech and is experienced more in action.
- This stage is in line with Piaget's sensory motor stage. At around two years of age, the child starts to express their thoughts verbally and their speech begins to reflect rationality.
- Vyogotsky believed that children are capable of handling thoughts using soundless speech, also known as Inner speech. During this period, the development of language and thinking becomes interdependent. The quality of inner speech plays a crucial role in the development of conceptual thinking and the reverse is also true-conceptual thinking impacts the quality of inner speech.

- Thought can be used without language when the vehicle of thinking is non-verbal, such as through visual or movement-related forms. Language, on the other hand, can be used without thought when it is used simply to express feelings or engage in social pleasantries. For example, saying "Good morning! How are you?" and responding with "Very well, I am fine" is a form of communication that does not necessarily involve deep thought.
- When the two functions–thought and language–overlap, they can be used together to produce verbal thought and rational speech, thereby contributing to higher-order thinking and effective communication.

7.7 Development of Language and Language Use

- In the absence of language, humans would not be able to communicate their ideas and feelings. Language is also essential for gaining access to what others think and feel. For example, as a child, when you first started saying 'ma…ma…ma', it not only gave you the motivation to continue repeating this activity but also became a joyous moment for your parents.
- Gradually, you learned to say 'ma' and 'papa', and later, you started combining two or more words to communicate your needs, feelings and thoughts. You also learned words appropriate for different situations and acquired the rules for constructing sentences.
- Initially, you learned your mother tongue at home, and later, formal language and other languages were learned at school. Looking back, you would realise that your journey from saying 'ma…ma…ma' to mastering many languages has been a fascinating process of language development.

Meaning and Nature of Language

- Language consists of a system of symbols that are organised by certain rules and it is used to communicate with one another. There are three fundamental characteristics of language
  (i) **Symbols** Symbols represent something or someone else. For example, we call the place where we live 'home', the place where we study 'school' and the food we eat 'food'. These words do not carry meaning by themselves but acquire meaning when they are associated with particular objects, events, or concepts. Over a time, we recognise those objects or events through their corresponding words (symbols).
  (ii) **Set of Rules** While combining two or more words, we follow a specific and accepted order, which is governed by certain rules. For instance, the phrase 'I am going to school' follows a specific word order, whereas 'School am going I' would not be considered a grammatically correct sentence in English.
  (iii) **Communication** Language is primarily used for communicating one's thoughts, ideas, intentions and feelings to others. It is not only restricted to verbal communication but also includes non-verbal communication, such as gestures or postures, which are essential components of body language. Sign language, used by people with severe hearing and speech impairments, is also considered a form of language.

Development of Language

- Language is a complex system unique to human beings. While psychologists have tried to teach sign language and the use of symbols to animals like chimpanzees, dolphins and parrots, it is observed that human language is much more complex, creative and spontaneous compared to the communication systems used by other animals.
- There is also a discernible pattern with which children all over the world learn the language or languages they are exposed to.
- When comparing individual children, there are differences in the rate of language development. However, when considering the general process of language acquisition across the globe, a predictable pattern emerges. Children move from having almost no use of language to becoming competent language users. This development follows specific stages.

Stages of Language Development

There are different stages through which language develops. These are

Infant Stage

- Newborn babies and young infants produce a variety of sounds, which gradually become modified and start resembling words.
- Crying is the first sound they make. Initially, the pattern of crying is the same across various situations.
- However, as infants grow, the pitch and intensity of their cries change according to different needs such as hunger, pain or sleepiness.
- These early cries gradually transform into cooing sounds, which are usually associated with happiness.

Babbling Stage

- At around six months of age, infants enter the babbling stage. Babbling involves the continuous repetition of various consonant and vowel sounds (e.g., 'da-aa-ba-').
- Around nine months of age, these sounds develop into more structured combinations, forming repetitive patterns known as Echolalia (e.g., 'dadadada').
- While the early babbling is random and accidental, later babbling patterns often seem to imitate the sounds of adult speech. By the time they are six months old, children show some understanding of a few words.

One-Word Stage

- Around the age of one year, most children enter the one-word stage. Their first words typically consist of one syllable.
- As they progress, they start combining one or more words to form simple sentences or phrases, known as Holophrases.
- These holophrases often represent entire thoughts or ideas using a single word, like 'milk' to indicate a request for milk.

Two-Word Stage

- Around 18 to 20 months, children enter the two-word stage. At this stage, they begin combining two words to express basic ideas or requests.
- These two-word combinations are often referred to as Telegraphic speech, as they consist primarily of nouns and verbs, similar to the brevity used in telegrams (e.g., 'got admission', 'send money').

Language Acquisition

- Nature vs. Nurture Most psychologists agree that both nature and nurture play an essential role in language acquisition. According to the behaviourist BF Skinner, language is learned in the same manner as other behaviours-through association, imitation and reinforcement. Language development, as per behaviourists, follows learning principles such as
  (i) **Association** The sight of an object, like a bottle, is associated with the word 'bottle'.
  (ii) **Imitation** Children learn words by imitating the words used by adults (e.g. when adults say 'bottle').
  (iii) **Reinforcement** Children receive positive reinforcement, such as smiles or hugs, when they correctly use a word.
- According to the principle of shaping, children progressively approximate the desired linguistic responses, leading to them speaking in a manner similar to adults. Regional variations in pronunciation and phrasing illustrate how different patterns of language use are reinforced in different areas.

Chomsky's View on Language

- Linguist Noam Chomsky proposed the nativist theory of language development, asserting that children are born with an innate ability to acquire language. Chomsky argued that the rate at which children acquire words and grammar, without explicit teaching, cannot be explained solely by learning principles. Children also generate sentences they have never heard before, indicating that they are not merely imitating.
- Chomsky also emphasised the concept of a critical period–a time when learning must take place for it to be successful. He believed that children are born with a universal grammar that allows them to learn any language to which they are exposed. In this view, language acquisition is a natural process that occurs given the right exposure, much like physical maturation.
- While Skinner's behaviourist theory explains how infants acquire the language they hear and how they add new words to their vocabularies, Chomsky's theory emphasises our inherent readiness to learn grammar, explaining why children acquire language so readily without direct teaching.

Bilingualism and Multilingualism

- Bilingualism refers to the ability to communicate proficiently in two languages.
- Multilingualism refers to the ability to communicate proficiently in more than two languages.
- The term mother tongue is commonly used to describe a person's native language-the language spoken from infancy, usually within the home environment. It is often considered the language with which one emotionally identifies, typically the language spoken by the mother or primary caregiver.

Language Use

- Language use refers to the ability to use language appropriately in different social contexts. It goes beyond simply knowing the vocabulary and grammar of a language.
- While knowledge of words and sentence structure is important, effective language use requires understanding how to communicate appropriately according to social norms and specific situations.
- When using language, individuals have various practical intentions such as making requests, asking questions, expressing gratitude or giving demands. For language to achieve its social purpose, it must not only be grammatically correct and meaningful but also contextually appropriate and suitable for the situation.
- Children often face challenges in using language in ways that are socially suitable. For example, they may struggle with choosing the right words or tone when making polite requests or expressing gratitude. Instead of making a polite request, children may unintentionally sound commanding or demanding.
- Additionally, children also have difficulty in taking turns during conversations. Unlike adults, who naturally understand when to speak and when to listen, children need to develop the social skills of turn-taking and maintain a balance between speaking and listening in conversations.

Quick Test 3

1. Who proposed that language decides the contents of thought?
2. What is the importance of cultivating different activities for improving creative thinking?
3. Name the basic principle of Osborn's Brainstorming Technique.
4. Mention one key difference between bilingualism and multilingualism.
5. Name the key stages of language development in children.
6. In which stage children enter around 1 year of age?

NCERT Folder

1. Explain the nature of thinking.

Ans. Thinking is the foundation for all cognitive (mental) activities or processes and is unique to human beings. It involves manipulation and analysis of information received from the environment. Thinking is a higher mental process using which we manipulate and analyse the acquired or existing information.

Such manipulation and analysis is done using ways like abstracting, reasoning, imagining, problem solving, judging and decision-making.

Thinking is mainly organised and goal directed. For example, every individual desires to reach the goal by planning, recalling the steps one has already followed in the past if the task is familiar or different strategies if the task is new.

Thinking is an internal mental process, which can be inferred from one's behaviour. For example, if you see a chess player engrossed in thinking for several minutes before making a move, you cannot observe what he is thinking. You can simply guess what he was thinking or what strategies he was typing to evaluate, from his next move.

2. What is a concept? Explain the role of concept in the thinking process.

Ans. A concept is a mental representation of a category and refers to a class of objects, ideas or events that share common properties.

Role of concept can be understood through the following points

- Concept formation helps us in organising our knowledge and thus helps us in accessing it with less time and effort. It is like organising things at our home.
- For example, children who are systematic and organised, arrange their things like books, bags and other items in specific places in their cupboard, so that in the morning, they can easily find a particular book or pencil box.
- In library, we also find that books are arranged as per subject areas and labelled, so that one can find them quickly with less effort.

  Thus, in order to make our thought process quick and efficient, we form concepts and categorise objects and events.

3. Identify obstacles that one may encounter in problem-solving.

Ans. Two main obstacles that one may encounter in problem solving are

(i) **Mental Set** It is the tendency to solve problems using previously tried methods or strategies, which can lead to mental rigidity. This prevents individuals from adapting to new approaches and hinders effective problem solving.

(ii) **Lack of Motivation** When individuals are not motivated, they may give up easily, especially when faced with challenges or failures. Motivation is essential for persevering through difficulties and continuing to search for solutions.

4. How does reasoning help in solving problems?

Ans. Reasoning is the process of gathering and analysing information to arrive at conclusions. It is also a form of problem solving. The goal is to determine what conclusion can be drawn from certain given information. There are different types of reasoning like deductive, inductive or analogy.

(i) **Deductive Reasoning** The kind of reasoning that starts with an assumption is called deductive reasoning. A general assumption is made that we know or believe to be true and then we draw specific conclusion based on this assumption.

(ii) **Inductive Reasoning** Reasoning that is based on specific facts and observation is called inductive reasoning. It is drawing a general conclusion based on particular observation. Most cases of scientific reasoning are inductive in nature.

(iii) **Analogy** It is another form of reasoning which involves four parts. A is to B as C is to D with the relation between the first two parts being the same as the relation between the last two parts. Analogies help us in solving problems. They help us in identifying and visualising the salient properties of an object or event.

5. Are judgement and decision-making interrelated processes? Explain.

Ans. Yes, judgement and decision-making are interrelated processes. In decision-making we choose one option among different alternatives based on cost and benefit of each alternative. Decision making is different from other types of problem solving. In decision making we already know the various solutions or choices one has to be selected.

In judgement and decision-making we draw conclusions, form opinions, evaluate events, objects, based on knowledge and available evidences. Sometimes we make judgements automatically without any effort. We also make changes to our judgements based on newly acquired information. Judgements are thus dependent on our beliefs and attitudes.

6. Why is divergent thinking important in creative thinking process?

Ans. Divergent thinking is important in the creative thinking process because it helps to generate a wide range of novel and original ideas. It promotes fluency, flexibility, originality and elaboration, allowing individuals to think of different solutions or answers to a problem.

By exploring various possibilities and combinations, divergent thinking facilitates the creation of new and unique concepts, which are essential for creativity.

7. How can creative thinking be enhanced?

Ans. Strategies to enhance memory

- **Originality** Originality can be developed by practicing fluency, flexibility, habit of associative thinking, exploring linkages, and fusing distinct or remote ideas.
- **Use of Imagination** Engaging more frequently in activities which require use of imagination and original thinking rather than routine work according to interest and hobbies.
- **Not to accept initial ideas** Never accepting the first ideas or solution. Many ideas die because we reject them thinking that the idea might be silly i.e. we have to first generate a number of possible ideas or solutions, then select the best from among them.
- **Getting feedback** By getting a feedback on the solutions we decide one from others who are less personally involved in the task.
- **Chance to Incubate** Giving ideas the chance to incubate means to allow time for incubation between production of ideas and the stages of evaluation of ideas, may bring in the good experience.
- **Diagram thinking** Sometimes ideas cluster like branches of a tree. It is useful to diagram our thinking so that we can follow each possible branch to its completion.
- **Developing independent thinking** Developing independent thinking in making judgements, figuring out things without any help or resources.
- **Self-confident** To be self-confident and positive. Never undermine your creative potential to experience the joy of your creation.

8. Does thinking take place without language? Discuss.

Ans. Thinking cannot take place without language. Benjamin Lee Whorf proposed that language decides the contents of thought. This view is called linguistic relativity hypothesis.

In its strong version, this hypothesis suggests that, the thinking of individuals is determined by the language and linguistic categories they use. This is called linguistic determinism.

But, experimental evidence shows that it is possible to have the same level or quality of thoughts in all languages depending upon the availability of linguistic categories and structures. Some thoughts may be easier in one language compared to another.

9. How is language acquired in human beings?

Ans. To achieve linguistic competence, children must master the four sub-systems of language

(i) **Phonology** The ability to understand and produce speech sounds.

(ii) **Semantics** The ability to understand words and the different combinations of words.

(iii) **Grammar** The ability to understand the rules by which words are arranged into sentences and the rules by which words can indicate tense and gender.

(iv) **Pragmatics** The ability to understand the rules of effective communication such as turn-taking, initiating and ending conversations and so on.

There are two contrasting views on how language is acquired. Some suggest that language acquisition is primarily biologically determined. This is typically a nativist position in the nature-nurture debate. Other position is the environmentalist position which views learning as the basis of language acquisition.Language development for behaviourists like B.F. Skinner follows the learning principles such as association, imitation, and reinforcement. They explain it in terms of operant conditioning. Regional differences in pronunciation and phrasing illustrate how different patterns are reinforced in different areas. The nativist view supported by Noam Chomsky argues that human beings' extraordinary capacity to learn and use language is based on certain innate mechanisms.

Chomsky suggested that children are born with powerful language acquisition device, LAD, which represents a knowledge of universal grammar. Children throughout the world seem to have a critical period that is from infancy to puberty where learning must occur if it is to occur successfully for learning language. Most psychologists accept that both nature and nurture are important in language acquisition.

Exam Pattern Questions

Objective Type Questions

Multiple Choice Questions (MCQs)

1. **If we think that hammer is used only to hit nails and nothing else. What is this problem called?**

(a) Functional fixedness (b) Mental set
(c) Analogy (d) Emotional disability

2. **What indicates variety in thinking in the divergent thinking abilities?**

(a) Fluency (b) Originality
(c) Elaboration (d) Flexibility

3. **Which hat in 'six thinking hats' technique covers thinking on what will work and why it will be beneficial?**

(a) White (b) Yellow (c) Black (d) Blue

4. **Feeling of excitement, even satisfaction kind of things are found in which stage of creative thinking?**

(a) Incubation (b) Verification
(c) Preparation (d) Illumination

5. **Who among these took years of experimentation with hundreds of failures before he produced the first bulb?**

(a) Albert Einstein (b) Issac Newton
(c) Thomas Alva Edison (d) Madam Curie

6. **Who among these suggested that thought not only determines language, but also precedes it?**

(a) Lev Vyogotsky (b) Jean Piaget
(c) Benjamin Lee Whorf (d) Osborn

7. **What involves continued repetition of a variety of consonants and vowel sounds?**

(a) Babbling (b) Cognition
(c) Thinking (d) Communication

8. **Which of the following attributes is related with divergent thinking?**

I. Fluency **II. Flexibility**
III. Originality **IV. Elaboration**

Codes

(a) I and II (b) II and III
(c) I, II and III (d) I, II, III and IV

9. **Which of the following statements are true regarding convergent thinking?**

I. It helps in producing novel and original ideas.
II. It is required to solve problems with only one correct answer.
III. It indicates variety in thinking and flexibility.
IV. It involves the mind converging to the correct solution.

Codes

(a) I and III (b) II and IV (c) I and II (d) III and IV

10. **Which of the following is correct for divergent thinking abilities?**

I. Flexibility indicates variety in thinking.
II. Elaboration helps in going into details and working out implications of ideas.
III. Fluency involves identifying the single most appropriate idea.
IV. Originality is the ability to produce rare and unusual ideas.

Codes

(a) I and II (b) II and III
(c) I, II and IV (d) I, III and IV

11. **What type of building block of thought is used when you imagine a cat sitting on a tree with its tail slightly raised and curved?**

I. Concept formation **II. Mental image**
III. Holistic thinking **IV. Analytical thinking**

Codes

(a) I and III (b) II and III (c) II and IV (d) Only II

12. **Which type of concept formation involves matching an unfamiliar object with already existing categories based on shared characteristics?**

I. Analytical thinking **II. Concept formation**
III. Divergent thinking **IV. Mental imagery**

Codes

(a) I and II (b) II and III (c) II and IV (d) III and IV

Assertion-Reason Questions

Directions (Q. Nos. 13-19) In the following questions, a statement of Assertion (A) is followed by a statement of Reason (R). Mark the correct choice from the options given below.

(a) Both A and R are true and R is the correct explanation of A.
(b) Both A and R are true, but R is not the correct explanation of A.
(c) A is true, but R is false.
(d) A is false, but R is true.

13. **Assertion** (A) An image is a mental representation of a sensory experience.

Reason (R) It can be used to think about things, places and events.

14. **Assertion** (A) Concept formation helps us in organising our knowledge.

Reason (R) It helps us in accessing it with less time and effort.

15. **Assertion** (A) Decision-making is a process that always involves detailed evaluation of all possible outcomes.

Reason (R) In decision-making, decisions are often made quickly and sometimes, not all outcomes are evaluated in detail.

16. **Assertion** (A) Reasoning is a form of problem-solving that involves the process of gathering and analysing information to reach a conclusion.

Reason (R) Reasoning helps in problem-solving by using mental operations and steps to evaluate different solutions and make conclusions.

17. **Assertion** (A) Inductive reasoning involves starting with a general assumption and drawing conclusions based on it.

Reason (R) Inductive reasoning begins with specific facts or observations and leads to general conclusions or theories.

18. **Assertion** (A) Children acquire language through natural exposure, without direct teaching.

Reason (R) According to behaviourists, children learn language through association, imitation and reinforcement by caregivers.

19. **Assertion** (A) Babbling in infants involves repetition of consonant and vowel sounds and later becomes more imitative of adult speech.

Reason (R) Babbling starts as random sounds and becomes purposeful when children start recognising words and their meanings.

Answers

1. (a) Functional fixedness
2. (d) Flexibility
3. (b) Yellow
4. (d) Illumination
5. (c) Thomas Alva Edison
6. (b) Jean Piaget
7. (a) Babbling
8. (d) I, II, III and IV
9. (b) II and IV
10. (c) I, II and IV
11. (d) Only II
12. (b) II and III
13. (b) Both A and R are true, but R is not the correct explanation of A.
14. (a) Both A and R are true and R is the correct explanation of A.
15. (d) A is false, but R is true.
16. (a) Both A and R are true and R is the correct explanation of A.
17. (d) A is false, but R is true.
18. (b) Both A and R are ture, but R is not the correct explanation of A.
19. (a) Both A and R are true and R is the correct explanation of A.

Subjective Questions

Very Short Answer Type Questions

1. Define thinking.

Ans. Thinking is the foundation for all cognitive (mental) activities or processes and is unique to human beings. It involves manipulation and analysis of information received from the environment.

2. How can you classify the concepts?

Ans. Concepts usually are classified based on hierarchies or levels of understanding. They are superordinate i.e. the highest level, basic i.e. an intermediate level and subordinate i.e. the lowest level.

3. How do people match prototypes?

Ans. In prototype matching, people decide whether an item is a member of a category, by comparing it with the most unique items of the category.

4. What is problem-solving?

Ans. Problem-solving is thinking that is goal-directed. It refers to cognitive processing directed at achieving a goal when the problem solver does not initially know a solution method.

5. Seema is a talented girl but she usually afraids while doing any science project as she is not motivated by her elders. What happens if people are not motivated?

Competency Based Que.

Ans. If people are not motivated, then all their skills and talents are of no use. Sometimes people give up easily when they encounter a problem or failure in implementing the first step.

6. Define deductive reasoning.

Ans. The kind of reasoning that starts with an assumption is called Deductive reasoning. A general assumption is made that we know or believe to be true and then we draw specific conclusion based on this assumption.

7. What is inductive reasoning?

Ans. Reasoning that is based on specific facts and observation is called inductive reasoning. It is drawing a general conclusion based on particular observation. Most cases of scientific reasoning are inductive in nature.

8. Give the meaning of effective surprise?

Ans. Burner calls creative thinking as effective surprise, i.e. if the product or idea is unusual, the response of most who experience it is one of instant surprise or of being shocked.

9. Define fluency.

Ans. Fluency is the ability to produce many ideas for a given task or a problem. The more ideas a person produces, the higher his fluency ability.

10. What is the significance of 'Six Thinking Hats'?

Ans. De Bono developed, 'Six Thinking Hats' technique to generate different models of thinking. The 'Six Thinking Hats' reflect different viewpoints from which an issue or problem is viewed. The technique can be used individually as well as in groups.

11. What happens in illumination stage?

Ans. Illumination stage is associated with the moment we normally associate with emergence of creative ideas. There usually is a feeling of excitement, even satisfaction, of having found a creative idea.

12. List three different viewpoints on language and thought.

Ans. The three different viewpoints with respect to language and thought are

(i) Language determines thought.

(ii) Thought determines language.

(iii) Thought and language have different origins.

13. What are the basic characteristics of language?

Ans. There are three basic characteristics of the language

(i) The presence of symbols

(ii) A set of rules to organise these symbols

(iii) Communication

14. Distinguish between bilingualism and multilingualism.

Ans. Bilingualism refers to attaining high level of skill in communicating through any two languages. While learning of more than two languages is referred to as multilingualism.

15. How is thinking represented?

Ans. Thinking depends on knowledge we already have, which is represented either in images or words. People usually think using images or words.

16. Ram is a chess player, he is thinking of his next move. What can you infer from this behaviour?

Competency Based Que.

Ans. Thinking is an internal mental process, which can be inferred from one's behaviour. If you see a chess player thinking, we cannot observe what he is thinking, but we can infer about his thinking and strategies from his next move.

17. Differentiate between vertical and lateral thinking.

Ans. Vertical thinking involves mental operations that move in a straight line back and forth between lower and higher level concepts, whereas lateral thinking involves looking for alternative ways of defining and interpreting problems.

18. Differentiate between Noam Chomsky and Skinner's views on language.

Ans. Skinner's stress on learning explains why infants acquire the language they hear and how they add new words to their vocabularies.

While Chomsky's stress on our built-in readiness to learn grammar explain why children acquire language so readily without direct teaching.

Short Answer Type Questions

1. Surbhi has been assigned a project on a social problem. To conduct her study she needs to know about the steps of problem solving. List steps of mental operations involved. Competency Based Que.

Ans. In problem solving there are two states i.e. initial state which is problem and there is an end state which is goal. These two states are connected by means of several steps of mental operations. Following are those steps

- Identify the problem
- Represent the problem
- Plan the solution: set sub-goods
- Evaluate all solutions
- Select one solution and execute it
- Evaluate the outcomes
- Rethink and redefine problems and solutions

2. What do you know about Osborn's Brainstorm Technique?

Ans. Osborn's Brainstorming Technique can be used to increase fluency and flexibility of ideas to open-ended situations. Brainstorming is based on the principle that producing ideas should be kept separate from the evaluation of their worth. The basic assumption is to let the minds think freely.

This helps in increasing the fluency of ideas and piling up alternatives. Brainstorming can be practised by playing brainstorming games with family members and friends keeping its principles in mind.

3. Explain the basic characteristics of the language in detail.

Ans. There are three basic characteristics of the language

(i) **Symbols** It represents something or someone else. For example we call the place where we live as 'home', where we study as 'school', the thing we eat is called 'food'. These words usually do not carry any meaning by themselves, but when these words are used along with some objects/events they attain meaning and we begin recognising those objects/events, etc with particular words (symbols).

(ii) **Rules** While combining two or more words we usually follow a definite and accepted order of presenting these words, which are called rules. One would most likely say "I am going to school" and not "School am going I".

(iii) **Communication** Language is used for communicating one's thought, ideas, intentions and feelings to others.

Many times we communicate using our body parts, called gestures or postures. This is called Non-verbal communication. Sign language is also a form of language. People having severe hearing and speech problems, communicate using signs.

4. Elucidate Noam Chomsky's views on development of language.

Ans. Noam Chomsky proposed that language development is a natural process, driven by an innate ability rather than learned through imitation. He believed children are born with a universal grammar, which enables them to acquire the grammar of any language they are exposed to. Chomsky argued that children rapidly learn language without direct teaching, and their ability to create sentences they've never heard supports the idea of an inbuilt linguistic framework. He also emphasised the existence of a critical period for language learning, where language acquisition occurs most effectively.

5. How is thinking influenced by our beliefs, values and social practices?

Ans. The way we think is influenced by our beliefs, values and social practices.

A study was conducted on American and Asian students by showing pictures of fish swimming in underwater.

The subjects were asked to look at the picture and later asked to describe what they saw. The American students focussed on the biggest, brightest, and most unique features (like the biggest fish). On the other hand, the Asian students focussed on the background (like the bottom was rocky, water was green).

Based on these finding, researchers concluded that Americans usually analyse each object separately which is called analytical thinking. Asian people (Japanese, Chinese, Koreans) think more about the relationship between objects and backgrounds, which is called Holistic thinking.

6. Explain 'Six Thinking Hats' technique.

Ans. Edward de Bono developed the 'Six Thinking Hats' technique to generate different models of thinking. These are

- **White hat** includes gathering information, facts figures and filling gaps in information.
- **Red hat** covers expression of feelings and emotions on the subject.
- **Black hat** represents judgement, caution and logic.
- **Yellow hat** covers thinking on what will work and why it will be beneficial.

- **Green hat** is for creativity, alternatives and changes.
- **Blue hat** represents thinking about the process and not the ideas as such.

7. Explain Lev Vyogotsky views on thoughts and language in detail.

Ans. Lev Vyogotsky, a Russian psychologist, proposed that thoughts and language develop in a child separately until about two years of age and then they merge. Before two years thought occurs before development of speech and is experienced more in action. This is called Piaget's sensory motor stage.

The child's sounds are more of an automatic reactions like crying when uncomfortable than thought based.

Around two years of age, the child expresses thought verbally and her/his speech reflects rationality. Now children are able to handle thoughts using soundless speech.

He believed that during this period the development of language and thinking become interdependent. The development of conceptual thinking depends upon the quality of inner speech and *vice-versa.*

Thought is used without language when the vehicle of thinking is non-verbal like visual or movement related.

People use language without thought when they express their feelings or exchange pleasantries. For example, when a person say "Good morning?" How are you? the other person answers without giving any thought. "Very well, I am fine."

When the two functions overlap, they can be used together to produce verbal thought and rational speech.

8. "Multilingualism and use of mother tongue are a way of life in India." Explain.

Ans. Learning of more than two languages is referred to as multilingualism. The term mother tongue has been defined as one's native language, the language spoken by the individual from the cradle, language ordinarily used at home, language spoken by the mother, etc. But generally the mother tongue is viewed as a language with which one identifies at the emotional level. It is possible for individuals to have multiple mother tongues.

The Indian social context is looked by grass root multilingualism which makes bilingualism/ multilingualism a feature or quality at the levels of individual as well as society. Most Indians use more than one language to communicate in various sphere of their daily life activities. Thus, multilingualism is a way of life in India. Studies reveal that bilingualism/multilingualism helps cognitive, linguistic and academic competence of children.

9. How is language helpful for socially suitable ways of communication?

Ans. Language use involves knowing socially suitable ways of communication. Knowledge of vocabulary and syntax of a language does not ensure proper use of language to achieve the purpose of communication in a variety of social situations.

When we use language we have different practical intentions like requesting, asking, thanking, demanding, etc. In order to effectively serve these social goals, language use must be practically correct or contextually appropriate besides being grammatical and meaningful.

Children often have difficulty with choice of appropriate utterances for politeness or for requests and their use of language conveys a demand or a command instead of a polite request. When children are engaged in conver- sations, they also have difficulty in taking turns in speaking and listening like adults.

10. "Thought is basic and necessary if language is to be understood." Justify. Competency Based Que.

Ans. Jean Piaget, a Swiss psychologists, suggested that thought not only determines language, but also precedes (comes before) it. He argued that children form an internal representation of the world through thinking.

A child's observation of other's behaviour and imitation of the same behaviour, involve thinking but not language. Language is just one of the means of thinking.

As actions become part of their qualities, language may affect children's range of symbolic thinking but it is not necessary for the origins of thought. Piaget believed that though language can be taught to children, it is important to understand words and require knowledge of the concepts i.e. thinking. Thus, thought is basic and necessary if language is to be understood.

11. "Inductive and deductive reasoning allows us to make judgement." Justify this statement. Competency Based Que.

Ans. In judgement, we draw conclusions, form opinions, evaluate events, objects, based on knowledge and available evidences.

For example, consider if a man is very talkative, like to mix with people, can convince other with ease, then he would be most suitable for a salesperson's job. Our judgement of this person is based on the specific characteristics of an expert salesperson.

Sometimes judgements are automatic and requires no conscious effort by the person and occur as a matter of habit.

For example, applying brakes on seeing red light. However, evaluating a novel or literary text requires reference to your past knowledge and experience. Thus, our judgements are not dependent on our beliefs and attitudes. We can change our judgements based on newly acquired information.

Long Answer Type Questions

1. Explain different building blocks of thought.

Ans. Thinking depends on knowledge we already have, which is represented either in images or words. People usually think using images or words. Different building blocks of thought are as follows

- **Mental Image** An image is a mental representation of a sensory experience. It can be used to think about things, places and events. We all have experience in reading a map in which we remember the different places and later we locate them in a physical map in the examination.
- **Concepts** A concept is a mental representation of a category and refers to a class of objects, ideas or events that share common properties. When we come across an object or event which we are familiar or unfamiliar, we try to identify the object or event by looking at its characteristics. We match it with the already existing category of objects and events and if matching is perfect, we give it the name of that category.
- **Concept Formation** It helps us in organising our knowledge and thus helps us in accessing it with less time and effort. It is like organising things at our home. Children who are systematic and organised, arrange their things like books, bag and other items in specific places in their cupboard, so that in the morning, they can easily find a particular book or pencil box. Thus, in order to make our thought process quick and efficient, we form concepts and categorise objects and events.

2. What do you know about process of creative thinking? Explain different stages involved in it.

Ans. The starting point in creative process is the need to think or bring out something new which starts the effort. The need for looking for new ideas and solutions arises from sensing problems and gaps in information. There are different stages in process of creative thinking which are as follows

- **Preparation Stage** Process of creative thinking begins with preparation stage. It requires one to understand the task or problem in hand, analyse the problem and become aware of the background facts and related information.
  The process raises curiosity and excitement to think more and more in different directions. The persons tries to look at the task or problem from different angles and viewpoints. Divergent thinking abilities play important role in this stage.
- **Incubation Stage** In this stage, when a person is trying to develop alternative ideas and try to view the problem or task from an unusual viewpoint, there may be a feeling of getting stuck. One may even get disgusted with failure and may leave the problem or task for sometime. Research shows that creative ideas may occur or strike when a person is doing something else, for e.g. going to sleep, waking up, taking bath or just walking along.
- **Illumination Stage** This stage is associated with the moment that we normally associate with emergence of creative ideas.
- **Verification Stage** This is the final stage when the worth or suitability of ideas or solutions are tested and judged. Here, convergent thinking plays its role in selecting the appropriate idea or solution that works.

3. Explain different viewpoints explaining the relationship between language and thought in detail.

Ans. The relationship between language and thought is explained through three main viewpoints

(i) **Language as Determinant of Thought** According to Benjamin Lee Whorf's linguistic relativity hypothesis, language determines the content of thought known as Linguistic determinism which suggest that the language we speak shapes how we think. For example, different languages may have distinct words for kinship terms and some languages have more or fewer words for colours. This can affect how individuals perceive and categorise concepts. However, experimental evidence suggests that thoughts can be similar across languages.

(ii) **Thought as Determinant of Language** Jean Piaget argued that thought precedes language and determines it. He suggested that children form an internal representation of the world through thinking, even before they acquire language. For example, children may imitate actions or observe behaviours without using language. Piaget believed that language helps to express thoughts but is not essential for the formation of thoughts.

(iii) **Different Origins of Language and Thought** Lev Vygotsky proposed that thought and language develop separately until around two years of age, after which they merge. Before this age, thought is more action-based and non-verbal. Around the age of two, language begins to reflect rational thought and the two functions-thought and language become interdependent. Vygotsky also noted that thinking can occur without language and language can sometimes be used without thought. As children grow, verbal thought and rational speech emerge through the interaction of these two functions.

4. "Thinking is the base of all cognitive activities of processes and is unique to human beings." Discuss. Competency Based Que.

Ans. In all human being, thinking is unique and is the base of all cognitive activities or processes. It involves manipulation and analysis of information received from the environment. For example, while seeing a painting, you are not simply focusing on the colour of the painting or lines or strokes, rather you are going beyond the given text in interpreting its meaning and you are trying to relate the information to your existing knowledge.

Understanding of the painting involves creation of new meaning that is added to your knowledge. Thinking, therefore, is a higher mental process through which we manipulate and analyse the acquired or existing information.

Such manipulation and analysis occur by means of abstracting, reasoning, imaging, problem solving, judging and decision-marking. Thinking is mostly organised and goal directed. All day-to -day activities ranging from cooking to solving a math problem have a goal. One desire to reach the goal by planning and recalling the steps that one has already followed in the past, if the task is familiar or inferring strategies if the task is new.

5. Lisa is doing a research work on language development, she finds out there are various stages through which language develops. Analyse these stages. Competency Based Que.

Ans. During her research work Lisa, finds out that there are various stages through which language develops. These stages are as follows

- **Infant Stage** Lisa finds out that newborn babies and young infants make different sounds, which slowly get modified to resemble words. Crying is the first sound they make. Initial crying is same across different situations. Slowly, the pattern of crying changes in its pitch and intensity is based on different moods like hunger, pain and sleepiness, etc. These different crying sounds slowly become more meaningful 'cooing sounds' which usually express happiness.
- **Babbling Stage** Lisa observes a six month baby who is supposed to enter babbling stage at this age. Babbling involves continued repetition of a variety of consonants and vowel sounds. Around nine months of age, these sounds get developed to strings of some sound combinations into repetitive patterns called **echolalia**. For example, 'dadadadadada'. While the early babblings are random or accidental in nature, the later babblings seem to be imitative of adult voices. Children show some understanding of a few words by the time they are six months old.
- **One-Word Stage** Lisa then observes a child of 1 year of age. Around this age, most children enter the one-word stage. Their first word usually contains one syllable. Slowly they move to one or more words which are combined to form whole sentences or phrases. Hence they are called **Holophrases**.
- **Two-Word Stage** Lisa finds out that around 18 to 20 months of age, children enter a two-word stage and begin or start to use two words together. The two-word stage is an example of telegraphic speech i.e. short sentences used in telegrams. i.e. got admission, send money, etc. They contain mainly nouns and verbs.

  Close to their third birthday, i.e. beyond two and a half years, children's language development gets focused on rules of the language they hear.

Case Based Questions

1. Read the case and answer the questions that follow.

Thinking depends on knowledge we already have, which is represented either in images or words (concepts). People usually think by means of mental images or words. For example, suppose you are travelling by road to reach a place, which you had visited long back. You would try to use the visual representation of the street and other places.

(i) What is the role of mental images in thinking according to the above content?

(ii) How does thinking depend on the existing knowledge we have?

Ans. (i) Mental images play a significant role in thinking as they allow individuals to form visual representations of places, events or objects. In the case of travelling to a place previously visited, mental images help in recalling the layout of streets and landmarks, guiding the person through the journey.

(ii) Thinking depends on the existing knowledge we have by using mental images or words (concepts) to process and make sense of information. When travelling to a familiar place, individuals rely on their mental images of the location, while in other situations, they use concepts formed by knowledge of categories (such as authors or themes when choosing a book).

2. Read the case and answer the questions that follow.

Your teacher asks you to imagine a cat sitting on a tree with its tail slightly raised and curved. You would most likely try to form a visual image of the whole situation, something similar to what the girl in the picture is doing. In another scenario, when you read a map, you remember the different places and subsequently locate them in a physical map in your examination.

While walking on the road you come across an unfamiliar quadruped of a very small size, with a face like a dog, wagging its tail and barking at strangers. As a result, you identified it as a dog.

(i) **Which process is used to manipulate and analyse the acquired or existing information? Discuss it.**

(ii) **Thinking is an internal mental process, which can be inferred from which type of behaviour? Give an example.**

Ans. (i) Thinking is used to manipulate and analyse the acquired or existing information.

Thinking is the foundation for all mental (cognitive) activities or processes. It is unique to human beings. It involves manipulation and analysis of information received from the environment.

(ii) Thinking is an internal process, which can be inferred from overt behaviour. For example, if you see a chess player engrossed in thinking for several minutes before making a move, you cannot observe what he is thinking. You can simply infer what he was thinking or what strategies he was trying to evaluate, from his next move.

3. Read the case and answer the questions that follow.

Sandy is a software engineer who faces frequent challenges in his work. He has to constantly solve technical problems related to software bugs, system failures and performance optimisation. One day, Sandy encounters a situation where a software bug is causing an application to crash repeatedly, even after several attempts to fix it using the same debugging steps. He tries to solve the problem using methods that have worked for similar issues in the past, but the issue persists. Frustrated, Sandy realises that his usual approach might not be effective this time. He takes a step back, redefines the problem and comes up with a new approach. After evaluating different solutions and testing them, he successfully resolves the issue.

(i) **What obstacle did Sandy face while solving the problem? How did he overcome it?**

(ii) **What role did reasoning play in solving Sandy's problem?**

Ans. (i) Sandy faced the obstacle of mental set. This occurs when a person becomes rigid in their approach, relying on methods that have worked in the past. Sandy overcame this by rethinking the problem, redefining it and trying a new approach. He evaluated different solutions before successfully resolving the issue.

(ii) Reasoning played a significant role as Sandy gathered information, evaluated different solutions and tested them logically to reach the correct conclusion. He used inductive reasoning to draw conclusions based on specific observations of the software's behaviour and applied them to fix the problem effectively.

4. Read the case and answer the questions that follow.

Ashish Panwar, a student of Class XI, participated in the first International Robotics Olympiad held at Glasgow. He won a bronze medal for assembling a five feet tall robot. Ashish's creativity and skills in robotics reflect how creative thinking can lead to extraordinary achievements. The process of building a robot required not just technical knowledge but also novel ideas and innovative problem-solving approaches, highlighting the application of divergent thinking. Divergent thinking helps individuals come up with various solutions and in Ashish's case, it helped him think outside the box and design something that others might not have considered.

(i) **In the given case, what kind of thinking helped Ashish to achieve the success? Which of the following defines the type of thinking Ashish used?**

(ii) **How does divergent thinking help in the process of creative thinking?**

Ans. (i) Ashish used divergent thinking. The following points define the type of thinking Ashish used

- He created a novel and original design for the robot.
- His thinking was open-ended, allowing him to explore various ideas to assemble the robot.
- Divergent thinking helped him come up with different solutions and aspects to focus on while building the robot.

(ii) Divergent thinking is essential in creative thinking because it encourages the generation of multiple ideas and solutions. In Ashish's case, divergent thinking allowed him to explore a wide range of approaches to assemble the robot. The ability to think flexibly and generate numerous ideas helped him identify the best solutions to challenges during the building process, ultimately leading to his success at the competition.

5. Read the case and answer the questions that follow.

Children enter different stages of language development as they grow. For example, around six months, babies start to babble, repeating sounds like 'da-aa-ba' or 'dadadada'. Initially, these sounds are random and not associated with any particular meaning. However, by the time they are one year old, children typically start using single words like 'ma' or 'papa'. By 18 to 20 months, they begin using two-word combinations such as 'want cookie' or 'big dog'. Over time, their language develops and they start learning the rules of grammar by the age of three, using longer and more complex sentences.

(i) **At what age do children usually enter the babbling stage and what sounds do they produce at this stage?**

(ii) **How does language development progress from the babbling stage?**

Ans. (i) Children enter the babbling stage around six months of age. At this stage, they produce repetitive consonant vowel sounds like 'da-aa-ba' or 'dadadada'.

(ii) After the babbling stage, children progress to the one-word stage around one year of age, where they start saying single words like 'ma' or 'papa'. By 18 to 20 months, they move on to the two-word stage, using combinations like 'want cookie' or 'big dog'.

SELF ASSESSMENT TEST

Objective Type Questions

1. Rearrangement of concepts to overcome a difficulty would mean

(a) reasoning
(b) problem-solving
(c) creative thinking
(d) None of these

2. Thinking is closely related to

(a) language
(b) feelings
(c) perception
(d) ideas

3. Noam Chomsky pioneered

(a) Nativist theory of language acquisition
(b) Linguistic relativity by pothesis
(c) Combination of conditioning theory
(d) Verbal learning theory

Very Short Answer Type Questions

1. What do you mean by creative thinking?

2. Define flexibility.

3. What is judgement?

4. Mention two major obstacles in sloving a problem.

5. Define mental set.

6. What is functional fixedness?

Short Answer Type Questions

1. Why is divergent thinking important in creative thinking process?

2. Briefly describe the meaning of the term analogy.

3. Define thinking. What are the building blocks of thinking?

4. Discuss the sequence involved in problem-solving.

Long Answer Type Questions

1. Discuss the meaning and nature of language. How it is acquired in human beings?

2. Explain the role of concept in the thinking process.

Case Based Questions

Read the case and answer the questions that follow.

Rohit is planning to give an entrance exam to join a famous college for design. People who have given the test earlier call it a 'creativity' test. They asked Rohit to study a bit of current affairs as there are some multiple-choice questions about them in the first part of the exam. They also told him to practice other types of questions like

- finding as many unusual uses as he could for ordinary objects like a grocery bag or the dining table
- finding a word that connects three seemingly unrelated words like low, lighting and off (one possible answer could be mood)

Rohit finds that many times the answers do not come to him immediately. He often finds a solution suddenly while doing something else like brushing his teeth before bed.

(i) What type of thinking is required to answer such questions? Explain.

(ii) If Rohit stops his exam preparation because he believes that he has too little time and too much competition, which barrier to creativity is he experiencing?

08

CHAPTER

The term motivation is derived from the Latin word movere which refers to the movement or activity. Motivation is one of the determinents of behaviour whereas emotions are the subjective feeling based on experiences.

▼ **YOUR STUDY GOALS**

▼ **YOUR PRACTICE GOAL**

- Objective Type Questions (19 Qs ; MCQs, A-R)
- Subjective Questions (9 VSAs, 9 SAs, 2 LAs, 4 Case Based)

Motivation and Emotion

8.1 Nature of Motivation

- The concept of **motivation**[1] focuses on explaining the factors that 'move' behaviour.
- Motives are used to explain most of our behaviours.
- For example, why do you go to school or college? There may be many reasons, such as wanting to learn, make friends, earn a diploma or degree for a good job or to make your parents happy.
- A combination of these reasons would explain why you choose to go for higher education.
- Motives help in making predictions about behaviour.
- A person will work hard in school, sports, business or music if they have a strong need for achievement.
- Motives are general states that help in making predictions about behaviour in many different situations.
- Instincts, drives, needs, goals and incentives come under the broad group of motivation.

1 **Motivation** It is a process that initiates, guides and maintains goal-oriented behaviours.

The Motivational Cycle

- Psychologists use the concept of need to explain the motivational properties of behaviour.
- The condition of need leads to drive. A drive is a state of tension or **arousal**[2] produced by a need and it supplies energy to random activity.
- When one of these random activities leads to a goal, it reduces the drive and the organism stops being active.
- The organism returns to a balanced state.

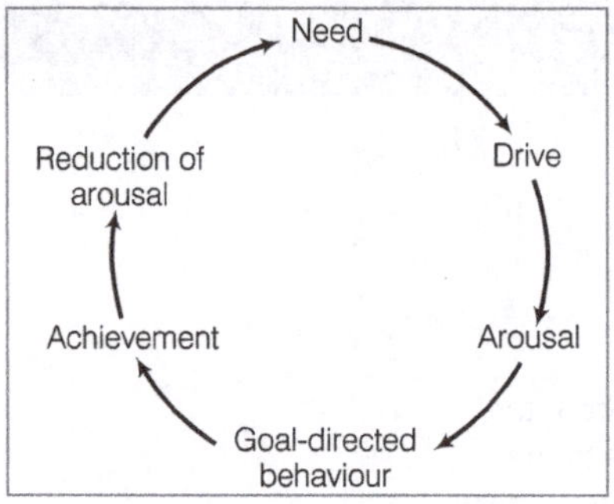

▲ *The Motivational Cycle*

8.2 Types of Motives

- There are two types of motives–biological and psychosocial.
  (i) **Biological Motives** Focus on the innate, biological causes of motivation like hormones, neurotransmitters and brain structures (such as the hypothalamus, limbic system). Examples include hunger, thirst and sex.
  (ii) **Psychosocial Motives** Focus on psychological and social (as well as environmental) factors and how they interact with each other to produce motivation. Examples include the need for achievement, affiliation, power, curiosity, exploration and self-actualisation motives.
- Both types are interdependent on each other.
- No motive is absolutely biological or psychosocial, but they occur in different combinations in individuals.

Biological Motives (Needs)

- Biological motives are also known as physiological motives because they are mainly guided by the physiological mechanisms of the body.
- Psychosocial motives are learned from the individual's interactions with environmental factors.
- The biological approach to motivation is the earliest attempt to understand the causes of behaviour.
- Most later theories carry traces of the biological approach.
- The approach following the concept of adaptive act holds that organisms have needs (internal physiological imbalances) that produce drive, arousing behaviour leading to certain actions toward achieving goals and reducing the drive.

2 **Arousal** It is the state of being physiologically alert, awake and attentive.

Instinct

- Instinct refers to inborn patterns of behaviour that are biologically determined rather than learned. For example, curiosity, flight, repulsion, reproduction and parental care.
- Instincts are innate (inborn/hereditary) tendencies found in all members of a species that direct behaviour in predictable ways.
- The term instinct most closely refers to an urge to do something.
- Instinct has an 'impetus' which drives the organism to do something to reduce that impetus.
- Basic biological needs explained using this approach include hunger, thirst and sex, which are essential for the individual's existence.

Hunger

- When someone is hungry, the need for food motivates them to obtain and consume food.
- The stimuli for hunger include stomach contractions (indicating an empty stomach), low glucose concentration in the blood, low protein levels and the amount of fats stored in the body.
- The liver also responds to the lack of bodily fuel by sending signals through nerve impulses to the brain.
- The aroma, taste or appearance of food can also create a desire to eat.
- All these factors combine with external factors (like the taste, colour, observing others eating and the smell of food) to help you understand you are hungry.
- Food intake is regulated by a complex feeding-satiety system located in the hypothalamus, liver and other parts of the body, along with external signs from the environment.

Thirst

- When we don't drink water for a while, the mouth and throat become dry, leading to dehydration of body tissues.
- Drinking water is necessary to wet a dry mouth, but a dry mouth does not always lead to drinking behaviour.
- The processes inside the body control thirst and the act of drinking water.
- Water must enter the tissues sufficiently to remove the dryness from the mouth and throat.
- Motivation to drink water is caused by the body's conditions like the loss of water from cells and a reduction in blood volume.
- When water is lost from bodily fluids, it leaves the cells and the anterior hypothalamus contains nerve cells called Osmoreceptors.
- These osmoreceptors generate nerve impulses when there is cell dehydration.

Sex

- Sex is one of the most powerful drives in both animals and human beings.
- The motivation to engage in sexual activity strongly influences human behaviour.
- Sex is different from other primary motives like hunger and thirst in several ways
  - (i) Sexual activity is not essential for an individual's survival.
  - (ii) Homeostasis (the process of maintaining stability within the body) is not the goal of sexual activity.
  - (iii) The sex drive develops with age.
- In lower animals, sexual activity depends on various physiological conditions.
- In humans, sex drive is closely regulated biologically, making it difficult to classify sex purely as a biological drive.

Psychosocial Motives

- Social motives are mostly learned or acquired through social groups like family, neighbours, friends and relatives.
- These are complex motives formed through the individual's interaction with their social environment.
- Some needs that arise through this approach are

Need for Affiliation

- Human beings generally want to maintain relationships with others as nobody likes to be alone all the time.
- When people notice similarities or like each other, they form groups.
- Group formation or collective behaviour is important in human life.
- People often seek to be close to others, to receive their help and to become members of their group.
- The desire to be close to others both physically and psychologically is called Affiliation.
- This need arises when people feel threatened, helpless, or happy.
- People with a high need for affiliation are motivated to seek the company of others and maintain friendly relationships.

Need for Power

- The need for power is the ability to influence the behaviour and emotions of others.
- The main goals of power motivation are to influence, control, persuade, lead and charm others and to improve one's reputation in the eyes of others.
- David McClelland (1975) described four ways of expressing the power motive
  - (i) People do things to feel power and strength from external sources, such as by reading stories about sports stars or associating with popular figures.
  - (ii) Power can also come from within, such as through building up the body and controlling one's urges.
  - (iii) People take actions individually to impact others, for example, by arguing or competing with others to influence them.
  - (iv) People use organisations, like political parties, to impact others. The individual might use the party to influence others.
- Depending on age and life experiences, one of these ways of expressing power may dominate.

Need for Achievement

- Achievement motivation refers to the desire to meet standards of excellence.
- For example, students work hard and compete for good grades to open doors for higher studies and better job prospects.
- Achievement motivation (also known as n-Ach) energises and directs behaviour, influencing how situations are perceived.
- Children learn achievement motivation from parents, role models and socio-cultural influences.
- People with high achievement motivation prefer moderately difficult and challenging tasks.
- They have a strong desire for feedback on their performance, to understand how they are doing and adjust their goals.

Curiosity

- Curiosity is behaviour driven by the motive to stay engaged in the activity itself.
  For example, people sometimes engage in activities without a specific goal but find pleasure in the experience.
- It is a motivational tendency to act without a clear, identifiable goal.
- The desire to experience something new or obtain information is a sign of curiosity.
- People often ask questions like, 'What will happen if the sky falls on us?' such questions stimulate intellectuals to search for answers.
- Studies show curiosity is not limited to humans; animals also exhibit curiosity.
- Curiosity is connected to the need for sensory stimulation, a basic motivational drive.

Exploration

- Our lack of knowledge about certain things motivates us to explore the world.
- This drive is very dominant in infants and small children.
- Children find satisfaction in exploring, which is reflected in their smiling and babbling.
- They become distressed when discouraged from exploring.

Quick Test 1

1. Who described four ways of expressing the power motive?
2. State any one biological need.
3. Explain the nature of motivation.
4. What is the motivational cycle?
5. Give one key difference between biological and psychosocial motives.

8.3 Maslow's Hierarchy of Needs

- Abraham H. Maslow provided a popular view on human motivation.
- He tried to show human behaviour by organising various needs in a hierarchy.
- His view on motivation is very well-known due to its theoretical and practical value, often referred to as the Theory of Self-actualisation.
- Maslow's model can be conceptualised as a pyramid.
- The bottom of the pyramid represents basic physiological or **biological needs**[3] that are essential for survival, such as hunger and thirst.
- Once these needs are satisfied, the next need arises - the need for safety, which includes physical and psychological protection.
- After safety needs are met, individuals seek the need to form relationships, to love and to be loved.
- Once the need for love is fulfilled, the individual then strives for esteem, which is the need to develop a sense of self-worth.
- The next higher need in the hierarchy is the need for self-actualisation, which is the desire for the fullest development of one's potential.
- A self-actualised person is self-aware, socially responsive, creative, spontaneous, open to new experiences, has a sense of humour and the ability to form deep interpersonal relationships.

▲ *Maslow's Hierarchy of Needs*

- Lower-level needs dominate an individual's focus until they are satisfied.
- Once lower-level needs are sufficiently met, higher-level needs become the individual's main focus.
- Very few people reach the highest level of self-actualisation, as most are more concerned with satisfying lower-level needs.

3 **Biological Needs** Some of the basis biological needs are hunger, thirst and sex, which are essential for the existence of the individual.

8.4 Nature of Emotions

- Emotions are a complex combination of arousal, subjective feelings and cognitive interpretation.
- Common emotions experienced daily include joy, sorrow, hope, love, excitement, anger and hate.
- For example, Swati is happy because her examination result has been declared and she has topped the class. She is feeling euphoric.
- Meanwhile, her friend Pranoy is sad because he did not perform well. Some of Swati's friends are jealous of her success.
- Jeevan, who has not met his expectations, feels angry with himself and upset that his parents will be disappointed.
- Emotions involve both physiological (bodily) and psychological reactions.

Classification of Emotions

- Emotion is a subjective feeling, meaning it is based on personal experiences and tastes and can vary from person to person.
- In psychology, six primary emotions are recognised–anger, disgust, fear, happiness, sadness and surprise.
- Izard proposed a set of ten basic emotions–joy, surprise, anger, disgust, contempt, fear, shame, guilt, interest and excitement.
- Combinations of these basic emotions result in other emotional blends.
- According to Plutchik, there are eight primary emotions and all other emotions are combinations of these primary ones.
- Plutchik arranged these emotions into four pairs of opposites

(i) joy-sadness
(ii) acceptance-disgust
(iii) fear-anger
(iv) surprise-anticipation

Intensity and Quality of Emotions

- Emotions vary in intensity (high or low) and quality (such as happiness, sadness, fear).
- Subjective factors and situational contexts influence how emotions are experienced.
- These factors include gender, personality and psychopathology (mental health conditions).
- Studies show that women experience all emotions, except anger, more intensely than men.
- These gender differences have been linked to social roles–men often face roles associated with competitiveness, while women are more associated with roles involving affiliation and care.

Quick Test 2

1. Name the model given by Abraham H. Maslow.
2. Name the Maslow's Hierarchy of Needs.
3. What are physiological needs according to Maslow?
4. Name any three primary emotions.
5. What is meant by self-actualization?

8.5 Expression of Emotions

- Emotion is an internal experience that cannot be directly observed by others.
- Emotions are inferred through verbal and non-verbal expressions.
- Verbal and non-verbal expressions act as channels for communicating emotions and help in understanding the feelings of others.

Culture and Emotional Expression

- The way emotions are experienced and expressed is influenced by culture.
- Research has focused on whether emotions are universal or culture-specific, particularly facial expressions.
- The face is a common channel for emotional communication, as it is visible and easily observed.
- Facial expressions can convey both the intensity and pleasantness or unpleasantness of an emotional state.
- Darwin's view supports the idea that facial expressions for basic emotions (joy, fear, anger, disgust, sadness and surprise) are inborn and universal.
- Bodily movements also help in expressing emotions. In theatres and dramas, body movements play a key role in emotional communication.
- Indian classical dances like Bharatanatyam, Odissi, Kuchipudi and Kathak use eyes, legs and fingers movement to express emotions like joy, sorrow, love and anger.
- Cultural differences exist in gaze behaviour; for example, Latin Americans and Southern Europeans make direct eye contact, while Asians, especially Indians and Pakistanis, prefer a peripheral gaze (looking away from the conversational partner).

Culture and Emotional Labelling

- Emotions differ in terms of how they are elaborated and labelled across cultures.
- The Tahitian language has 46 different words for the English word 'anger'.
- In North America, people provide 40 different labels for the facial expression of anger and 81 for contempt (disregard).
- The Japanese have multiple labels for emotions–10 for happiness, 8 for anger and 6 for disgust.
- Ancient Chinese literature identifies seven basic emotions–joy, anger, sadness, fear, love, dislike and liking.
- Ancient Indian literature recognises eight emotions: love, mirth (amusement), energy, wonder, anger, grief, disgust and fear.
- In Western literature, emotions like happiness, sadness, fear, anger and disgust are considered basic, while surprise, contempt, shame and guilt are not universally accepted as basic emotions.
- Some emotions are universally expressed and understood across cultures, while others are specific to certain cultures.
- Culture plays a significant role in both the expression and experience of emotions. Display rules, which are culture-specific, determine when and how emotions can be expressed and the intensity with which they can be displayed.

8.6 Managing Negative Emotions

- Emotions are an essential part of daily life and interpersonal relationships.
- Effective emotion management is key to social functioning in modern society.
- Tips for managing emotions include
  - **Enhance Self-awareness** Be aware of your own emotions and try to understand the 'how' and 'why' behind them.
  - **Appraise the Situation Objectively** Emotions are influenced by how events are perceived. If an event is seen as disturbing, the body's sympathetic nervous system is activated, causing stress. The way you perceive events determines your emotional response.
  - **Self-monitoring** Regularly assess past achievements and emotional states. Positive self-assessment can lead to a better sense of well-being.
  - **Self-modelling** Reflect on your best past performances and use them as inspiration to improve in the future.
  - **Perceptual Reorganisation and Cognitive Restructuring** View situations from a different perspective and restructure negative thoughts to promote positive feelings.
  - **Be Creative** Find activities or hobbies that interest and amuse you.
  - **Develop Good Relationships** Surround yourself with positive, cheerful friends, who can improve your mood.
  - **Empathy** Understand and value the feelings of others. Meaningful relationships are built on mutual empathy and support.
  - **Participate in Community Service** Helping others, such as working with intellectually challenged children, can help you understand your own emotions and improve emotional well-being.

Managing Your Anger

- Anger is a negative emotion that can make you lose control over your actions.
- The main cause of anger is frustration when goals or desires are blocked.
- Anger is not automatic or caused by others. It is a choice you make based on your thoughts.
- Since anger results from your thinking, it can be controlled by changing your thoughts.

Key Points in Anger Management

- **Recognise the power of your thoughts** Your thoughts influence your emotions, so by controlling your thoughts, you can control anger.
- **Realise that you alone can control it** You are the only one who can manage your anger.
- **Avoid self-talk that makes anger worse** Don't dwell on negative thoughts or magnify your feelings.
- **Don't assume bad intentions of others** Avoid thinking others have hidden motives.
- **Resist irrational beliefs** Don't allow distorted or unrealistic thoughts to drive your anger.
- **Express anger constructively** Find healthy ways to express anger. Control how intense and how long you stay angry.
- **Look inward for anger control** Focus on controlling your reactions, not blaming others.
- **Give yourself time to change** Changing your anger habits takes time and effort.

8.7 Enhancing Positive Emotions

- Emotions help us to adapt to the world around us and are vital for survival and well-being.
- Negative emotions like fear or anger help to prepare us to act quickly in danger, but too much of these emotions can harm our health.
- Positive emotions, such as hope, joy, optimism, satisfaction and gratitude, improve our emotional well-being and give us energy.
- Positive emotions help us to think creatively, cope with problems and bounce back from difficulties.
- People who experience positive emotions are better at finding new ideas and solutions to problems compared to those experiencing negative emotions.

Ways to Improve Positive Emotions

- **Personality Traits** Optimism, hopefulness and a positive self-regard help to boost positive emotions.
- **Finding Meaning** Look for positive meaning in difficult situations.
- **Quality relationships** Having supportive relationships with friends and family helps to improve emotional health.
- **Engage in meaningful work** Feeling productive and gaining mastery in activities increases positive emotions.
- **Faith and purpose** A strong sense of faith and purpose in life can offer social support and hope.
- **Positive interpretations** Try to view most daily events in a positive light.

Quick Test 3

1. Name any one tip to achieve the desired balance of emotions.
2. State any one strategy to manage anxiety.
3. Which cultural form of dance uses body movements to express emotions in India?
4. What are 'display rules' in emotional expression?
5. Name one strategy to manage examination anxiety.
6. What is the full form of PTSD?
7. How do positive emotions benefit us?

NCERT Folder

1. Explain the concept of motivation.

Ans. The term motivation is derived from the Latin word *movere*, referring to movement of activity. Motives are used to explain most of our behaviours, for example, the motive behind going to college might be, to get a degree and then a job, or make your parents happy, etc.

Motives help in making predictions about behaviour.

Hence, motives are the general states that enable us to make predictions about behaviour in many different situations i.e. motivation is one of the determinants of behaviour. Instincts, drives, needs, goals and incentives come under the broad group of motivation.

2. What are the biological bases of hunger and thirst needs?

Ans. Hunger It motivates people to obtain and consume food. Studies show that many events inside and outside the body may cause hunger or prevents it.

The stimuli for hunger include stomach contractions, which indicate that the stomach is empty, a low concentration of glucose in the blood, a low level of protein and the amount of fats stored in the body.

The aroma, taste or appearance of food may also result in a desire to eat.

The changes in the metabolic functions of the liver result in a feeling of hunger. The liver sends a signal to a part of the brain called Hypothalamus.

The two regions of hypothalamus involved in hunger are the Lateral Hypothalamus (LH) and the Ventro-Medial Hypothalamus (VMH).

LH is considered to be the excitatory area. The VMH is located in the middle of the hypothalamus, which is otherwise known as Hunger-controlling area which prevents the hunger drive.

Thirst When we don't take water for a period of several hours, the mouth and throat become dry, which leads to dehydration of body tissues.

Motivation to drink water is mainly caused by the conditions of the body like loss of water from cells and reduction of blood volume.

When water is lost by bodily fluids, water leaves the interior of the cells. The anterior hypothalamus contains nerve cells called Osmoreceptors, which generate nerve impulses in case of cell dehydration.

These nerve impulses act as a signal for thirst and drinking. When thirst is regulated by loss of water from the osmoreceptors, it is called Cellular-dehydration thirst.

3. How do the needs for achievement, affiliation and power influence the behaviour of adolescents? Explain with examples.

Ans.
- **Need for Achievement** Achievement motivation refers to the desire of a person to meet standards of excellence.

  The sources from which, children learn achievement motivation include parents, other role models and socio-cultural influences. Persons high in achievement motivation tend to prefer tasks that are moderately difficult and challenging.

  For example, adolescents work hard to get into best engineering, medical or other universities, so that they can achieve higher goals in their future.

- **Need for Affiliation** It involves motivation for social contact. Need for affiliation is aroused when individuals feel threatened or helpless and also when they are happy. People high on this need are motivated to seek the company of others and to maintain friendly relationships with other people.

  For example, it is during adolescent age, children make long-term friends. If someone observes after becoming adult, most of our friends are from adolescent age. Even many love relationships emerge during adolescent age.

- **Need for Power** It is an ability of a person to produce desired effects on the behaviour and emotions of another person. The various goals of power motivation are to influence, control, persuade, lead and charm others and most importantly to enhance one's own reputation in the eyes of other people.

  For example, during adolescent age, children often try to become class leaders, school house leaders, participate in college elections, etc. This shows the need for power among adolescents.

4. What is the basic idea behind Maslow's hierarchy of needs? Explain with suitable examples.

Ans. Abraham H Maslow gave one of the most popular views on human motivation. The basic idea behind his hierarchy of needs was that he tried to show a picture of human behaviour by arranging the various needs in a hierarchy. His viewpoint about motivation is very popular because of its theoretical and applied value which is popularly known as the 'Theory of Self-actualisation'.

His model can be understood through the following points

- Maslow's model can be conceptualised as a pyramid in which the bottom of this hierarchy represents basic physiological or biological needs which are basic to survival such as hunger, thirst, etc.
- Only when these needs are met, the need to be free from threatened danger arises. This refers to the safety needs of physical and psychological nature.
- For example, Poorest of poor people mainly focus on getting three meals a day and drinking water. It is only after the fulfillment of these needs, they look for some shelter or home to keep themselves safe.
- Then comes the need to seek out other people, to love and to be loved. After these needs are fulfilled, the individual strives for esteem i.e. the need to develop a sense of self-worth.
- The next higher need in the hierarchy shows an individual's motive towards the fullest development of potential i.e. self-actualisation.
- For example, after having proper food, home, people try to make friends in the society and then try to attain some kind of power in the society by contesting for colony association president, etc.
- Lower level needs in the hierarchy dominate as long as they are unsatisfied. Once they are sufficiently satisfied, the higher needs occupy the individual's attention and effort.
- In general, very few people reach the highest level because most of the people are concerned more with the lower level needs. For example, we generally see that not many people from the colony become society's association president, it is just couple of individuals.

5. How does culture influence the expression of emotions?

Ans. Most basic emotions are inborn and do not have to be learned. Psychologists largely have a notion that emotions, especially facial expressions, have strong biological ties. But on comparing different cultures we see that learning plays an important role in emotions. This happens in two ways.

(i) Cultural learning influences the expression of emotions more than what is experienced, for example, some cultures encourage free emotional expression, whereas other cultures teach people through modelling and reinforcement, to reveal little of their emotions in public.

(ii) Learning has a great importance to do with the stimuli that produce emotional reactions. It has been shown that individuals with excessive fears of elevators and automobiles learnt these fears through modelling, classical conditioning or avoidance conditioning.

The process involved in emotions have been known to be influenced by culture.

Most of this research has been carried out on the facial expression of emotions. Facial expression is the most common channel of emotional communication.

6. Why is it important to manage negative emotions? Suggest ways to manage negative emotions.

Ans. It is important to manage negative emotions because a lot of negative emotions like fear, anxiety, disgust etc. develop in our daily life to a considerable extent. Such negative emotions, if allowed to prevail for a long time are likely to affect our psychological and physical health adversely.

There are a number of ways which help to manage negative emotions. These are given below

- **Enhance Self-awareness** Be aware of your own emotions and feelings. Try to gain understanding into the 'how' and 'why' of your feelings.
- **Appraise the Situation Objectively** Emotion is preceded by evaluation of the event. If the event is experienced as disturbing, sympathetic nervous system is activated and you feel stressed. If you do not experience the event as disturbing, then there is no stress.
- **Do Some Self-monitoring** This involves constant or periodic evaluation of past achievements, emotional and physical states, real and imaginative experiences. A positive appraisal would improve your faith in yourself and lead to improved feeling of wellness and satisfaction.
- **Engage in Self-modeling** Be the ideal for yourself. Observe the best parts of your past performance and use them as an inspiration and motivation to perform better in the future.
- **Perceptual Reorganisation and Cognitive Restructuring** Try viewing the events differently and visualise the other side of the coin. Restructure your thoughts to enhance positive and reassuring feelings and eliminate negative thoughts.
- **Be Creative** Find and develop an interest or a hobby. Engage in an activity that interests and amuses you.
- **Develop and Nurture Good Relationships** Choose your friends carefully. In the company of happy and cheerful friends, you will feel happy in general.
- **Have Empathy** Try understanding other's feelings. Make your relationships meaningful and valuable.

Exam Pattern Questions

Objective Type Questions

Multiple Choice Questions (MCQs)

1. The word is derived from Latin word movere is ……

(a) Moments (b) Movement (c) Motivation (d) Movie

2. Which of the following is a state of tension or arousal produced by a need?

(a) Instinct (b) Drive (c) Emotion (d) Motive

3. What is the common human instinct among the following?

(a) Curiosity (b) Reproduction
(c) Parental care (d) All of these

4. Which of the following area is stimulated due to which animals are able to eat?

(a) Ventro-medial hypothalamus
(b) Lateral hypothalamus
(c) Liver
(d) Pancreas

5. Which of the following needs indicates trying to make friends?

(a) Need for achievement trying to make friends
(b) Need for power
(c) Need for affiliation
(d) None of the above

6. Which of the following is not included in psychological needs?

I. Need for affiliation II. Need for power
III. Need for achievement IV. Need for sex

Codes

(a) Only I (b) Only II
(c) Only II and III (d) Only IV

7. Which of the following statements are true regarding personality assessment?

I. A person's behaviour in a variety of situations can provide us with meaningful information about his/her personality.
II. Indirect techniques can be scored in an objective manner.
III. Direct methods of personality assessment cover the unconscious part of our behaviour.
IV. Psychological testing requires great skill and training.

Codes

(a) I and III (b) I and IV (c) II and III (d) II and IV

8. Which of the following statements are true regarding social motives?

I. Need for affiliation is aroused when individuals feel threatened or helpless.
II. Need for power is based on the ability to influence others through external sources.
III. Achievement motivation energises and directs behaviour based on personal goals.
IV. Social motives are primarily biological and independent of social interactions.

Codes

(a) I, II and III (b) II, III and IV
(c) I and IV (d) III and IV

9. Which of the following are true about Maslow's Hierarchy of Needs?

I. Physiological needs are the most basic and fundamental needs in the hierarchy.
II. Self-actualisation represents the highest level of human needs.
III. The need for belongingness and love is considered more essential than the need for esteem.
IV. Once lower-level needs are satisfied, higher-level needs emerge as dominant.

Codes

(a) I, II and IV (b) I and III
(c) II and IV (d) III and IV

10. Shweta has joined the National Cadet Corps. Identify the type of group she is now a member of.

I. Primary II. Secondary
III. Informal IV. Formal

Codes

(a) I and IV (b) III and IV (c) II and IV (d) II and III

11. Which of the following is true for secondary groups?

I. They are large and include impersonal relationships.
II. They involve more formal interactions based on shared goals or activities.
III. Secondary groups are always informal in nature.
IV. They often lack emotional intimacy but are essential for achieving specific objectives.

Codes

(a) I and II (b) II and IV (c) I and III (d) III and IV

Assertion-Reason Questions

Directions (Q. Nos. 12-19) In the following questions, a statement of Assertion A is followed by a statement of Reason R. Mark the correct choice from the options given below.

(a) Both A and R are true and R is the correct explanation of A.
(b) Both A and R are true, but R is not the correct explanation of A.
(c) A is true, but R is false.
(d) A is false, but R is true.

12. **Assertion** (A) Psychologists use the concept of need to explain the motivational properties of behaviour.

Reason (R) A need is lack or deficit of some necessity.

13. **Assertion** (A) Emotions are a complex pattern of arousal, subjective feeling and cognitive interpretation.

Reason (R) Subjective factors and situational contexts do not influence the experience of emotions.

14. **Assertion** (A) Emotions such as joy, sadness and anger are universally recognised across cultures.

Reason (R) Facial expressions for these emotions are inborn and universal, as supported by research in emotional communication.

15. **Assertion** (A) Gender differences in emotional intensity suggest that men and women experience emotions equally.

Reason (R) Research shows that women experience all emotions except anger more intensely than men, while men experience higher intensity and frequency of anger.

16. **Assertion** (A) Inoculation against stress can help prepare individuals to face stressful situations with better control.

Reason (R) Inoculation involves preparing for stressful situations by rehearsals and role-playing, which boosts confidence and reduces stress.

17. **Assertion** (A) Biological motives are primarily driven by physiological imbalances in the body.

Reason (R) Psychosocial motives are influenced by an individual's interactions with the environment and social factors.

18. **Assertion** (A) The need for affiliation motivates individuals to form groups and seek social contact.

Reason (R) Individuals with high need for affiliation prefer solitude and avoid interactions with others.

19. **Assertion** (A) Curiosity and exploration are motivated by the need for sensory stimulation and novelty.

Reason (R) Sensory stimulation and exploration are basic motives that lead to goal-directed behaviour with a clear purpose.

Answers

1. (c) Motivation
2. (b) Drive
3. (d) All of these
4. (b) Lateral hypothalamus
5. (c) Need for affiliation
6. (d) Only IV
7. (b) I and IV
8. (a) I, II and III
9. (a) I, II and IV
10. (c) II and IV
11. (b) II and IV
12. (b) Both A and R are true, but R is not the correct explanation of A.
13. (c) A is true, but R is false.
14. (a) Both A and R are true and R is the correct explanation of A.
15. (d) A is false, but R is true.
16. (a) Both A and R are true and R is the correct explanation of A.
17. (a) Both A and R are true and R is the correct explanation of A.
18. (c) A is true, but R is false.
19. (c) A is true, but R is false.

Subjective Questions

Very Short Answer Type Questions

1. What is the focus of biological motives?

Ans. Biological motives focus on the innate biological causes of motivation like hormones, neurotransmitters and brain structures like hypothalamus, limbic system, etc.

2. What is the focus of psychosocial motives?

Ans. Psychosocial motives focus on psychological and social along with environmental factors and how they interact with each other to produce motivation.

3. Determine the use of osmoreceptors.

Ans. The anterior hypothalamus contains nerve cells called Osmoreceptors, which generate nerve impulses in case of cell dehydration. These nerve impulses act as a signal for thirst and drinking water.

4. What are the signs of curiosity?

Ans. Curiosity is a motivational tendency to act without any specific identifiable goal. The tendency to seek for a novel experience, gain pleasure by obtaining information, etc. are signs of curiosity.

5. What do you mean by paralanguage?

Ans. Non-verbal aspects of the voice like pitch and loudness of voice, and temporal characteristics of speech are called paralanguage.

6. How is sex different from other primary motives like hunger and thirst?

Ans. Sexual activity is not necessary for an individual's survival like other primary motives i.e. hunger and thirst. Homeostasis i.e the tendency of the organism as a whole to maintain constancy (unchanging) or to attempt to restore equilibrium if constancy is disturbed, is not the goal of sexual activity.

7. Differentiate between feeling and mood.

Ans. Feeling indicates the pleasure or pain dimension of emotion, which usually involves bodily functions. Mood is an affective state of long duration but of lesser intensity than emotion.

8. Why are lie detectors called Polygraphs?

Ans. Lie detectors are also called Polygraphs because they graphically record several bodily reactions simultaneously which measure the bodily arousal of the individual.

9. How do positive emotions help people?

Ans. Positive emotions give us a greater ability to cope with bad circumstances and quickly return to a normal state. They help us to set up long-term plans and goals and form new relationships.

Short Answer Type Questions

1. Explain the role of bodily movements in communication of emotions.

Ans. Bodily movements facilitate the communication of emotions. Theatres and drama provide an excellent opportunity to understand the impact of body movements in communicating emotions. The roles of gestures and proximal behaviours are also significant. In Indian classical dances, emotions are expressed with the help of movements of eyes, legs and fingers. The dancers are trained extremely in the grammar of body movement and non-verbal communication to express joy, sorrow, love, anger and various other forms of emotional states.

2. Parul met some victims of natural disaster during her medical career. She came to know about some people were suffering from Post-Traumatic Stress Disorder (PTSD). Explain about Post-Traumatic Stress Disorder (PSTD).

Competency Based Que.

Ans. In Post-Traumatic Stress Disorder (PTSD), the person tends to re-experience the event (loss due to a disaster) through flashbacks and get devastating thoughts about the event even after a substantial period of time.

This condition makes a person emotionally disturbed and the person fails to adopt an appropriate coping strategy in regular activities. Emotions manifest in uniquely recognisable patterns with maladaptive behaviour (like depression) and autonomic arousal.

3. Enumerate different way of improving positive emotions.

Ans. There are different ways to improve positive emotions like personality traits of optimism, hopefulness, happiness and a positive self-regard.

- Finding positive meaning in urgent circumstances.
- Having quality connections with others and supportive network of close relationships.
- Being engaged in work and gaining mastery.
- A faith that provides social support, purpose and hope, leading a life of purpose.
- Positive interpretations of most daily events.

4. Discuss about Autonomic Nervous Sysem.

Ans. The ANS (Autonomic Nervous System) is divided into two systems. They are sympathetic and parasympathetic. These two systems function together in a reciprocal (give and take) manner. In a stressful situation, the sympathetic system prepares the body to face the situation. It strengthens the internal environment of the individual by controlling the fall in heart rate, blood pressure, blood sugar, etc.

It brings out a state of physiological arousal that prepares the individual for fight or flight response in order to face the stressful situation. As the threat is removed, the parasympathetic system gets active and restores and conserves energy and brings the individual back to a normal state. Though acting in an opposite manner, the sympathetic and parasympathetic systems enhance each other in completing the process of experience and expression of emotion.

5. What do you know about the verbal and non-verbal channels of communication?

Ans. The verbal channel of communication is composed of spoken words and other vocal features of speech like pitch and loudness of the voice. These non-verbal aspects of the voice and temporal characteristics of speech are called 'Paralanguage'. Other verbal channels include facial expression, kinetic (gesture, posture, movement of the body) and proximal (physical distance during face-to-face interaction) behaviours.

Facial expression is the most common channel of emotional communication. The amount and kind of information conveyed by the face is easy to understand as the face is exposed to the full view of others.

Facial expressions can convey the intensity as well as the pleasantness or unpleasantness of the individual's emotional state. Facial expressions play an important role in our everyday lives.

There has been some research evidence supporting Darwin's view that facial expressions for basic emotions (joy fear, anger, disgust, sadness and surprise) are inborn and universal.

6. Differentiate between negative and positive emotions.

Ans. Differences between negative and positive emotions are as follow

	Negative Emotion	Positive Emotion
(i)	Negative emotions like fear, anger or disgust prepare us mentally and physically for taking immediate action towards the stimulus that is threatening. For example, if there was no fear we would have caught a poisonous snake in our hand.	Positive emotions such as hope, joy, optimism, satisfaction and gratitude, energise us and enhance our sense of emotional well-being.
(ii)	Though negative emotions protect us in such situations but excessive or inappropriate use of these emotions can become life threatening to us, as it can harm our immune system and have serious consequences for our health.	When we experience positive affect, we display a greater preference for a large variety of actions and ideas. We can think of more possibilities and options to solve whatever problems we face and thus, we become proactive.
(iii)	People with a negative emotion ignore the good and pay attention to the bad in people, situations, events, etc.	Individuals who experience positive emotions will pay attention to the good, rather than bad in people, situations, events, etc.

7. Emotion is a subjective feeling and the experience of emotions varies from person to person. Discuss.

Competency Based Que.

Ans. In psychology, attempts have been made to identify basic emotions. It has been noted that at least six emotions are experienced and recognised everywhere. These are anger, disgust, fear, happiness, sadness and surprise.

Izard has proposed a set of basic emotions i.e. joy, surprise, anger disgust, contempt fear, shame, guilt, interest and excitement with combinations of them resulting in other emotional blends.

According to Plutchik, there are eight basic or primary emotions. All other emotions results from various mixtures of these basic emotions. He arranged these emotions in four pairs of opposites i.e. joy-sadness, acceptance-disgust, fear-anger and surprise-anticipation. Emotions vary in their intensity (high-low) and quality (happiness, sadness, fear). Subjective factors and situational contents influence the experience of emotions. These factors are gender, personality and psychopathology of certain kinds.

8. The process involved in emotions have been known to be influenced by culture. Explain it with giving appropriate example. **Competency Based Que.**

Ans. Current research has dealt more specifically with the issue of universality or culture specificity of emotions. Most of this research have been carried out on facial expression of emotions as the face is open to easy observation, is relatively free from complexity and provides a link between subjective experience and overt expression of an emotion.

An emotion may be communicated through other non-verbal channels as well. For example, gaze behaviour, paralanguage and proximal behaviour. The emotional meaning conveyed *via* gesture (body language) varies from culture to culture. For example, in China, a handclap is an expression of worry or disappointment and anger is expressed with laughter. Silence has also been found to convey different meaning for different culture. For example, in India deep emotions are sometimes communicated *via* silence. This convey embarrassment during communication in Western countries.

9. "Anger is the biggest enemy of a person." Justify. Explain different ways to effectively manage anger.

Competency Based Que.

Ans. Anger is a negative emotion. It carries the mind away or in other words, the person looses control on behavioural functions during the state of anger.

The major source of anger is the frustration of motives. Anger is a result of your thinking and hence is controllable by your own thoughts only. Some key points in anger management include

- Recognise the power of your thoughts.
- Realise that you alone can control it.
- Do not engage in 'self-talk that burns'. Do not magnify negative feelings.
- Do not attribute intentions and hidden motives to others.
- Resist having irrational beliefs about people and events.
- Try to find constructive ways of expressing your anger. Have control on the degree and duration of anger that you choose to express.

Long Answer Type Questions

1. Explain the basic biological needs of humans using physiological approach.

Ans. The basic biological needs of humans, explained using the physiological approach, include

- **Hunger** is triggered by signals such as stomach contractions, low glucose levels in the blood, and a lack of fats and proteins in the body. These stimuli, along with external cues like the smell, taste, and appearance of food, motivate individuals to eat. The feeding-satiety system, located in the hypothalamus and liver, regulates food intake.
- **Thirst** arises from the dehydration of body tissues, causing a dry mouth and throat. The body controls the thirst mechanism through osmoreceptors in the anterior hypothalamus, which send nerve impulses when cells lose water. Drinking water replenishes the body's fluids, helping to restore balance.
- **Sexual** motivation is a powerful biological drive, although it differs from hunger and thirst. Unlike these needs, sexual activity is not essential for individual survival and it does not aim to restore homeostasis. Sexual drive develops with age and is regulated biologically, although it can be influenced by psychological and social factors as well.

2. Explain in detail about lie detectors and the process involved in it.

Ans. Lie detectors are also called Polygraphs because they graphically record several bodily reactions simultaneously which measure the bodily arousal of the individual. Typically, a lie detector measures changes in blood pressure, heart rate, breathing rate and depth and the Galvanic Skin Response (GSR) which indicates variations in the electrical conductivity of the skin. In lie detection, the individual being tested is first asked a series of neutral (control) questions to establish a baseline. Simple questions are followed by specific questions that are designed to evoke responses from a guilty knowledge supposedly indicating the individual's involvement in the crime being investigated. The lie detector or the polygraph records the changes in neurophysiological activities that occur while the suspected individual answers these questions.

Though the polygraph makes several objective recordings, the interpretation of these records depends heavily on the subjective judgement by the examiner. It is also probable that several unrelated factors like fear, pain or anxiety being felt by the individual during the test may affect her/his level of arousal. It is possible for the individual to lie with it. The validity of polygraph results is doubtful but these are still used by law-enforcing agencies for lie detection.

Case Based Questions

1. Read the case and answer the questions that follow.

Ravi is a college student who has been feeling an intense urge to go out and interact with his friends after a long period of staying at home due to the pandemic. He finds himself seeking the company of others and feels uncomfortable being alone. This need to be around people is motivated by his desire to maintain social bonds and avoid isolation. He is also highly motivated to work hard to achieve high grades because he believes good academic performance will enhance his future career prospects. Additionally, Ravi experiences frequent curiosity, often asking questions about various subjects and seeking new experiences to satisfy his intellectual desires. At times, his curiosity leads him to explore new hobbies and interests. Ravi's behaviour reflects both biological and psychosocial motives that influence his actions.

(i) In the given case, what are the two main types of motives Ravi is experiencing?

(ii) What is the difference between biological and psychosocial motives as seen in the case?

Ans. (i) Ravi is experiencing biological motives (such as the need for social interaction) and psychosocial motives (such as the need for achievement and curiosity).

(ii) Biological motives are driven by internal physiological processes (like the need for food, water, and social interaction for survival), while psychosocial motives are influenced by social and environmental factors, such as the need for affiliation, achievement or curiosity. In Ravi's case, his need for social interaction is primarily a biological motive, while his curiosity and achievement motivation are psychosocial motives.

2. Read the case and answer the questions that follow.

Swati is very happy. Her examination result has been declared today and she has topped the class. She is feeling euphoric. However, her friend Pranoy is feeling sad, as he has not done well. Among her friends, some are feeling jealous of Swati's achievement. Jeevan, who has not performed up to his expectation, is angry with himself; he feels unhappy that his parents would be very disappointed. Emotions involve physiological as well as psychological reactions.

(i) In the given case, how does Swati feel and what emotions do her friends experience?

(ii) What type of emotions are involved in the case?

Ans. (i) Swati feels euphoric and happy about her examination result. Her friends experience a range of emotions

- Pranoy feels sad because he did not do well.
- Some of her friends feel jealous of Swati's achievement.
- Jeevan feels angry with himself and unhappy about disappointing his parents.

(ii) The emotions involved in the case are a mixture of joy, sadness, anger and jealousy, which are common basic emotions experienced in response to Swati's achievement and her friends' reactions.

3. Read the case and answer the questions that follow.

Anita is a theatre artist who performs in various plays. She uses her body movements, facial expressions and gestures to communicate emotions to the audience. In her performances, she often portrays emotions like joy, sorrow and anger through her movements and expressions. Anita has received training in different classical dance forms like Bharatanatyam and Kathak, which have helped her understand the nuances of emotional expression through body language. During one of her performances, she noticed that the audience responded differently to her expressions based on their cultural background. People from Latin American cultures maintained eye contact during the performance, while people from Asian backgrounds preferred looking away.

(i) In the given case, Anita is using which forms of communication to express emotions?

(ii) What cultural difference did Anita notice in the audience's response?

Ans. (i) Anita uses non-verbal communication to express emotions through her body movements, facial expressions and gestures.

(ii) Anita observed that people from Latin American cultures maintained eye contact during the performance, while people from Asian cultures, especially from India, preferred a peripheral gaze (looking away from the conversational partner) during the interaction.

4. Read the case and answer the questions that follow.

Suresh is a student preparing for an upcoming exam. He experiences a lot of anxiety when thinking about the exam and often finds himself stressed out. Suresh knows that a certain level of anxiety is essential to motivate him, but the anxiety sometimes becomes overwhelming. He decides to adopt some strategies to manage his anxiety. He prepares well in advance, familiarising himself with the exam pattern and frequently asked questions. To reduce his anxiety, Suresh also engages in positive thinking, focusing on his strengths and using relaxation techniques like deep breathing and muscle relaxation. He believes these strategies will help him stay calm and perform better during the exam.

(i) What strategies is Suresh using to manage his anxiety?

(ii) What is the role of anxiety in Suresh's exam preparation?

Ans. (i) Suresh is using the following strategies to manage his anxiety

- **Preparation** He prepares well in advance by familiarising himself with the exam pattern.
- **Positive thinking** He focuses on his strengths and remains positive.
- **Relaxation techniques** He uses deep breathing and muscle relaxation to stay calm.

(ii) Anxiety plays a motivational role in Suresh's exam preparation. A certain level of anxiety motivates him to perform his best. However, excessive anxiety can become an obstruction to his optimal performance, so managing anxiety is important for effective performance.

SELF ASSESSMENT TEST

Objective Type Questions

1. Want, desire, need, hunger refer to

(a) intelligence (b) cognitive behaviour (c) motives (d) abnormal behaviour

2. Motives arouse behaviour and direct it towards an

(a) appropriate goal (b) inference (c) prediction (d) None of these

3. A self-actualised person is ....

(a) self-aware (b) social responsive (c) creative (d) All of these

4. Children acquire achievement motivation during ....

(a) infancy (b) childhood (c) puberty (d) adolescence

Very Short Answer Type Questions

1. What is responsible for sexual motivation?

2. What are psychosocial motives?

3. Define affiliation.

4. Define emotion.

Short Answer Type Questions

1. Briefly discuss the role of learning in emotions.

2. What is cultural and emotional labeling? Explain.

3. Describe strategies that may be useful for achieving the desired balance of emotion.

Long Answer Type Questions

1. Define anger. Discuss strategies to manage anger.

2. Describe different ways to improve positive emotions.

3. How to manage anger?

Case Based Questions

Read the case and answer the questions that follow.

Garima is a highly driven eleventh grader. She wants to become an oncologist (cancer expert) in the future. She became interested in the field when, as a thirteen-year-old who had just learned about cell division. She grew more fascinated when she found that science had no exact answers about what causes and cures the disease. She knows that she will have to work really hard to achieve this. This has grown into a full-blown obsession and Garima routinely spends her free time reading medical journals and keeping up with current research on the disease. Her parents want her to slow down and "be a teenager." With that in mind, they asked her to choose between a family trip to Manali or a trek with friends to Kasauli as a two-week break during her summer holidays. Garima got angry and fought with her parents for trying to distract her from her studies.

(i) 'Garima got very angry and fought with her parents for trying to distract her from her studies.' This statement is supported by which hypothesis?

(ii) What are Psychosocial motives and explain the type of motive mentioned in the above case?

SAMPLE PROJECT

PROJECT FILE ON LEARNING

Name : ....

Class : ....

Roll No. : ....

Subject : ....

School : ....

Submitted by ....

Submitted to ....

Sample Project

Acknowledgement

I would like to extend my sincere and heartfelt obligation towards all those who have helped me in making this project. Without their active guidance, help, cooperation and encouragement, I would not have been able to present the project on time.

I am extremely thankful and pay my gratitude to my teacher Mr/Ms .... for his/her valuable guidance and support for completion of this project.

I extend my gratitude to my Principal Mr/Ms .... for the moral support extended during the tenure of the project.

I also acknowledge with a deep sense of reverence, my gratitude towards my parents, other faculty members of the school and friends for their valuable suggestions given to me in completing this project.

Date........... ....

Name of Student

Certificate

This is to Certify that the project work

.... is the bonafide

work of .... (Name of the student) who

carried out the work under my supervision

....

Name and Signature of
Teacher/Supervisor

Contents

LEARNING

Learning is a psychological process. It is a very important part in human behaviour. It refers to a range of changes that take place as a result of one's experience. Learning may be defined as "any relatively permanent change in behaviour or behavioural potential produced by experience".

Objectives of Learning

The main objectives of "Learning" is to understand how living beings go through the process of learning and to know about the effect of learning on behavioural changes. It also gives us insights on how certain techniques like conditioning can be used to alter the behavioural changes both in animals and humans.

Features of Learning

There are different features for the process of learning. These are discussed as follows:

Learning by Experience

We experience an event occuring in a certain sequence during different occasions. If an event happens then it might be followed by some other events. If some action is repeatedly done and if it gives satisfaction, this experience will lead to the formation of habit. Sometimes a single experience can lead to learning.

For example, a child being burnt by using matchbox will learn to be carefull while using the matchbox

Temporary Behavioural Changes

In the process of learning, behavioural changes that occur due to learning are relatively permanent. Changes in behaviour might occur due to the effects of tiredness, repeated monotonous work and drugs. These changes are not considered as learning.

Habituation

It is a case of change in one's behaviour. The change is because of the continuous exposure to agents that arouse some activity or action. This phenomenon is called habituation. It is not due to learning.

Conditioning : The Simplest Form of Learning

Conditioning, in psychology, a behavioral process whereby a response becomes more frequent or more predictable in a given environment . In other words, conditioning is the process of training a person or animal to do something or to behave in a certain way in a particular situation. Conditioning is a form of learning in which either a given stimulus (or signal) becomes increasingly effective in evoking a response or a response occurs with increasing regularity in a well-specified and stable environment.

Classical Conditioning

Classical conditioning is a type of learning that had a major influence on the school of thought in psychology known as behaviorism. It is discovered by Russian physiologist Ivan Pavlov. Classical conditioning is a learning process that occurs through associations between an environmental stimulus and a naturally occuring stimulus.

How Does Classical Conditioning Work?

Classical conditioning basically involves forming an association between two stimuli resulting in a learned response. There are three basic phases of this process:

Phase 1: Before Conditioning

The first part of the classical conditioning process requires a naturally occuring stimulus that will automatically elicit a response. Salivating in response to the smell of food is a good example of a naturally occuring stimulus. During this phase of the processes, the unconditioned stimulus (UCS) results in an unconditioned response (UCR).

For example, presenting food (the UCS) naturally and automatically triggers a salivation response (the UCR). At this point, there is also a neutral stimulus that produces no effect - yet. It isn't until this neutral stimulus is paired with the UCS that it will come to evoke a response. Let's take a closer look at the two critical components of this phase of classical conditioning.

The unconditioned stimulus is one that unconditionally, naturally, and automatically triggers a response. For example, when you smell one of your favorite food, you may immediately feel very hungry. In this example, the smell of the food is the unconditioned stimulus. The unconditioned response is the unlearned response that occurs naturally in response to the unconditioned stimulus. In our example, the feeling of hunger in response to the smell of food is the unconditioned response.

Phase 2: During Conditioning

During the second phase of the classical conditioning process, the previously neutral stimulus is repeatedly paired with the unconditioned stimulus. As a result of this pairing, an association between the previously neutral stimulus and the UCS is formed. At this point, the once neutral stimulus becomes known as the conditioned stimulus (CS). The subject has now been conditioned to respond to this stimulus.

The conditioned stimulus is previously neutral stimulus that, after becoming associated with the unconditioned stimulus, eventually comes to trigger a conditioned response. In our earlier example, suppose that when you smelled your favorite food, you also heard the sound of a whistle. While the whistle is unrelated to the smell of the food, if the sound of the whistle was paired multiple times with the smell, the sound would eventually trigger the conditioned response. In this case, the sound of the whistle is the conditioned stimulus.

Phase 3: After Conditioning

Once the association has been made between the UCS and the CS, presenting the conditioned stimulus alone will come to evoke a response even without the unconditioned stimulus. The resulting response is known as the conditioned response (CR). The conditioned response is the learned response to the previously neutral stimulus. In our example, the conditioned response would be feeling hungry when you heard the sound of the whistle

Classical Conditioning :

Case Study on Pavlov's Dog Experiment

In the first part of the experiment, a dog was kept in the box as shown in the figure to conduct experiment. A simple surgery was conducted, and one end of a tube was inserted in the dog's jaw and the other end of tube was put in a measuring glass. This was used to measure the amount of saliva dog secreted.

In the second part of the experiment, the dog was kept hungry and placed in harness. A bell was rang and immediately after the sound, food(meat powder) was served to dog. The dog was allowed to eat it. This routine was continued for next few days i.e immediately after ringing the bell, food was given to the dog. After a number of such trials, a test trail was conducted in which, everything was repeated except that food was not served to dog after ringing the bell. The dog still secreted saliva after listening to the sound of the bell, expecting its food to be served, because dog thought bell and food were connected. This connection between bell and food resulted in obtaining a new response by the dog, i.e secreting saliva to the sound of bell. This has been called conditioning.

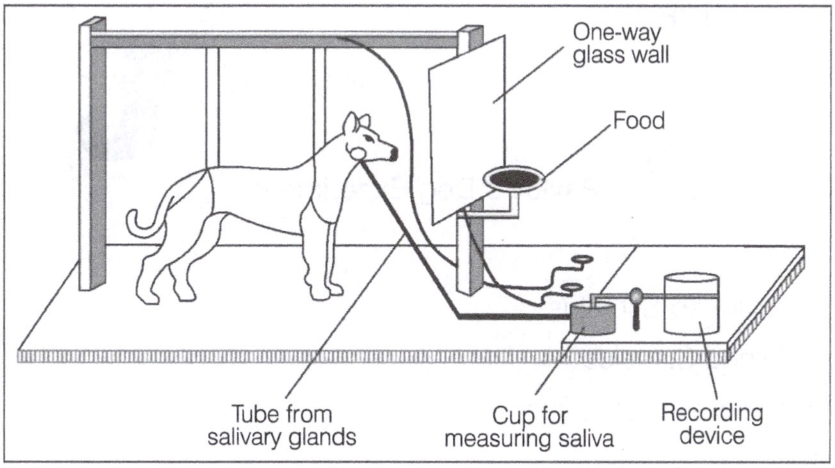

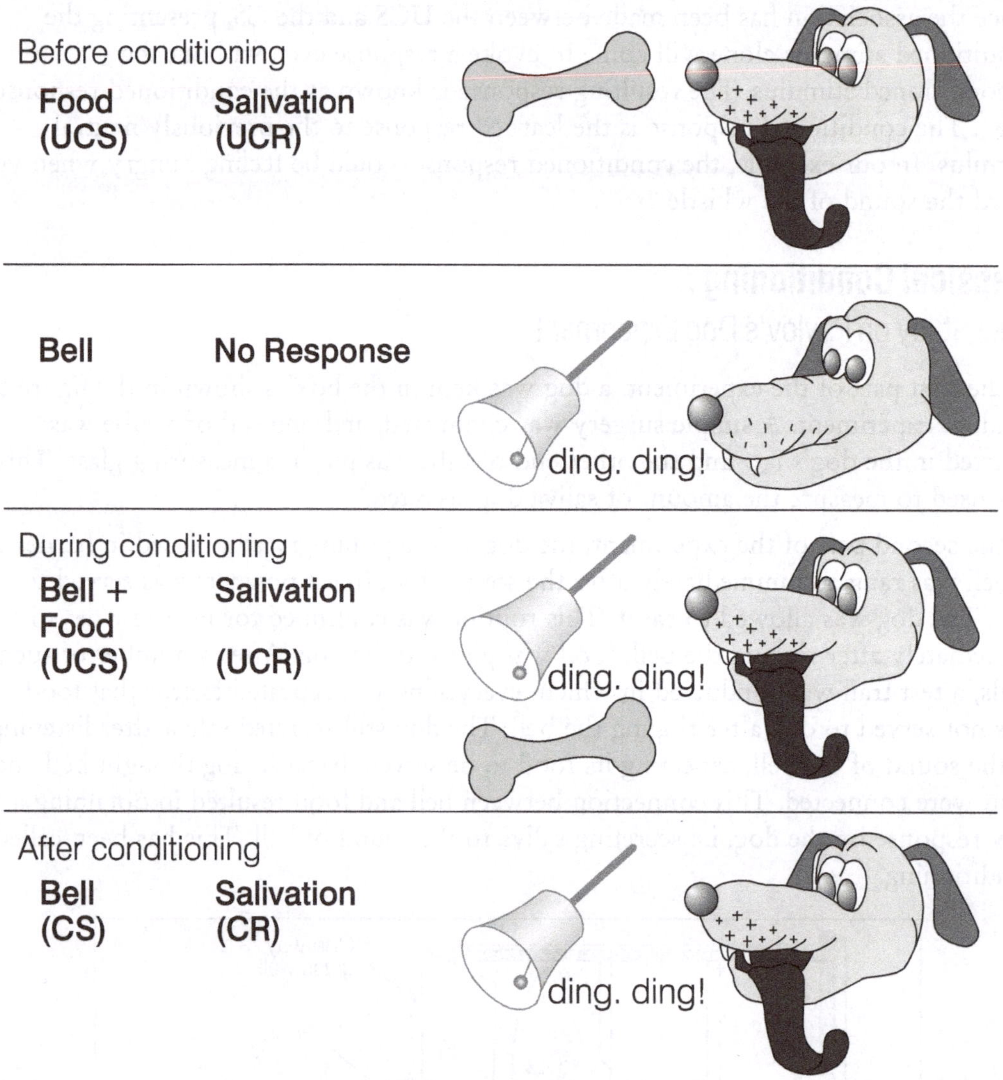

Pavlov's Dog Experiment

where,

UCS - Unconditioned Stimulus

CS - Conditioned Stimulus

UCR - Unconditioned Response

CR - Condition Response

Classical Conditioning :

Case Study on Little Albert Experiment

The Little Albert Experiment is most famous as being a prime example of an unethical psychology study. In the experiment a 9 months old infant known as Little Albert was presented with various stimuli such as a monkey, masks, a rat and a rabbit. While Albert showed no fear of any of these stimuli, one particular stimuli did startle him and cause him to cry: a hammer striking a steel bar just behind his head.

Its no wonder Little Albert was upset by this particular stimuli. But the 'researchers' didn't stop there, at 11 months old Albert was presented with the rat in combination with the hammer striking the steel bar again, this was performed 7 times over the following 7 weeks, upsetting Albert on every occasion. As with Pavlov's dogs over the 7 weeks an association between the neutral (the rat) and potent stimulus (hammer striking) created and association and now when Albert was shown just the rat he would cry and try to crawl away.

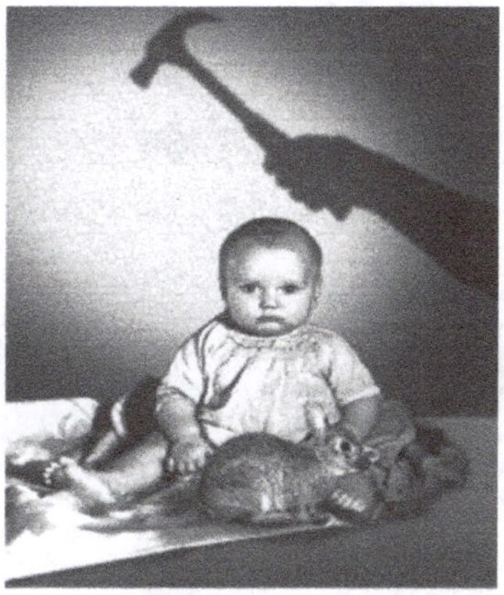

Little Albert Experiment

Watson's Little Albert Experiment (Classical Conditioning)

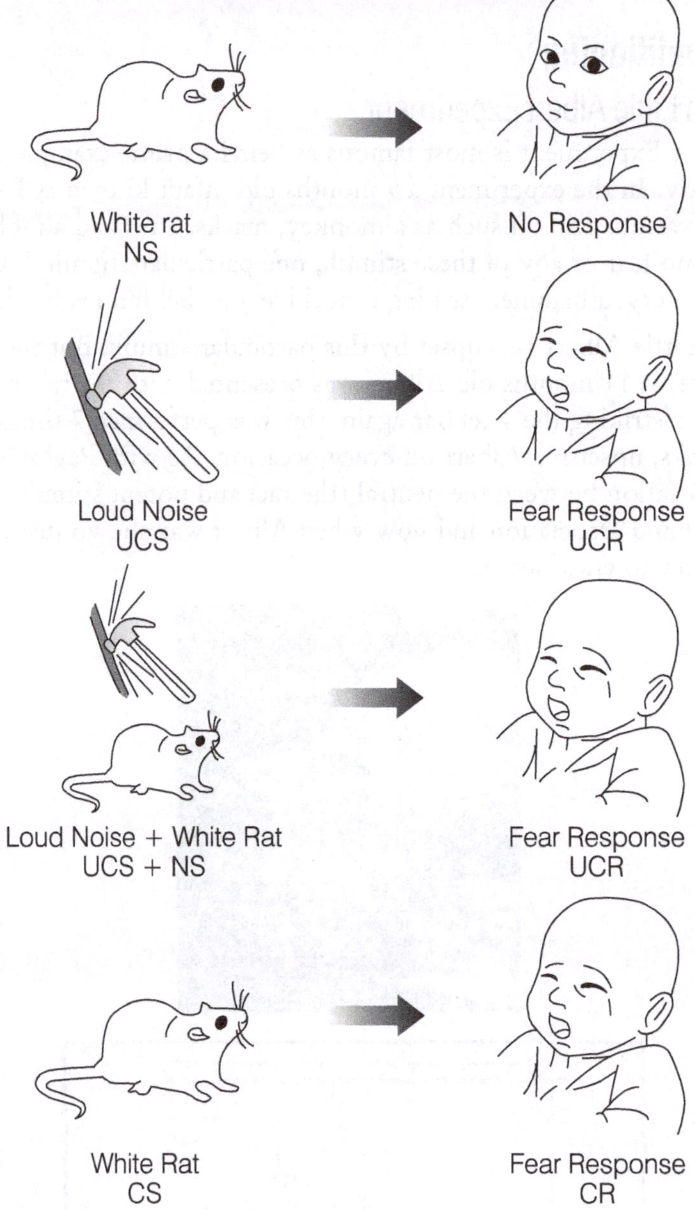

NS - No Response

UCS - Unconditioned Stimulus

CS - Conditioned Stimulus

UCR - Unconditioned Response

CR - Condition Response

Viva Voce Questions

1. *Define learning.*

Ans. Learning may be defined as "any relatively permanent change in behaviour or behavioural potential produced by experience".

2. *What might bring temporal behavioural changes?*

Ans. Changes in behaviour might occur due to the effects of tiredness, repeated monotonous work and drugs. These are temporary in nature.

3. *What is habituation? Give an example.*

Ans. It is a case of change in one's behaviour. The change is because of the continuous exposure to agents that arouse some activity or action. Biting nails while watching horror movie.

4. *What is conditioning?*

Ans. Conditioning is the process of training a person or animal to do something or to behave in a certain way in a particular situation.

5. *What is classical conditioning?*

Ans. Classical conditioning basically involves forming an association between two stimuli resulting in a learned response.

6. *Give an example of naturally occuring stimulus.*

Ans. Salivating in response to the smell of food is a good example of a naturally occuring stimulus.

7. *What does UCS and UCR stands for?*

Ans. UCS - unconditioned stimulus ; UCR - unconditioned response.

8. *What is food and salivation in conditioning experiment?*

Ans. Food is unconditioned stimulus and salivation is unconditioned response.

9. *What is unconditioned response?*

Ans. The unconditioned response is the unlearned response that occurs naturally in response to the unconditioned stimulus.

10. *Give an example of unconditioned response.*

Ans. For example, the feeling of hunger in response to the smell of food is the unconditioned response.

11. *Give an example of conditioned stimulus in your daily life.*

Ans. For example, listening lunch bell in the school, automatically stimulates hunger.

12. *Which animal was used in Pavlov conditioning experiment?*

Ans. Dog

13. *What happened to dog after performing classical conditioning experiment on it?*

Ans. The dog secreted saliva after listening to the sound of the bell, expecting its food to be served, because dog thought bell and food were connected, through classical conditioning.

14. ***What was Little Albert experiment?***

Ans. In the Little Albert experiment a 9 months old infant known as Little Albert was presented with various stimuli such as a monkey, masks, a rat and a rabbit in order to generate fear.

15. ***What was the outcome of Little Albert experiment?***

Ans. After repeating the experiment for over 7 weeks, whenever Albert was shown a rat, he would cry and crawl away.

16. ***What is the researcher's name who conducted Little Albert experiment?***

Ans. Watson

17. ***Why was Little Albert experiment unethical?***

Ans. The experiment has shown cruelty to a little infant, by generating fear striking a hammer on steel bar just behind his head.

18. ***In modern times, do you think experimenting with animals is also unethical?***

Ans. Yes, experimenting with animals is also unethical, because it is a form of cruelty towards animals.

19. ***Do you think government should keep restrictions on such kind of experiments?***

Ans. Yes, government should regulate such kind of experiments.

20. ***How important is conditioning in our daily lives?***

Ans. Using conditioning teachers and parents can shape the behaviours of children in a right manner. So that they can grow up as well behaved.

SAMPLE
QUESTION PAPERS (1-3)

SAMPLE QUESTION PAPER 1

A Highly Simulated Sample Question Paper for CBSE Class XI

(Solved)

PSYCHOLOGY

General Instructions

- All questions are compulsory except where internal choice has been given.
- Question Nos. 1-14 in Section A carry 1 mark each.
- Question Nos. 15-19 in Section B are Very Short Answer Type-I questions carrying 2 marks each. Answer to each question should not exceed 30 words.
- Question Nos. 20-23 in Section C are Short Answer Questions Type-II carrying 3 marks each. Answer to each question should not exceed 60 words.
- Question Nos. 24-27 in Section D are Long Answer Type I questions carrying 4 marks each. Answer to each question should not exceed 120 words.
- Question Nos. 28 & 29 in Section E are Long Answer Type question carrying 6 marks. Answer to this question should not exceed 200 words.
- Question Nos. 30–33 in Section F are based on two cases given. Answer to each one-mark question should not exceed 20 words. Answer to each two-mark question should not exceed 30 words.

Time : 3 hours **Max. Marks : 70**

Section A

1 Ivy remembers watching the solar eclipse in amazing detail. She is certain, she can remember exactly what she was wearing, who she was with, what music was playing on a nearby radio and even the breed of dog which ran past her just before the eclipse. This is an example of .... (1)

I. Flashbulb memory
II. Eidetic image
III. Procedural memory
IV. Semantic memory

Codes

(a) Only I (b) II and III
(c) I and II (d) I and IV

2 A rabbit is in a cage with a red button. Regardless of how the rabbit interacts with the button, a trap door releases a food pellet every twenty minutes. This reinforcement schedule would be classified as .... (1)

(a) fixed-interval (b) variable-ratio
(c) fixed-ratio (d) continuous

3 The information related to very recent incidents or very distant events is stored in .... (1)

(a) short-term memory (b) long-term memory
(c) sensory memory (d) working memory

4 Which of the following factors affect learning? (1)

I. Motivation of the learner
II. Maturation of the learner
III. Teaching strategies
IV. Physical and emotional health of the learner

Codes

(a) I and II (b) II and III
(c) I, II and III (d) All of these

5 Mr. Jones is in the habit of offering extra-credit points on the next exam to students who contribute to class discussions. What kind of reinforcement strategy is Mr. Jones using to encourage class participation? (1)

(a) Positive reward
(b) Positive punishment
(c) Negative reward
(d) None of the above

6 Which of the following gives us information about our body position, movement and acceleration? (1)

I. The vestibular system
II. The kinesthetic system
III. Smell
IV. Taste

Codes

(a) Only I (b) I and II
(c) II and III (d) III and IV

7 Identify the correct statement in the contexts of Bronfenbrenner Model of Development. (1)

(a) Microsystem consists of relations between family, peers, teachers and neighbourhood.
(b) Exosystem includes immediate environment setting.
(c) Macrosystem includes the culture in which the individual live.
(d) All of the above

8 Rajan has been appointed as a new Hindi teacher in a school. In order to develop rapport with students, he has to understand behaviour of the students. He will utilise .... method for understanding their behaviour. (1)

(a) correlational (b) experimental
(c) observational (d) survey

9 When she studies for a Psychology exam, Melodee always tries to think of ways in which the information she is trying to learn relates to her own life. It is an example of which of the following? (1)

(a) The self-reference effect
(b) The spacing effect
(c) Overlearning
(d) Enhanced interference

10 Which of the following thoughts best represents intrinsic motivation? (1)

(a) "Susan is a member of Debate Club. If I want to be like Susan, I need to join Debate Club also."
(b) "I should help my neighbour carry in his groceries, since people ought to be kind to one another."
(c) "I shouldn't steal from my workplace, since I'll probably get caught."
(d) "I wish this teacher would slow down, but I don't think I should ask her to. It'd be rude."

11 In the following question, a statement of Assertion (A) is followed by a statement of Reason (R). Mark the correct choice. (1)

Assertion (A) Training aids in encouraging and achieving self-development and self confidence.

Reason (R) It helps a person to handle stress, tension, frustration and conflict.

Codes

(a) Both A and R are true and R is the correct explanation of A
(b) Both A and R are true, but R is not the correct explanation of A
(c) A is true, but R is false
(d) R is true, but A is false

12 Reading disorder is a developmental disorder characterised by the accuracy, speed and comprehension of reading being significantly below standards expected for which of the following? (1)

(a) Chronological age
(b) IQ
(c) Schooling experience
(d) Both (a) and (b)

13 Research has shown that there is .... between the accuracy of a person's memory and their confidence in the accuracy of that memory. (1)

(a) virtually no correlation
(b) a strong positive correlation
(c) a strong negative correlation
(d) a curvilinear relationship

14 In the following questions, a statement of Assertion (A) is followed by a statement of Reason (R). Mark the correct choice. (1)

Assertion (A) If pressure due to stress continue, one may suffer from mental overload.

Reason (R) This suffering from high levels of stress can rapidly cause individuals to lose their ability to make sound decisions. It leads to poor concentration and reduces short-term memory capacity.

Codes

(a) Both A and R are true and R is the correct explanation of A
(b) Both A and R are true, but R is not the correct explanation of A
(c) A is true, but R is false
(d) A is false, but R is true

Section B

15 Priya studies in Class XIth of the Saint Ann School. She is suffering from motivational and emotional problems. In order to get relief from her problem she should visit which type of psychologist. Explain the work of that psychologist. (2)

16 What is the difference between divided and selective attention? (2)

Or

What is the difference between field dependent and field independent people?

17 Lona saw a newborn baby in hospital who was doing some actions. What are these actions called? (2)

18 Neeru is in a development stage (4-7 years) and she thinks a lot about herself. In simple words she can be called self-centered. Name her development stage and throw light on egocentrism. (2)

19 What are the ethical guidelines that a psychologist needs to follow while conducting a psychological enquiry? (2)

Section C

20 Arun wants to conduct a survey research and he opted interview technique to complete his task. Why Arun has chosen interview technique? State its significance. (3)

21 Mansi is doing a research work on old age people. She finds that there are many challenges at this stage but the most common is dependency. Why dependency mostly affects the old age people? (3)

Or

Richa was studying the changes during middle adulthood. Which type of physical and cognitive ablities change during middle adulthood? Provide examples to explain these changes.

22 Gloria is suffering from anxiety and depression since a long time. Her mother tries to find out about her mental state. Discuss about her problems. (3)

23 Define the challenges of marriage, parenthood and family faced by adults. (3)

Section D

24 What are significant features of modern human beings? Discuss the environmental factors that influence development. (4)

25 Adolescence is a stage marked by variety of conflicts including those about one's identity. Elaborate upon how identity development is a major concern of this age and what are the factors that influence it. (4)

26 What do you know about the verbal and non-verbal channels of communication? (4)

27 Describe various stages of creative thinking. (4)

Or Is it important to consciously interpret and label emotions in order to explain them? Discuss giving suitable example.

Section E

28 How is retrieval related forgetting different from forgetting due to interference? (6)

Or Define Mnemonics? Suggest a plan to improve your own memory.

29 When do conflicts occur? Explain the basic forms of conflicts. How do you resolve conflicting situations? (6)

Or Explain in detail about lie detectors and the process involved in it.

Section F

Read the passage and answer the questions that follow.

Observation is a very powerful tool of psychological enquiry. It is an effective method of describing behaviour. In our daily life, we remain busy with observing numerous things throughout the day. Many times, we do not take notice of what we are seeing or what we have seen. We see but we do not observe. We remain aware of only a few things that we see daily. Have you experienced such a thing? You may also have experienced that if you carefully observe a person or event for some time, you come to know many interesting things about the person or the event.

A scientific observation differs from day-to-day observation in many respects.

30 What is observational research? What is its goal? (1)

31 Describe the limitations of psychological enquiry. (2)

Read the passage and answer the questions that follow.

Scenario 1 You happened to remember certain event. The memory of event is very arousing or surprising. The memories of this event are like images frozen in memory and tied to particular places, dates, and times.

Scenario 2 There is no memories reported pertaining to early childhood particularly during the first 4 to 5 years. However, you have observed that there is a dramatic increase in the frequency of memories just after early adulthood, i.e. in your twenties.

Scenario 3 Your brother is a typist. This mean, he also knows the particular letters on the keyboard. However, when asked to label it, he cannot correctly label blank keys in a drawing of a keyboard.

32 How is informations processed through short-term and long-term memory system? (1)

33 What evidence do we have to say that memory is a constructive process? (2)

Answers

FULLY SOLVED

1 (a) Only I

2 (a) fixed-interval

3 (b) long-term memory

4 (d) All of these

5 (a) Positive reward

6 (a) Only I

7 (d) All of the above

8 (b) experimental

9 (a) The self-reference effect

10 (b) "I should help my neighbour carry in his groceries, since people ought to be kind to one another."

11 (a) Both A and R are true and R is the correct explanation of A

12 (d) Both (a) and (b)

13 (a) virtually no correlation

14 (a) Both A and R are true and R is the correct explanation of A

15 Priya studies in class XIth of the Saint Ann School and she is suffering from motivational and emotional problems. In order to get relief from her problem she should visit counselling psychologists.

The counselling psychologists work with persons who suffer from motivational and emotional problems.

A counselling psychologist involves in vocational rehabilitation programmes, or helping persons in making professional choices or in adjusting to new and difficult situations of life.

16 When we can attend two different things at the same time, it is called divided attention. Whereas, selective attention is concerned mainly with the selection of a limited number of stimuli or objects from a large number of stimuli.

Or Field dependent people perceive the external world in its totality i.e. in a global or holistic manner. On the other hand, field independent people perceive the external world by breaking it into smaller units i.e. in an analytic or differentiated manner.

17 The actions which newborn babies do are called as reflexes. These govern the movement of newborns. These are automatic, built-in responses to stimuli. They are genetically-carried, survival mechanisms and are the building blocks for subsequent motor development.

18 Neeru is in a preoperational development stage. This stage is characterised by children having a tendency of centration. A salient feature of preoperational thought is egocentrism (self focus) i.e. children see the world only in terms of their own selves and are not able to appreciate others' point of view. Children because of egocentrism, engage in animism (philosophical) thinking that all things are living, like oneself.

19 Some ethical guidelines that a psychologist needs to follow while conducting a psychological enquiry

- **Voluntary Participation** The person on whom the study has to be conducted has the choice whether to participate or not in the study.
- **Informed Consent** The participants should be informed about the nature of the study and its impact upon them before it starts.
- **Sharing the Results** The researcher has to share the results of the study with the participants to fulfill their expectations.

20 The interview technique is best suited while conducting a survey research. Arun has chosen this technique due to following significance.

- The interview method helps in obtaining in-depth information.

- It is flexible and adaptable to individual situations and can often be used when no other method is possible or adequate.
- It can be used even with children and non-literate persons.
- However, interviews require time. Often getting information from one person may take an hour or more which may not be cost-effective.

21 Dependency is the common issue/challenge found among old age people. It is because old adults may depend on their children for financial support and to overcome their loneliness (after children have moved out). This might trigger-off feelings of hopelessness and depression in some people. In old age, feeling of loss of energy, and dwindling of health and financial assets, lead to insecurity and dependency. The elderly tend to look towards others to lean on and to care for them. Indian culture favours dependency of elderly on their children, for old age needs caring. In fact, parents in most oriental cultures rear their children with the fond hope that they will care for them during old age. It is important to give the elderly sense of security and belonging, a feeling that people care for them (especially in the time of crisis) and to remember that we all have to grow old one day.

Or

Richa will find different behavioural changes during the study of middle adulthood along with changes in physical and cognitive abilities. During middle adulthood, physical abilities decline due to natural ageing, leading to changes like vision deterioration, hearing loss, and weight gain. Cognitive abilities also change, with long-term memory declining more than short-term memory. For example, a middle-aged person may recall a phone number instantly but forget it after a few days.

However, wisdom often improves with age. Individual differences exist, meaning not all adults experience the same level of cognitive or physical decline.

22 Anxiety is a condition that an individual develops in case of failure to adopt an appropriate ego defence i.e. defending one's own self-respect or self importance. As Gloria is suffering from anxiety, she finds it difficult to concentrate or to make decisions even for trivial matters. Gloria once failed to stick to a defence of rationalisation for her immoral act i.e. cheating. She developed intense fear about the outcomes of such an act.

The state of depression affect on individual's ability to think rationally, feel realistically and work effectively. Gloria is suffering from depression as she has developed a variety of symptoms like difficulty in falling asleep, increase level of Pscyhomoter (movement and thinking related), agitation or retardation, decrease in ability to think or concentrate and loss of interest in personal or social activities, etc.

23 The The challenges of marriage, parenthood and family faced by adults are as follows

- Adults have to make adjustments when entering in a marriage life like, to knowing the other person if not known earlier, coping with each other's likes, dislikes, tastes and choices.
- If both the partners are working, adjustments are required regarding sharing and performing roles and responsibilities at home.
- In addition to getting married, becoming a parent can be a difficult and stressful transition in young adults, even though it is usually accompanied by the feeling of love for the baby.
- Parenting experience is affected by different situations such as the number of children in the family, the availability of social support, and the happiness or unhappiness of the married couple.
- Death of a spouse or divorce creates a family structure in which a single parent either the mother or the father has to take up the responsibility of the children.
- In recent times, women are increasingly seeking employment outside the home thus creating another type of family in which both parents work. The stressors when both parents are working are quite the same as of a single working parent, namely, taking care of children, their schoolwork, illness and coping with workload at home and in the office, etc.

24 Three important features of modern human beings are

(i) A bigger and developed brain with increased capacity for cognitive behaviours like perception, memory, reasoning, problem solving and use of language for communication.

(ii) Ability to walk upright on two legs.

(iii) A free hand with a workable opposing thumb.

The environmental factors that influence development are as follows

- Genes set the limit and within that limit the environment influences development.
- Genes also play an important role in determining the type of environment their children will encounter.
- Sandra Scarr (1992) believes that the environment which is provided by parents for their children depends to some extent on their own genetic predisposition.
- Children themselves choose certain environments based on their genotype. These interactions with environment keep changing from infancy through adolescence. Environmental influences are as complex as the genes one inherit.

FULLY SOLVED

FULLY SOLVED

25 A well-developed identity is comprised of goals, values and beliefs to which a person is committed. It is the awareness of the consistency in self over time, the recognition of this consistency by others (Erikson, 1980). The process of identity development is both an individual and social phenomenon Identity is formed through a process of exploring options or choices and committing to an option based upon the outcome of their exploration. Failure to establish a well-developed sense of identity can result in identity confusion. Those experiencing identity confusion do not have a clear sense of who they are or their role in society.

Factor that effect identity in adolescence are

- **Society** Society can act as a positive and negative force in adolescence identity. The concept of collectivism, in which we view ourselves in relation to others within our society, is just as important as individualism. Finding a group that shares aspects of our identity and either helps us accept or change how we identify ourselves helps us throughout our lives.
- **Family and Loved Ones** Throughout our early developmental years, we may embody the title of son, daughter, brother or sister. How strongly we identify with these labels is influenced by variables like the size and type of family we belong to and the level of support or conflict that we receive from our family effect the identity in adolescence .
- **Ethnicity ,Race and Culture** Many people have a strong sense of pride when it comes to these factors. However, how our environment reacts to features like our skin color, heritage or cultural customs can either strengthen or weaken our sense of pride in that aspect of adolescence identity.
- **Media** The internet provides a wealth of information and communication that we can use as a guide for social comparison and to find others who share our collective identity. However, too much information and exposure can make us question aspects of our identity. Exposure to media in any form is just as influential in shaping adolescence identity as our family, friends and society.

26 The verbal channel of communication is composed of spoken words and other vocal features of speech like pitch and loudness of the voice. These non-verbal aspects of the voice and temporal characteristics of speech are called 'paralanguage'. Other non-verbal channels include facial expression, kinetic (gesture, posture, movement of the body) and proximal (physical distance during face-to-face interaction) behaviours.

Facial expression is the most common channel of emotional communication. The amount and kind of information conveyed by the face is easy to understand as the face is exposed to the full view of others.

Facial expressions can convey the intensity as well as the pleasantness or unpleasantness of the individual's emotional state. Facial expressions play an important role in our everyday lives.

There has been some research evidence supporting Darwin's view that facial expressions for basic emotions (joy fear, anger, disgust, sadness and surprise) are inborn and universal

27 Creative thinking is characterised by the ability to perceive the world in new ways. It is a way of looking at problems or situations from a fresh perspective. It is referred to as 'thinking outside of the box'. The four stages in creative thinking are

(i) **Preparation** This involves formulating the problem and gathering information about its. Identifying sources of inspiration and acquiring knowledge about the protect or problem at hand. This is often an internal process (thinking deeply to generate and engage with ideas) as well as an external one (going out into the world to gather the necessary data, resources, materials and expertise).

(ii) **Incubation** Next, the ideas and information gathered in stage 1 marinate in the mind. As ideas slowly simmer, the work deepens and new connections are formed. During this period of germination, the artist takes their focus off the problem and allows the mind to rest. While the conscious mind wanders, the unconscious engages in what Einstein called "combinatory play": taking diverse ideas and influences and finding new ways to bring them together.

(iii) **Illumination** Following the period of incubation the creative ideas occur suddenly. Consequently the obscure thing becomes clear. This sudden flash of solution is known as illumination and is similar to 'aha (eureka)' experience. For example, Archimedes found solution to the crown problem.

(iv) **Verification** Though the solution is found in illumination stage, it is necessary to verify whether that solution is correct or not. Hence in this last stage evaluation of the solution is done. If the solution is not satisfactory the thinker will go back to creative process from the beginning. If it is satisfactory, the same will be accepted and if necessary, minor modification may also be made in solution.

Or Yes, it is important to consciously interpret and label emotions in order to explain them as the expression of emotions varies from culture to culture. There are some basic emotions that are common to all cultures and yet there are other emotions that are culture specific. The identification and experience of emotions also vary across cultures and display rules exist to modify the intensity of expression of emotions.

For example, the Tahitian language has 46 labels for anger that may be used in different contexts. The

North Americans can produce up to 40 different facial expressions for anger while the Japanese have 10 labels for various facial expressions of happiness and 8 levels to express anger. While some emotions like love, anger, grief and wonder are deemed to be universal and present across Indian, Chinese and Western cultures, other emotions like surprise, contempt and shame are not considered as basic to everyone and the degree of their presence varies individually as well as culturally.

Therefore, it is important to interpret and label emotions in order to understand and explain them.

28 Retrieval forgetting takes place due to inability to retrieve previously learnt knowledge, information or experience from long-term memory. This occurs when retrieval stimuli or cues are missing which were earlier present while encoding the memory. Decay theory states that retrieval forgetting can be due to memory being faded or erased over time when a new memory is created over an old memory. Retrieval practices help to correct retrieval forgetting.

Interference forgetting takes place when one memory interferes with the ability to remember another memory. This happens when information stored in long-term memory becomes confused with another similar type of information which would have combined during encoding process of memory which is now distorting or interfering with one another. Proactive interference makes an old information or task to interfere with the ability to remember a new information or task. Retroactive interference makes a new information or task to interfere with the ability to remember a previously learnt information or task. Rehearsal practices helps to avoid interference of memories.

Or Mnemonics are processes to enhance memory by using images or emphasising the organisation of the learnt behaviour. In order to improve memory, two easy methods can be used based on the kind of material to be learnt. These are

(i) **Words** Words can be learnt by relating them to form sentences. For example the words are-shoe, pen, teacher, books, table. These words can be arranged as-I was gifted a new pair of shoes and a pen by my teacher. However, after looking at my dirty books, she asked me to stand on the table. This method helps to learn the words easily.

(ii) **Chapters** Chapters or lessons can be learnt by first reading and then writing them. This enables continuous recall of information. After enough practice, most chapters can be recalled.

There are different plans to improve memory. One of such plans is engaging in deep level processing. If one wants to memorise any information well, he should engage in deep level processing. Deep processing would involve asking as many questions related to the information as possible, considering its meaning and examining its relationships to the facts one already knows. In this way, the new information will become a part of his existing knowledge frame work and the chances that it will be remembered are increased.

29 Conflict occurs whenever a person must choose between contradictory (opposite) needs, desires, motives or demands. There are three basic forms of conflicts, such as

(i) Approach-approach conflict comes from having to choose between two positives and desirable alternatives.

(ii) Avoidance-avoidance conflict comes from choosing between two negatives or mutually undesirable alternatives.

(iii) Approach-avoidance conflict comes from being attracted to and repelled by the same goal or activity. The central characteristic of this conflict is ambivalence i.e. a mixture of positive and negative conflicts.

An example of this form of conflict is : a person wanting to buy a new motorbike but not wanting to make monthly payments. Many of life's important decisions have approach-avoidance dimensions.

A major source of frustration lies in motivational conflict. In life, we are often influenced by a number of competing forces that propel us in different directions. Such situations demonstrate the condition of conflict. Hence, the simultaneous existence of multiple wishes and needs characterise conflict.

Conflicting situations should be resolved after giving enough consideration of the pros and cons of each of the choices. We need to understand that conflicts cause frustration, which in turn, can lead to aggression.

For example, a young man who wants to be a musician but is pursing a course in management due to parental pressure and is not able to perform as per the expectations of his parents may turn aggressive upon being questioned on his poor performance in the course.

Or Lie detectors are also called polygraphs because they graphically record several bodily reactions simultaneously which measure the bodily arousal of the individual. Typically, a lie detector measures changes in blood pressure, heart rate, breathing rate and depth, and the Galvanic Skin Response (GSR) which indicates variations in the electrical conductivity of the skin. In lie detection, the individual being tested is first asked a series of neutral (control) questions to establish a baseline. Simple questions are followed by specific questions that are designed to evoke responses from a guilty knowledge supposedly indicating the individual's involvement in the crime being investigated. The lie detector or the polygraph records the changes in neurophysiological activities that occur while the suspected individual answers these questions.

Though the polygraph makes several objective recordings, the interpretation of these records depends heavily on the subjective judgement by the examiner. It is also probable that several unrelated factors like fear, pain or anxiety being felt by the individual during the test may affect her/his level of arousal. It is possible for the individual to lie with it. The validity of polygraph results is doubtful but these are still used by law-enforcing agencies for lie detection.

30 The term observational research is used to refer to several different types of non-experimental studies in which behavior is systematically observed and recorded.

The goal of observational research is to describe a variable or set of variables. More generally, the goal is to obtain a snapshot of specific characteristics of an individual, group, or setting.

31 The limitations of psychological enquiry are

- **Lack of true zero point** Psychological measurements do not have a zero point. The scores that are assigned to individuals in psychological studies are not absolute in nature but have relative value.
- **Relative nature of psychological tools** Psychological tests need to be developed, modified and adapted according to the context of study. For example, test developed for urban children is not suitable and cannot be applied on tribal children.

32 The information is processed through short-term and long-term memory systems in the following ways

- **Short-term Memory** It refers to the system that holds small amount of information for a brief period of time. According to Atkinson and Shiffrin, the information is primarily encoded acoustically and unless it is rehearsed continuously, the information gets lost within 30 seconds. The STM is fragile but not as fragile as sensory registers where information decays automatically in less than a second.
- **Long-term Memory** The information that survives in short term memory enters the long-term memory system. Once information enters here, it is never forgotten as it gets encoded semantically i.e in terms of the meaning that any information carries .Thus, it is a permanent storehouse of all the information.

33 Memory is a constructive process as the information that is stored undergoes modification according to past knowledge and schema. Schema refers to active organisation of past reactions and experiences.

Bartlett pointed that the memorised information is influenced by the meaning that is assigned to the stimulus material. It cannot remain in isolation from other cognitive processes after it is committed to the memory system.

SAMPLE QUESTION PAPER 2

A Highly Simulated Sample Question Paper for CBSE Class XI

(Unsolved)

PSYCHOLOGY

General Instructions

- All questions are compulsory except where internal choice has been given.
- Question Nos. 1-14 in Section A carry 1 mark each.
- Question Nos. 15-19 in Section B are Very Short Answer Type-I questions carrying 2 marks each. Answer to each question should not exceed 30 words.
- Question Nos. 20-23 in Section C are Short Answer Questions Type-II carrying 3 marks each. Answer to each question should not exceed 60 words.
- Question Nos. 24-27 in Section D are Long Answer Type I questions carrying 4 marks each. Answer to each question should not exceed 120 words.
- Question Nos. 28 & 29 in Section E are Long Answer Type question carrying 6 marks. Answer to this question should not exceed 200 words.
- Question Nos. 30–33 in Section F are based on two cases given. Answer to each one-mark question should not exceed 20 words. Answer to each two-mark question should not exceed 30 words.

Time : 3 hours **Max. Marks : 70**

Section A

1 Sarita is an accomplished Singer in the Indian cinema. Name the need which best represents this case in the Maslow`s hierarchy of needs. (1)

I. Motivation II. Emotion
III. Inclination IV. Diversion

(a) I and II (b) II and III
(c) III and IV (d) II and IV

2 Receiving an electric shock would be an example of a .... whereas being frightened would be an example of a .... (1)

(a) stimulus, response
(b) punishment, reward
(c) reaction, emotion
(d) reinforcement, stimulus

3 Naturalistic observation can be conducted in .... (1)

(a) Hospitals (b) Homes
(c) Schools (d) All of these

4 What are the activities of teaching associated with its interactive stage? (1)

I. Determining learning outcomes.
II. Presenting the content interspersed with questions.
III. Providing feedback and probing
IV. Motivating and monitoring student tasks

Codes

(a) I, II and III (b) II, III and IV
(c) III and IV (d) II and IV

5 In a famous study by Simons and Chabris (1999), the researchers made participants watch a short video of six people (three wearing white and three wearing black) passing basketball amongst themselves. The participants were tasked with counting how many times the people in white shirts made passes. The researcher found that half of the participants who watched the video and counted the passes, completely missed the gorilla, shown in between the video. Using your understanding of the above case, identify that activity that the participants were engaged in. (1)

(a) Sustained Attention Task
(b) Selective Attention Task
(c) Divided Attention Task
(d) None of the above

6 The factors that operate with deep levels of processing are (1)

I. Distinctiveness
II. Sameness
III. Elaboration
IV. Physical contours

Codes

(a) I and II (b) IV and III
(c) II and IV (d) I and III

7 Which of the following is/are true regarding reinforcement? (1)

I. A reinforce is defined as any stimulus or event which increases the probability of the occurrence of a desired response.
II. The type-positive or negative, frequency, quality and schedule or reinforcer are determinants of conditioning.
III. Positive reinforcement provides a desirable stimulus while negative reinforcement taking away an undesirable stimulus.
IV. Reinforcement is an important part of operant or instrumental conditioning.

Codes

(a) Only I is true
(b) I and II are true
(c) I, II and III are true
(d) I, II, III and IV are true

8 In an experiment, the stimuli were presented to the subjects in certain order and after the presentation of stimuli, their order was disturbed. In the test phase, the subjects were needed to set them in the presented order.
.... methods is used in this expriment. (1)

(a) Recognition (b) Relearning
(c) Reconstruction (d) Recall

9 .... can happen when memories become progressively reconstructed over time to fit in with our pre-existing concepts and ideas. (1)

(a) Interference (b) Trace decay
(c) Distortions (d) Decoding

10 A young child hears the bell of an ice cream truck approaching in the summer time. This truck has come to her neighbourhood every day for weeks but usually comes earlier in the afternoon. This makes her salivate and get excited. She then runs into the house and asks her dad for some money, her father gives her the money in order to stop her from crying. This seems to happen on a daily basis.

From your understanding of the case, identify the classical conditioning. (1)

(a) Unconditioned stimulus
(b) Conditioned stimulus
(c) Unconditioned response
(d) Conditioned response

11. In the following question, a statement of Assertion (A) is followed by a statement of Reason (R). Mark the correct choice. (1)

Assertion (A) In a maze learning experiment, rats which were reinforced from the beginning and those which were not reinforced until the eleventh day of the experiment, did not show any difference in learning and performance.

Reason (R) It is possible for learning to remain dormant for a considerable length of time before it is manifested in behaviour.

Codes

(a) Both A and R are true and R is the correct explanation of A
(b) Both A and R are true, but R is not the correct explanation of A
(c) A is true, but R is false
(d) A is false, but R is true

12 Making some orienting reflexes i.e. getting accustomed to the event is involved in which of the following phenomenon? (1)

(a) Habituation (b) Reinforcement
(c) Extinction (d) Transfer effect

13 Bindu is a remarkable singer and she has won many accolades. She is known as a child prodigy. Which of the following terms best describe Bindu's abilities? (1)

(a) Talent
(b) Giftedness
(c) Naturalistic Intelligence
(d) Interest

UNSOLVED

14 In the following question, a statement of Assertion (A) is followed by a statement of Reason (R). Mark the correct choice. (1)

Assertion (A) Spatial intelligence is used while navigating in space, forming, transforming and using mental images.

Reason (R) Spatial intelligence is involved in perceiving the formation of images in three dimensions.

Codes

(a) Both A and R are true and R is the correct explanation of A

(b) Both A and R are true, but R is not the correct explanation of A

(c) A is true, but R is false

(d) R is true, but A is false

Section B

15 Explain any four factors influencing the formation of identify during adolescence. Support your answer with examples. (2)

16 Due to some family and personal issue, Rishi was not able to concentrate on his studies as a result of which he decided to leave his exam. You are friend of Rishi, how you can motivate him to take the exam? (2)

Or

Lucy is a student of class XIth. She has given very bad performance in the several class tests due to which her motivation level has deteriorated. In this context define motivation.

17 Raghav has been given a list word translations of foreign language, that he is to memorise. He realises that it is much easier to memorise the list, if he just creates the image of the word and its meaning in his mind. What method do you think Raghav is using here to enhance his memory? Elaborate. (2)

18 Shrikant is in his childhood, as a result of which he is facing many physical and mental changes. Write the main characteristics of this age group. (2)

19 How the Attention Deficit Hyperactivity Disorder (ADHD) can be treated? (2)

Section C

20 Does physiological arousal precede or follow an emotional experience? Explain. (3)

21 Anya is going to study condition of children exposed to devastation by tsunami, war or vehicular pollution, etc. She decided to use case study method for it. Define this method and how she will conduct her study. (3)

Or

Parul met some victims of natural disaster during her medical career. She came to know about some people were suffering from Post-Traumatic Stress Disorder (PTSD). Explain about Post-Traumatic Stress Disorder (PSTD).

22 Mr. Tyagi is a psychology teacher of the class 11th. He directs students to perform classical conditioning experiment. In this context, explain the classical conditioning and also mention types of unconditional stimuli. (3)

23 Dia, a 9-year-old, was given two identical clay balls of different shapes. She was able to understand that both balls have the same amount of clay. What does Dia's ability to recognise that both balls contain the same amount of clay despite their different shapes demonstrate about her cognitive development? How does this show a shift from preoperational to concrete operational thinking? (3)

Section D

24 Mr. Arvind is a psychology teacher in school 'Y'. He gave a project to students on the topic 'People and their motives'. All the students have conducted data from their locality.

On the basis of this case, define motive and discuss different types of motives in detail with example. (4)

Or An individual passes through different stages of the development. In develop mental stage, a person shows distinct characteristics. In this context, explain the Bronfenbrenner's Model of Development.

25 A good role model is very important for a growing up child. Discuss the kind of learning that support it. (4)

26 How can we identify students with learning disabilities? (4)

27 Is it important to consciously interpret and label emotions in order to explain them. Discuss giving suitable examples. (4)

Section E

28 From her childhood Mona is suffering from learning disability because of which she is not able to compete with her classmates. Explain some of the important symptoms of Mona and how she can come out of it. (6)

Or In a society, people have different types of attention. The attention of Raghvendra is concerned mainly with the selection of a limited number of stimuli or from a large number of stimuli. Which type of attention is possessed by the Raghvendra and explain the factor which affect this attention?

29. Discuss in brief the various types of observation. (6)

Or Explain in brief the concept of variable.

UNSOLVED

Section F

Read the case and answer the questions that follow.

Devansh is student of the class 11. He has opted for a science stream after class 10th. He lives along with his three brother and sisters. He is youngest among them. He does not pay much attention to studies and extra-curricular activities.

Due to his lack of interest in studies his performance in studies in class is poor. Every person in his family ranging from siblings to parent tries to motivate him for studies but Devansh did not listened them. His family is worried about his attitude. His parents also discussed this issue with his teacher during parent teacher meeting but not able to arrive at the solution.

His parents again try to motivate him to do studies in proper ways so that he can make his dream true. His parents try to find out what is his goal of his life or what he want to become in his life. After listening these questions, Devansh replies that he wanted to become sportsperson and he is not interested in studying science subject as he is not able to comprehend them.

30 In what ways, Devansh can be motivated to study science subject? (1)

31 Why Devansh was not showing interest in studying science subject? (2)

Read the case and answer the questions that follow.

Parker is a child psychologist who works on the theory of Jean Piaget. When he observes children of infancy stage he founds different activities done by these infants. During his research work, he observed that the child during infancy experiences the world through senses and interactions with objects i.e. through looking, hearing, touching, mouthing and grasping. The newborn lives in the present. If something is out of sight, it is out of mind of children at this stage.

For example, once Parker hid a toy in front of a child with which the child was playing. The young infant did react as if nothing has happened, i.e. she did not search for the toy. The child assumed the toy did not exist. Parker recalls the theory of Jean Piaget that children at this stage have lack object permanence i.e. the awareness that the objects continue to exist when not perceived.

Gradually by 8 months of age, the child starts pursuing the object partially covered in her/his presence. As per this theory, vocalisation begins with the infant's babbling, sometime between 3 to 6 months of age. Jean Piaget stressed that children actively construct their understanding of the world. Information does not simply enter their minds from the environment. As children grow, additional information is acquired and they adapt their thinking to include new ideas, as this improves their understanding of the world.

32 Skill learning process goes different phases. Discuss it. (1)

33 How children observes the world through senses and interaction with object during the infancy stage? (2)

SAMPLE QUESTION PAPER 3

A Highly Simulated Sample Question Paper for CBSE Class XI

(Unsolved)

PSYCHOLOGY

General Instructions

- All questions are compulsory except where internal choice has been given.
- Question Nos. 1-14 in Section A carry 1 mark each.
- Question Nos. 15-19 in Section B are Very Short Answer Type-I questions carrying 2 marks each. Answer to each question should not exceed 30 words.
- Question Nos. 20-23 in Section C are Short Answer Questions Type-II carrying 3 marks each. Answer to each question should not exceed 60 words.
- Question Nos. 24-27 in Section D are Long Answer Type I questions carrying 4 marks each. Answer to each question should not exceed 120 words.
- Question Nos. 28 & 29 in Section E are Long Answer Type question carrying 6 marks. Answer to this question should not exceed 200 words.
- Question Nos. 30–33 in Section F are based on two cases given. Answer to each one-mark question should not exceed 20 words. Answer to each two-mark question should not exceed 30 words.

Time : 3 hours **Max. Marks : 70**

Section A

1 Mary is a 23 year old single parent who is working for minimum wage. Mary is trying to satisfy which need? (1)

I. Social II. Esteem

III. Self-actualisation IV. Physiological

Codes

(a) Only I (b) Only II

(c) II and III (d) Only IV

2 .... memory is related to first-hand experience whereas as .... memory is related to knowledge about the world. (1)

(a) Semantic, episodic (b) Episodic, semantic

(c) Implicit, explicit (d) Xplicit, implicit

3 One reason that people comply with social pressure is to gain approval or avoid rejection. This is called .... (1)

(a) social control

(b) social influence

(c) normative social influence

(d) social facilitation

4 Which of the following is an element of emotional intelligence? (1)

I. Entrepreneurial competence

II. Self-motivation

III. Empathy

IV. Handing relationships

Codes

(a) I and II

(b) II and III

(c) II, III and IV

(d) III and IV

5 For the entire semester, Rohit have been playing and having fun every day. His studies are not doing well. However, he believe, he can secure an 'A' grade for the exam next week. What is the mistake that the Rohit has committed here with respect to critical thinking? (1)

(a) Wishful thinking

(b) Ego centrism

(c) Self-confident thinking

(d) Moral Subjectivism

UNSOLVED

6 Shandra is convinced that her neighbour, Joe, is cruel to his dog. She notices every time Joe shouts at the dog or jerks its lead but she doesn't seem to notice the times when Joe plays with the dog or gives it treats. This is an example of .... (1)

I. misinformation
II. anterograde amnesia
III. proactive interference
IV. confirmation bias

Codes
(a) Only I
(b) I and II
(c) Only III
(d) Only IV

7 Out of the following, which one of the statements is wrong in the context of characteristics of sentiments? (1)

I. Emotions are the basis of sentiments.
II. Sentiments are innate.
III. Sentiments get older with the passage of time and they may even change their state.
IV. Most of the animals do have sentiments because they do not have intellectual comprehension.

Codes
(a) Only I (b) Only II
(c) I and II (d) II and III

8 **Lecturer** : You all should focus on this section. It's a critical section that requires a lot of thought and review.

Peter : Ah, I know everything. This section is not a problem for me.
I don't need to learn this.

Peter has committed here .... with respect to critical thinking. (1)

(a) group bias
(b) moral subjectivism
(c) self-serving bias
(d) relativistic thinking

9 In the following questions, a statement of Assertion (A) is followed by a statement of Reason (R). Mark the correct choice. (1)

Assertion (A) If your teacher embarrasses you for asking a question in class, it is less likely that you would ask questions in class in future.

Reason (R) Negative reinforcement reduces the occurrence of a behaviour.

Codes
(a) Both A and R are true and R is the correct explanation of A
(b) Both A and R are true, but R is not the correct explanation of A
(c) A is true, but R is false
(d) A is false, but R is true

10 Ashok is very fond of playing cricket and he is very good at it too. He is the captain of his college team. He spends long hours playing or watching cricket and never gets tired or bored. Which personal factor is affecting the learning in this case? (1)

(a) Maturation
(b) Motivation
(c) Self-concept
(d) Levels of aspiration

11 In the following questions, a statement of Assertion (A) is followed by a statement of Reason (R). Mark the correct choice. (1)

Assertion (A) A mentally retarded child feels difficulties in learning basic academic skills.

Reason (R) A mentally retarded child has difficulty in focussing attention.

Codes
(a) Both A and R are correct and R is the correct explanation of A
(b) Both A and R are correct, but R is not the correct explanation of A
(c) A is true, but R is false
(d) R is true, but A is false

12 Journalist Jayram was so passionate about K-drama and Korean culture all through his college years that he ended up moving to Seoul, South Korea, to work as an English teacher. He says that he is extremely happy there, having made a lot of local friends. When asked if he misses India, he replied, "Not really. I find myself feeling very disconnected from that part of my life. I have settled down very well in this place and want to build my life here. It feels like I have come home." From your understanding of the above-mentioned case, identify the type of Jayram's contact with another culture (1)

(a) Direct; Voluntary (b) Indirect; Voluntary
(c) Direct; Involuntary (d) Indirect; Involuntary

13 The fact that you may notice a disgusting smell when you first walk into a room but stop noticing it if you stay in the room for a while illustrates .... (1)

(a) synesthesia (b) selective attention
(c) sensory attention (d) sensory adaption

14 When Loftus and Palmer asked observers of a filmed car accident how fast the vehicles were going when they 'smashed' into each other, the observers developed memories of the accident that (1)

(a) omitted some of the most painful aspects of the event.
(b) were more accurate than the memories of the subjects who had not been immediately questioned about what they saw.
(c) were influenced by whether or not Loftus and Palmer identified themselves as police officers.
(d) portrayed the event as more serious than it actually had been.

Section B

15 In a school, a competition was conducted to know the memory capacity or ability of the students. Result of the experiment shows that people have different capacity or ability of the memory. Identify the reason behind different memory power of the students. (2)

16 Discuss about knowledge representation in the form of images in detail. How do mental models help in this process? (2)

Or

What is trace decay? What are the shortcomings of this theory?

17 Dristi is a psychology student of school X. She is quite curious about his memory power or capacity. She visited her teacher and asked him how she can measure her memory power? In this context, discuss different method of measuring memory. (2)

18 Monica loves to have fast food everyday. Being aware of its ill effects on her body, she promised herself that she would buy a book of her choice if she managed to restrain herself from eating fast food for a month. Identify and explain the behaviour being exhibited by Sanjana. (2)

19 Neeraj wants to crack NEET entrance exam in his first attempt. For this he asked tips from his senior and teachers. Most of them have suggested him to emphasise on developing creative thinking which can help in increase the probability of cracking the exam. In this context, define creative thinking and also discuss process of creative thinking. (2)

Section C

20 Sometimes stimuli simultaneously enter receptors and create a kind of 'bottleneck' situation. This concept was pounded by which theory and also explains this theory. (3)

21 "Environment of the child has a major role in the development of the child". Support your answer with examples. (3)

Or

At the present time, substance abuse has become common in adolescents. Due to substance abuse they are facing lot of problems. Identify the main reason behind it and also how we can prevent adolescent from this problem.

22 The school administration is organising a research programme for students of class 11th. Before commencing research trip, Raju (Head of whole trip) has been given responsibility to explain all the ethical issues associated with research. Explain different ethical issues involved in research. (3)

23 If you are used to hearing your milkman knock at the door every morning at 5:30 A.M., you may mistake any knock at that time for him, even if it's someone else. How does this example show the effect of expectations on what we perceive? How might this affect our ability to see things as they truly are? (3)

Section D

24 Emotion is a subjective feeling and the experience of emotions varies from person to person. Discuss. (4)

25 Explain how the processes of stimulus generalisation and stimulus discrimination are considered opposite. (4)

26 Explain the difference between negative reinforcement and punishment and provide several examples of each based on your own experiences. (4)

27 How does continuous reinforcement promote a desired behaviour? Discuss. (4)

Or

A group of researchers is interested in observing mice ringing a bell. As a positive reinforcement, they offer cheese. If the mice fail to do so, they provide a small electric shock. After some time, they change their reinforcement schedule. What reinforcement schedule have they most likely chosen? Discuss.

Section E

28 Explain how BF Skinner's principle of operant conditioning is being used in classroom incentive programs to encourage appropriate behaviour in students. (6)

Or

What is the difference between a reflex and a learned behaviour?

29 How do we distinguish figure as per Gestalt psychologists? (6)

Or

Explain different theories proposed for selective attention.

Section F

Read the passage and answer the question.

This is a story of three students Ruby, Radhika and Shankar who were enrolled in an Undergraduate Psychology Program in a University. Ruby was the admission officer's dream. She was selected for the program as she had perfect entrance test scores, outstanding grades and excellent letters of recommendation. But when it was time for Ruby to start coming up with ideas of her own, she disappointed her professors. On the other hand, Radhika did not meet the admission officer's expectations. She had good grades but low entrance exam scores. However, her letters of recommendation described her as a creative young woman. She could design and implement research work with minimal guidance at college. Shankar ranked somewhere in between the two students. He was satisfactory on almost every traditional measure of success. But rather than falling somewhere in the middle of his class at college, Shankar proved to be an outstanding student. His strength lay in the ability to not only adapt well to the demands of his new environment but also to modify the environment to suit his needs.

30 Identify the theory of intelligence which best explains the intelligence of all the three students in the story. (1)

31 To what extent our intelligence is the result of hereditary in nature and environment? (2)

Read the passage and answer the questions that follow.

Anuradha is a student of class 11 of a renowned school in city X. One day, she was going to school with her driver to give her exam. On the way, after few minutes of drive, she found that an accident has taken place between truck and bicycle. The injured people are lying there and no one has come for their help. Anuradha directs her driver to stop the car near the accident. When she and her driver came out of car they noticed that one of injured person has died while other one is seriously injured. Anuradha's driver requests her to sit in car and go to school, and do not meddle in this case. Her driver was worried about the police behavior. Anuradha declined to follow the direction of her driver instead she asked him to help her in taking injured people to the hospital. Again, driver warns her about unfavourable consequence which she can face from police.

32 Identify the problems which were faced by Anuradha. (1)

33 Why Anuradha's driver was showing reluctance in helping injured people? (2)

UNSOLVED

Answers

Sample Paper 2

1 (a) I and II
2 (a) stimulus, response
3 (d) All of these
4 (b) II, III and IV
5 (a) Sustained Attention Task
6 (d) I and III
7 (d) I, II, III and IV are true
8 (c) Reconstruction
9 (c) Distortions
10 (b) Conditioned stimulus
11 (a) Both A and R are true and R is the correct explanation of A
12 (a) Habituation
13 (a) Talent
14 (a) Both A and R are true and R is the correct explanation of A

Sample Paper 3

1 (d) Only IV
2 (b) Episodic, semantic
3 (c) normative social influence
4 (c) II, III and IV
5 (a) Wishful thinking
6 (d) Only IV
7 (b) Only II
8 (c) self-serving bias
9 (c) A is true, but R is false
10 (b) Motivation
11 (b) Both A and R are true, but R is not the correct explanation of A
12 (b) Indirect; Voluntary
13 (d) sensory adaption
14 (d) portrayed the event as more serious than it actually had been.